Teaching Thoreau's *Walden*
and Other Works

Approaches to Teaching
World Literature

Joseph Gibaldi, series editor

**For a complete listing of titles,
see the last pages of this book.**

Approaches to Teaching Thoreau's *Walden* and Other Works

Edited by

Richard J. Schneider

The Modern Language Association of America
New York   1996

©1996 by The Modern Language Association of America
All rights reserved. Printed in the United States of America

Library of Congress Cataloging-in-Publication Data

Approaches to teaching Thoreau's Walden and other works / edited by
    Richard J. Schneider.
        p.   cm. — (Approaches to teaching world literature : 55)
    Includes index.
    ISBN 0-87352-733-X (cloth). — ISBN 0-87352-734-8 (paper)
    1. Thoreau, Henry David, 1817–1862—Study and teaching.
    2. Thoreau, Henry David, 1817–1862. Walden. 3. Walden Woods
    (Mass.)—In literature. 4. Solitude in literature. 5. Nature in
    literature. I. Schneider, Richard J. II. Series.
    PS3054.A63   1996
    818'.303—dc20   95-51533
    ISSN 1059-1133

Cover illustration of the paperback edition: Asher B. Durand, *Kindred
Spirits*, 1849. Oil on canvas. Collection of The New York Public Library,
Astor, Lenox and Tilden Foundations

Set in Caledonia and Bodoni. Printed on recycled paper

Published by The Modern Language Association of America
10 Astor Place, New York, New York 10003-6981

CONTENTS

Thoreau beyond the Conventional Classroom

PREFACE TO THE SERIES

In *The Art of Teaching* Gilbert Highet wrote, "Bad teaching wastes a great deal of effort, and spoils many lives which might have been full of energy and happiness." All too many teachers have failed in their work, Highet argued, simply "because they have not thought about it." We hope that the Approaches to Teaching World Literature series, sponsored by the Modern Language Association's Publications Committee, will not only improve the craft—as well as the art—of teaching but also encourage serious and continuing discussion of the aims and methods of teaching literature.

The principal objective of the series is to collect within each volume different points of view on teaching a specific literary work, a literary tradition, or a writer widely taught at the undergraduate level. The preparation of each volume begins with a wide-ranging survey of instructors, thus enabling us to include in the volume the philosophies and approaches, thoughts and methods of scores of experienced teachers. The result is a sourcebook of material, information, and ideas on teaching the subject of the volume to undergraduates.

The series is intended to serve nonspecialists as well as specialists, inexperienced as well as experienced teachers, graduate students who wish to learn effective ways of teaching as well as senior professors who wish to compare their own approaches with the approaches of colleagues in other schools. Of course, no volume in the series can ever substitute for erudition, intelligence, creativity, and sensitivity in teaching. We hope merely that each book will point readers in useful directions; at most each will offer only a first step in the long journey to successful teaching.

Joseph Gibaldi
Series Editor

PREFACE TO THE VOLUME

Because the strategies for teaching Thoreau have recently come to depend heavily on intertextuality, this volume in the Approaches to Teaching World Literature series expands the usual format to include consideration of more than one text by a single author. It is difficult to teach the structure of *Walden* without referring to Thoreau's Journal or the lessons he learned from having published *A Week on the Concord and Merrimack Rivers*. Thoreau's idea of wildness makes little sense without comparing his experiences in *Walden* with those in the more truly wild landscapes of *The Maine Woods* or *Cape Cod*. Nor can one consider the social views expressed in *Walden* without taking into account "Civil Disobedience," "Life without Principle," and the John Brown essays. This volume is thus an attempt to acknowledge intertextuality as a necessity in all but the briefest attempts to teach Thoreau. The plan of the book is not only to focus on *Walden* and to include a representative sampling of teaching suggestions for different levels and types of undergraduate literature courses and for different critical approaches but also to bow significantly in the direction of Thoreau's other works, both as comparisons with *Walden* and as possible additions to a syllabus.

There are many people to whom I am indebted for their assistance at various stages in the preparation of this volume. The Thoreau scholars and teachers who contributed to this book have been generous with their time and flexible in responding to editorial needs. I am grateful to Joseph Gibaldi of the MLA for taking an interest in my suggestion that this book be included in the Approaches series, for being willing to expand the scope of the book beyond *Walden*, for presenting the project to the MLA's Publications Committee, and for his advice and patience throughout the process. Sonia Kane and her colleagues at the MLA office handled editorial negotiations with tact and wisdom. Martin Bickman deserves thanks for his especially thorough editorial suggestions on the first draft. I owe a particular debt to Walter Harding and Michael Meyer for their comprehensive bibliographical work on Thoreau, on which I depended heavily.

Locally I have had generous support from the administration and from the Faculty Development Committee of Wartburg College, which provided financial help in mailing and phone costs and in travel to professional meetings. I am also grateful to Olivia Coil, secretary in Wartburg's humanities office, and to her excellent staff of students for their skilled assistance in typing and correspondence.

Personally I am indebted, as always, to Lawrence Willson, who taught me how to read Thoreau; to Walter Harding, who encouraged my continued study of Thoreau; to my wife, Mary, and my children, Eric, Heidi, and Rick, for their continued patience; and to all my students who keep reminding me that Thoreau still has a very real effect on their lives.

Richard J. Schneider
Wartburg College

Introduction: Thoreau's Challenge to Teachers

During the 1960s Thoreau was so popular in college courses that one parody of freshman composition courses advised, "Chances Are, You'll Read Thoreau" (Meyer, *Lives to Live* 186). In the 1990s chances are even better that students will read Thoreau, in even more places in the curriculum and for a wider range of reasons.

Thoreau's popularity in the 1960s rested primarily on his political radicalism and on his advocacy of the simple life. Interest in him waned somewhat during the 1970s, but in the late 1980s and early 1990s Thoreau has emerged with new popularity and versatility. His concept of passive resistance found renewed relevance in the events of China's Tiananmen Square and in the collapse of Communist governments throughout Eastern Europe in 1989 and the early 1990s. His pioneering interest in the unity of nature supports the ecology movement's urgent attempt to dissuade the human species from presiding over "the end of nature." Part of that attempt also includes Thoreau's emphasis on the simple life, which becomes increasingly important as our natural resources are consumed and our landfills overflow.

For these reasons it is not surprising that a 1990 MLA survey of college teachers (B. Huber 40) found that Hawthorne and Thoreau were the authors most frequently mentioned as being particularly important among those regularly taught in nineteenth-century American literature courses (56% and 49%, respectively). Furthermore, *Walden* was mentioned more frequently than any other single work of nineteenth-century American literature. At a time when the canon of American literature is in tremendous flux, Thoreau's place in it seems firmer than ever.

The challenge of teaching Thoreau, then, is not whether to teach Thoreau but how to make most effective use of his obvious appeal amid the variety of possible course structures, critical theories, and pedagogical methods. The MLA survey findings for Thoreau involved only courses on nineteenth-century American literature, but a student might as readily encounter Thoreau in a wide variety of other courses. My own survey of college professors indicates that he continues to be taught regularly in freshman composition courses. The survey also indicates that Thoreau is taught regularly in introduction to literature courses, in special literary topic courses, and in interdisciplinary courses.

Titles of special topic[s] courses include American Humor; Agrarianism in American Literature; Asia in American Literature; The Invention of Liberty; Work and Play in Literature; Literature, Language, and Rebellion; and Early American Poetry. Titles of interdisciplinary courses include Visionary Thinkers, Men and Nature, The American Landscape, Literature and Science, Concepts of Selfhood, and there are the interdisciplinary courses in great books and in the humanities. There is also a growing number of courses on the previously neglected topic of American prose nature writing, which necessarily include Thoreau.

To illustrate Thoreau's potential uses in the curriculum, I refer briefly to my own experience teaching Thoreau in four different courses, all within the curriculum of one small liberal arts college. In a standard American literature survey, I stick to *Walden*, "Civil Disobedience," and a few Journal passages. In a team-taught humanities course for freshmen, I use selections from *Walden* to represent Romantic views of nature and individualism. In an interdisciplinary course for seniors, The American Landscape, I use "Walking" to represent American tendencies to view nature symbolically and spiritually, and I use "The Succession of Forest Trees" to set up a discussion of ecology with specific reference to the Yellowstone fires of 1989.

The above courses are usually classroom-bound, but in a senior seminar on Thoreau during a short May term, I am able to get the students outdoors to gain a better feel for Thoreau's exploration of nature. During the three-hour class session we meet, weather permitting, in various parks and woods in the area. We spend the first hour discussing one of Thoreau's works, the second hour walking individually or in small groups to gather information for the students' nature journals; then for the third hour we gather again to share what we have seen and to continue our discussion of Thoreau's writing.

No matter what the setting, however, instructors in my survey found that certain qualities of Thoreau's writing especially attract student interest, while other qualities frequently seem to cause students problems. Of most interest to students is Thoreau's affirmation of the integrity of the individual conscience, and second is his ecological approach to nature, especially his defense of the wilderness. Students are also interested in Thoreau's feisty personality and nonconformism, his involvement in political and social reform, his reflective attitude, his difficulty in finding a vocation, and his attempt to simplify his lifestyle. Each of these qualities can be a useful point of entry into Thoreau's texts, because each indicates what students seem to see of themselves in Thoreau.

Among the problems that students find in reading Thoreau, the most frequently mentioned by teachers is his superior stance, what one survey respondent described as his "arrogance" and another as his "bullying tone." How can he criticize others' desire for material success and social acceptance when he himself failed to experience either?, some students ask. Related problems are his apparent hypocrisy (living in the woods but taking dinner with his mother or the Emersons), his emphasis on chastity, and what students perceive as his philosophical complexity. There is also the problem of his style: the sometimes complex syntax, the allusions and puns, and the unfamiliar or archaic words.

Since most students will encounter the virtues and problems of Thoreau's writing through *Walden*, this volume focuses most heavily on that work. It should ideally be taught in its entirety, of course, but respondents to my survey indicated that most instructors of lower-level classes and a significant number of instructors of survey courses use only selected chapters. The chapters most often selected suggest an interesting pattern of instructors' emphases or expectations (and those of anthology editors) about reader responses to the various parts of the book. According to the survey, the formal structure of *Walden* as perceived by college instructors is essentially a three-part structure that focuses on the symbol of the pond. In the "plot" of *Walden* (undergraduates often view it as if it were a novel) there appear to be three crucial chapters: "Where I Lived, and What I Lived For," "The Ponds," and "Spring"; interest in other chapters clusters around these three.

The further Thoreau strays from the central symbol of the pond into his cabin or into the world of human affairs, the less interest instructors seem to anticipate in their students. The three chapters least-often selected are "Visitors," "Housewarming," and "Former Inhabitants; and Winter Visitors." When Thoreau steps inside his cabin, few seem inclined to follow him. The exception is "Economy," which might best be viewed as a special case, a prologue like Hawthorne's "Customs House" chapter in *The Scarlet Letter*, which establishes thematic motifs but is not really a part of the "main plot." Alternatively, "Economy" might be seen as a diagnosis of social and spiritual problems for which the rest of the book suggests cures.

While my survey indicates the chapters that instructors find most fruitful to teach, one should also consider Richard Dillman's caution in this volume. Dillman suggests that "Economy" and "Where I Lived, and What I Lived For" are the two most difficult chapters for students to understand. One survey respondent said bluntly that students "*hate* the 'Economy' chapter at first." Such comments suggest that instructors should work carefully on these two chapters to ensure that student interest continues into the rest of the book.

A large part of students' difficulty with the early chapters of *Walden* is Thoreau's purposeful establishment of a dialogic strategy: Everything his neighbors think is good he will demonstrate is bad. As I suggest further in my essay in this volume, most undergraduates have probably not ventured beyond dialogic thinking in their educations by the time they read *Walden*, so they cannot resist taking sides. Some find Thoreau's criticism of society's values reprehensible and hypocritical, some admire his rebellious spirit, but few are indifferent. Without careful guidance and encouragement, even fewer go beyond complete rejection or acceptance to follow Thoreau into a questioning of both sides of the dialogue as the book progresses.

Perhaps, then, one of the most important things a teacher can do in introducing *Walden* or any of Thoreau's other works is to nudge students into considering Thoreau's struggle to achieve what cognitive psychologists call multiplistic thinking: the recognition that there may be some value to both sides of a dialogue and that there may be no absolute right or wrong view of an issue. For this purpose the chapter "Higher Laws" provides the most obvious example. How can Thoreau say, "I love the wild not less than the good" (*Walden* 210; see my note about sources on p. 22) when several pages later he also says, "Nature is hard to be overcome, but she must be overcome" (221), thus seeming to assert an opposition between the "wild" (nature) and the "good" (the impulse to transcend nature)? The struggle to accept, even to love, both sides of such a basic opposition is what *Walden* is about.

Thoreau presents all his writings as an exploration of the uncertainty that is life itself, and he invites us to learn to love this uncertainty too. He reminds us in "Spring" that "[a]t the same time that we are earnest to explore and learn all things, we require that all things be mysterious and unexplorable" (317–18). If students can be nudged into seeing *Walden* and Thoreau's other works as journeys toward an acceptance of the wonderful yet frightening uncertainties of life, into seeing that they themselves have "several more lives to live" (323) then some genuine education will have occurred in their movement from dialogic toward multiplistic thinking.

One volume cannot hope to cope adequately with all the ways in which students can be guided into the exploration of Thoreau's writing or with all the kinds of courses in which Thoreau can be appropriately included; nor will a teaching technique that works for one teacher necessarily work for another. However, the aim of this volume is to provide models and suggestions to help teachers guide their students down some of the many paths that Thoreau's writing invites us to explore. While all these essays are grounded to some extent in critical theory, the emphasis is—as I think Thoreau would wish it to be—on practical classroom strategies and issues.

An editor can only hope, however, that the readers of this book will heed Thoreau's advice and "accept such portions as apply to them. I trust that none will stretch the seams in putting on the coat, for it may do good service to him whom it fits" (4).

Part One

MATERIALS

Classroom Texts

Respondents to my survey indicate that the text of *Walden* most often used in undergraduate courses, particularly survey courses, is that in *The Norton Anthology of American Literature* (Baym et al.). Like most current anthologies, the Norton includes the complete text of *Walden*, as well as several of Thoreau's essays and a sampling of his Journal entries. Many of the major publishing companies have anthologies of American literature, each of which is used by fewer professors. Of these collections, the most obviously different from the Norton is *The Heath Anthology of American Literature* (Lauter et al.). Although the Heath contains less Thoreau—only four chapters, for example, from *Walden* ("Where I Lived," "Higher Laws," "Spring," and "Conclusion"), its drastic expansion of the canon to include marginalized voices invites fruitful comparisons of Thoreau with other writers who have lived "border lives" in American society. (See Meem's and Johnson's comments in this volume.)

All the anthologies contain "Civil Disobedience," sometimes under the title "Resistance to Civil Government." Which title is more defensible has been much debated, but this volume follows Fritz Oehlschlaeger's recent argument in favor of the former title.

The range of freshman readers containing either selections from *Walden* or "Civil Disobedience" is too wide to be included here. However, for those who want to teach Thoreau in an interdisciplinary course, several anthologies of nature writing may be useful. *The Wilderness Reader* (Bergon) and *This Incomperable Lande* (T. Lyon) include only American writers; the latter has an excellent annotated bibliography. *The Norton Book of Nature Writing* (Finch and Elder) and *The Literature of Nature: The British and American Traditions* (Begiebing and Grumbling) include British and European in addition to American writers.

For professors who prefer a separate paperback edition of *Walden*, there are at least fifteen available at this writing. The most frequently used is the Norton Critical Edition, Walden *and "Civil Disobedience"* (Rossi), which has recently been updated to include new critical essays. If one does not need the critical essays of the Norton edition, the Princeton paperback edition (Shanley), which is introduced by Joyce Carol Oates, is an affordable version of the standard *Walden* text approved by the Modern Language Association's Committee on Scholarly Editions. The Penguin Walden *and "Civil Disobedience"* (Meyer) is also popular, having good annotations and a low price. The Riverside edition (Paul) is another frequently used edition. *The Variorum* Walden *and "Civil Disobedience"* (Harding), although out of print, is a useful resource for teachers because of its annotations, as is *The Annotated* Walden (Stern), a hardbound edition with plentiful illustrations.

Volumes containing *Walden* amid a wider selection of Thoreau's works include *The Portable Thoreau* (Bode) and the Modern Library edition of Walden *and Other Writings* (Howarth). Both contain the complete *Walden*, as well as selections from Thoreau's other books, and the Journal. Both are useful for those who wish to give students a sampling of Thoreau's range. However, the selections in them tend to be idiosyncratic: Bode's book contains a wide selection of poems; Howarth's contains no poems and makes unannounced mergings of chapters from *A Week on the Concord and Merrimack Rivers*. These two collections are thus unlikely to satisfy a teacher hoping to capture the full scope of Thoreau's writings.

To capture that scope, perhaps the best single volume is the Library of America's volume containing the complete texts of *A Week, Walden, The Maine Woods*, and *Cape Cod* (*Thoreau:* A Week [Sayre]), which contains the complete texts of all four books. Possible supplements to these works would be *Great Short Works of Henry David Thoreau* (Glick), *The Natural History Essays* (Sattelmeyer), and *The Essays of Henry David Thoreau* (Dillman). Two readily available paperbacks of selections from Thoreau's Journal are the Signet *Selected Journals of Henry D. Thoreau* (Bode), and the Dover *The Heart of Thoreau's Journals* (Shepard). A more recent selection, *Henry David Thoreau: An American Landscape* (Rothwell) focuses on Journal entries about nature. *A Year in Thoreau's Journal: 1851* (Peck) provides the option of focusing on just one complete year from the Journal. Some combination of these books should prove workable to professors devoting an entire course to Thoreau. However, we still need a more comprehensive single compilation of Thoreau's short works and Journal selections to supplement the Sayre volume.

The multivolume Princeton University Press edition of *The Writings of Henry D. Thoreau* is the standard edition of all the works Princeton has published so far. Walter Harding and William Howarth served as editors in chief for early volumes of the Princeton edition; the current editor in chief is Elizabeth Hall Witherell. (These volumes are listed separately, by title, under Thoreau in the works-cited list.) Unless otherwise indicated, references to Thoreau's works throughout this book are to that edition.

For those parts of the Journal not yet published in the Princeton edition, the standard edition remains *The Writings of Henry David Thoreau* (1906) in either the Manuscript, or Walden, edition, as it is known, or the two-volume Dover reprint (1962). However, *The Correspondence of Henry David Thoreau* (Harding and Bode, 1958) supersedes the 1906 Walden edition of *Familiar Letters*. For Thoreau's poetry the best current edition is *Collected Poems of Henry Thoreau* (Bode). Thoreau's manuscript titled "The Dispersion of Seeds" and some of his other late natural history writings have recently been published for the first time, under the title *Faith in a Seed* (Dean).

Biographical Works

The standard biography of Thoreau is Walter Harding's *The Days of Henry Thoreau*, which is the place to start for the facts of Thoreau's life. Raymond Borst's recent *The Thoreau Log* provides a valuable supplement to Harding's work by presenting a day-by-day listing of Thoreau's activities, about which we have a remarkably large amount of information because of the author's Journal and the journals of his contemporaries. Richard Lebeaux's *Young Man Thoreau* and *Thoreau's Seasons* present an interesting two-volume psychological biography that contains many important insights. Robert D. Richardson's *Henry David Thoreau: A Life of the Mind* is the best account of Thoreau's intellectual development. Using Thoreau's reading as a touchstone, Richardson presents a fascinating exploration of the growth of the writer's mind. In *Thoreau's Reading*, Robert Sattelmeyer discusses Thoreau's reading more briefly and provides a useful bibliographical catalog of everything Thoreau is known to have read.
Brief accounts of Thoreau by his contemporaries are collected in *Thoreau: Man of Concord* (Harding), recently republished as *Thoreau As Seen by His Contemporaries*; especially influential have been the views of Ralph Waldo Emerson (mostly favorable but condescending) and James Russell Lowell (emphatically unfavorable). Book-length accounts by people who knew Thoreau that can provide teachable personal anecdotes include those by William Ellery Channing, Annie Russell Marble, Horace Hosmer, and Edward Emerson.

For those teaching Thoreau for the first time, either of the two recent brief introductions to his life and writing, Richard J. Schneider's *Henry David Thoreau* and Edward Wagenknecht's *Henry David Thoreau: What Manner of Man?*, is a good place to start. F. O. Matthiessen's pioneering study in *The American Renaissance* focuses on Thoreau as a writer and continues to be essential reading for students and teachers. The closest thing to a comprehensive critical biography is still Sherman Paul's excellent *The Shores of America*, but at present no book fully synthesizes the wealth of material we have on Thoreau's life with critical assessments of his works.

For additional materials on Thoreau, there are two recent annotated bibliographies: *The New Thoreau Handbook* (Harding and Meyer) and Michael Meyer's section on Thoreau in *The Transcendentalists: A Review of Research and Criticism* (Myerson). For subsequent works consult the ongoing bibliographies in the *Thoreau Society Bulletin*, the *MLA Bibliography*, *American Literary Scholarship: An Annual*, or the *Bibliography of American Literature*.

General Studies of Thoreau and His Times

Because of the availability of the Harding and Meyer and the Meyer bibliographies, this bibliographic essay and the following essays do not attempt to be comprehensive but focus on materials especially useful for the classroom, either as student assignments or as background for teachers, and on the best of recent materials.

Thoreau's writing has always created controversy and should continue to do so in the classroom. Therefore teachers may find useful Meyer's *Several More Lives to Live*, which chronicles the pendulum swings of Thoreau's reputation in various periods of American history. For students, classic appreciations of Thoreau that should still spark interest are E. B. White's essays and Stanley Edgar Hyman's "Henry Thoreau in Our Time." More recent brief appreciations are Robert Bly's "The Greatness of Thoreau," Joyce Carol Oates's "The Mysterious Mr. Thoreau," and David Shi's "Thoreau for Commuters." For negative appraisals of Thoreau that are sure to spur discussion, see George Hochfield's "Anti-Thoreau" or portions of Richard Bridgman's book *Dark Thoreau*. Leon Edel's earlier brief study of Thoreau in the University of Minnesota pamphlet series on American writers is also decidedly negative.

Both students and teachers will need some background on Thoreau's place in the intellectual movements of his time, especially European and British Romanticism and American transcendentalism. For Romanticism see Perry Miller's early assessment "Thoreau in the Context of International Romanticism." A recent reassessment of the topic is Lorrie Smith's "Walking from England to America: Re-viewing Thoreau's Romanticism." Books that focus on Thoreau's Romanticism include James McIntosh's *Thoreau as Romantic Naturalist*, Frederick Garber's *Thoreau's Redemptive Imagination*, and Robert Weisbuch's *Atlantic Double Cross*.

To understand Thoreau's relation to American transcendentalism, students and teachers might turn first to Ralph Waldo Emerson's works, especially *Nature*, "The American Scholar," "The Divinity School Address," "Self-Reliance," "The Transcendentalist," and, of course, "Thoreau." Joel Porte's *Emerson and Thoreau* examines in detail the philosophical relation between the two transcendentalists. Alexander Kern's essay "The Rise of Transcendentalism, 1815–1860" provides a useful brief introduction to Thoreau's place in transcendentalism, as does Lawrence Buell's more recent chapter on transcendentalism in the *Columbia Literary History of the United States*. In his comprehensive study *Literary Transcendentalism*, Buell has also written an important assessment of Thoreau as transcendentalist. Some students might find interesting the connection between transcendentalism and Oriental religions explored in Arthur Christy's *The Orient in American Transcendentalism*. Two helpful anthologies of critical essays on transcendentalism are Brian Barbour's *American Transcendentalism* and Philip Gura and Joel Myerson's *Critical Essays on American Transcendentalism*.

Two paperback anthologies of the transcendentalists' writings might also prove useful: Hochfield's *Selected Writings of the American Transcendentalists*, for its general introduction to transcendentalism, and Miller's *The American Transcendentalists*, for its juxtaposition of selections from Thoreau with those from other transcendentalists. Miller's earlier *The Transcendentalists: An Anthology* provides more extensive selections.

To understand Thoreau's writing, one needs to understand his goals as a student of language and as a professional writer. An important study of the difference between Emerson's and Thoreau's symbolic uses of language is Charles Feidelson's *Symbolism and American Literature*. For Thoreau's interest in language theory, see Annette Woodlief's "The Influence of Theories of Rhetoric on Thoreau," Richard Dillman's "The Psychological Rhetoric of *Walden*" (as well as his three articles in the *Bucknell Review*), Kevin J. H. Dettmar's "Ransacking the Root Cellar: The Appeal to/of Etymology in *Walden*," and Michael West's important essay "Scatology and Eschatology: The Heroic Dimensions of Thoreau's Wordplay." The most comprehensive discussion of the topic is Gura's *The Wisdom of Words*. The most recent discussion of Thoreau's rhetoric, focusing on his narrative voice, is Henry Golemba's *Thoreau's Wild Rhetoric*.

Several books explore Thoreau's career as a professional writer. Stephen Adams and Donald Ross discuss Thoreau's revision process in *Revising Mythologies*. Steven Fink focuses on Thoreau's pre-*Walden* attempts to establish himself as a writer in *Prophet in the Marketplace*, and Michael Gilmore examines Thoreau's ambivalent relation to the economics of publishing in *American Romanticism and the Marketplace*.

Because Thoreau's writing is widely viewed as representing criticisms of American nineteenth-century culture that were in the air in his day, many studies of the relation between literature and nineteenth-century American culture include him. Two classic studies still worth reading are R. W. B. Lewis's *The American Adam* and Leo Marx's *The Machine in the Garden*. Among the host of other studies, those by Sacvan Bercovitch, Irving Howe, Alfred Kazin, and Larzer Ziff stand out as particularly thought-provoking; they all wrestle with the conflict between Thoreau's personal and social impulses. Buell explores Thoreau's relation to New England village culture in *New England Literary Culture*. Robert Gross's essay "'The Most Estimable Place in All the World'" is also helpful on the subject of Thoreau's relation to his social background. In *Beneath the American Renaissance*, David S. Reynolds sees Thoreau as using a subversive form of popular humor to criticize American culture.

What currently attracts the most student interest in Thoreau is his expression of the American preoccupation with nature. Although most books and essays on Thoreau necessarily address this issue, some focus on his abilities as naturalist and ecologist. Useful histories of the idea of ecology are Donald Worster's *Nature's Economy* and Max Oelschlaeger's *The Idea of Wilderness: From Prehistory to the Age of Ecology*. Roderick Nash's critiques of the American ambivalence about nature, such as *Wilderness and the American Mind* and *The Rights of Nature*, also present Thoreau as an important figure. Two studies about Thoreau as a pioneer ecologist are by Philip Whitford and Kathryn Whitford and by William J. Wolf. For Thoreau in the tradition of natural history writing, see John Hildebidle's *Thoreau: A Naturalist's Liberty*. Philip Hicks in *The Development of the Natural History Essay in American Literature* discusses Thoreau's influence on subsequent nature writers, as do Paul O. Williams in "The Influence of Thoreau on the American Nature Essay" and Scott Slovic in his chapter on Thoreau in *Seeking Awareness in American Nature Writing*. See also Cecilia Tichi's *New World, New Earth* for a discussion of Thoreau in the context of American attitudes toward nature.

Thoreau used the techniques of various branches of science to create an organic approach to nature. His abilities as a naturalist have not always been admired. For a sampling of the controversy over his skills, see the essays by Fanny Eckstorm (who attacks Thoreau) and Mary P. Sherwood (who defends him). A balanced general view of Thoreau's scientific abilities is provided by Harding's "Walden's Man of Science." See also Nina Baym's "Thoreau's View of Science." For studies of Thoreau's interest in specific branches of science, see Lawrence Willson's "Thoreau and New England's Weather" (meteorology), Kathryn Whitford's "Thoreau and the Woodlots of Concord" (plant succession), and Schneider's "Reflections in Walden Pond" (optics). Further discussion of Thoreau's interest in optics can be found in Judith P. Saunders's "'A Different Angle.'" Richardson's discussions of Thoreau's interest in Louis Agassiz and Charles Darwin in *Henry David Thoreau: A Life of the Mind* help put Thoreau in the context of the scientific controversies of his time. Two other recent essays are especially important in relating Thoreau's interest in science to his philosophical development: Robert Sattelmeyer and Richard Hocks's essay "Thoreau and Coleridge's *Theory of Life*" and William Rossi's "Roots, Leaves, and Method: Henry Thoreau and Nineteenth-Century Natural Science."

Thoreau viewed nature artistically as well as scientifically. Although he did not always speak favorably of the visual arts, it is nonetheless clear that he was influenced by both the paintings in galleries and the illustrations in popular magazines. The earliest significant assessment of this interest is Norman Foerster's "Thoreau as Artist." Since then, prompted by the art historian Barbara Novak's association of Thoreau with luminist painters in *American Painting of the Nineteenth Century* and in *Nature and Culture*, a spate of articles has explored the luminist connection. See Barton Levi St. Armand's "Luminism in the Work of Henry David Thoreau," John Conron's "'Bright American Rivers,'" Kevin Radaker's "'A Separate Intention of the Eye,'" and the references to Thoreau in John Wilmerding's *American Light*. Schneider's "Thoreau and Nineteenth-Century American Landscape Painting" extends the discussion to a wider range of painting styles.

The other most obvious topic of interest to students is Thoreau's social and political criticism. Two good introductions to Thoreau's social views are Shi's *The Simple Life*, which compares Thoreau with other American figures who advocated a simple lifestyle, and Mary Elkins Moller's *Thoreau in the Human Community*, which discusses Thoreau's personal relations with those closest to him. Students may also find interesting Frank Levering and Wanda Urbanska's *Simple Living: One Couple's Search for a Better Life*, a recent account of a married couple who sought a more meaningful life by leaving Los Angeles to run a fruit orchard in the Blue Ridge Mountains. Douglas Anderson considers Thoreau's ideas about family life in *A House Undivided: Domesticity and Community in American Literature*. For Thoreau's views of architecture and the social and psychological ideas they imply, see Edward Foster's *The Civilized Wilderness*, Robert Harrington's chapter "The Woods of Walden" in *Forests*, and the essays by Richard Masteller and Jean Carwile Masteller and by Paul McCarthy. For a consideration of gender roles in Thoreau's work, see Ann Douglas's *The Feminization of American Culture*, David Leverenz's *Manhood in the American Renaissance*, and Harding's "Thoreau's Sexuality."

Thoreau seems to have shared the concerns and at least some of the prejudices of American society regarding minority racial and ethnic groups. For his view of the Irish immigrants, for instance, see George Ryan's essay. Recently, however, it is Thoreau's view of Native Americans that has attracted the most attention. The fullest discussion of this topic is in Robert Sayre's *Thoreau and the American Indians*, but see also Richard Fleck's *Henry Thoreau and John Muir among the Indians*. Briefer studies include essays by Linda Frost, Philip Gura ("Thoreau's Maine Woods Indians"), Linck C. Johnson ("Into History"), Lauriat Lane ("Thoreau's Autumnal Indians"), Donald M. Murray, and Jarold Ramsey.

No books deal specifically with Thoreau's response to slavery, but a good selection of essays is available. In "Thoreau and Radical Abolitionism" Wendell Glick considers the question of why Thoreau did not formally join the abolitionist movement despite his sympathies with it and his involvement in the Underground Railroad. In "Thoreau and John Brown," Truman Nelson suggests that the slavery issue led Thoreau to abandon passive resistance. In "Thoreau's Rescue of John Brown from History," Meyer discusses how much Thoreau knew about John Brown's use of violence, and in "Thoreau and Black Emigration," he explores the possibility that Thoreau approved of the mass exportation of African Americans as a solution to slavery. See also background material in Deborah McDowell and Arnold Rampersad's *Slavery and the Literary Imagination*.

Thoreau's interest in slavery was part of his overriding concern about the relation between the individual and the state. Taylor Stoehr compares Thoreau's view on this topic with those of his Concord neighbors, Emerson and Alcott, in *Nay-Saying in Concord*. James Duban discusses the roots of Thoreau's political thought in Christianity, especially Unitarianism, in "Conscience and Consciousness: The Liberal Christian Context of Thoreau's Political Ethics." Two interesting essays on Thoreau's view of government are Lewis Lipsitz's "If, As Verba Says, the State Functions as a Religion" and William Herr's "A More

Perfect State." For the debate on whether Thoreau was an anarchist, see the essays by Richard Drinnon, Eunice Schuster, and John Broderick ("Thoreau's Proposals for Legislation"). For provocative negative views of Thoreau's politics, see the essays by Heinz Eulau and Vincent Buranelli. Ralph Ketcham, in his "Reply," defends Thoreau against Buranelli's attack. Barry Kritzberg provides a convenient brief chronicle of Thoreau's main political concerns in "Thoreau, Slavery, and Resistance to Civil Government." Meyer's *Several More Lives to Live* contains a comprehensive survey of shifting attitudes, both pro and con, toward Thoreau's political views.

Thoreau's understanding of the relation between politics and economy pervades his writings. For many years the standard discussion of Thoreau's economic views has been Leo Stoller's *After* Walden. Recently it was joined by Leonard Neufeldt's *The Economist*, a reassessment of the cultural roots of Thoreau's economic ideas. For briefer discussions of Thoreau's economic views, see the essays by Francis Dedmond and by Thomas Woodson. For historical background on the agricultural economy of Concord and on Thoreau's view of farming, see Gross's "Culture and Cultivation" and "The Great Bean-Field Hoax." Herbert Smith in "Thoreau among the Classical Economists" and Dillman in "Thoreau's Human Economy" both discuss how Thoreau was influenced by classical economists.

Critical Commentary on *Walden*

Most of the books and essays listed above necessarily include historical background or critical commentary on *Walden*. There is, however, also a large body of criticism specifically on *Walden*. An excellent bibliographical guide to such criticism is Woodlief's "*Walden*: A Checklist of Literary Criticism through 1973." Unfortunately no comprehensive single checklist exists for criticism on *Walden* after 1973.

Thoreau kept many of his preliminary manuscripts, from which his process of composition and revision can be studied. In his pioneer study *The Making of* Walden, J. Lyndon Shanley demonstrates the seven stages of revision that Thoreau took the book through between 1846 and 1854. Sattelmeyer provides an excellent updated discussion of Thoreau's revisions in "The Remaking of *Walden*." Both these studies are required reading for anyone teaching *Walden*, as well as important reading for upper-level undergraduates.

Modern criticism of *Walden* begins with Matthiessen's chapters on Thoreau in *The American Renaissance*. Since Matthiessen, the best book-length studies of *Walden* are Charles R. Anderson's *The Magic Circle of* Walden and Stanley Cavell's *The Senses of* Walden. Anderson's is a close formalist reading of the book following in Matthiessen's footsteps; Cavell's is a brief, difficult, but rich, philosophically based study of *Walden* as a book as much about its own writing as about nature. Strongest among more recent books about *Walden* is Martin Bickman's *Volatile Truths*, which convincingly presents *Walden* as Thoreau's ongoing search for truth. Other recent books on *Walden* are Gordon Boudreau's *The Roots of* Walden *and the Tree of Life* and William C. Johnson's *What Thoreau Said:* Walden *and the Unsayable*.

For students, perhaps the most teachable essay-length introduction to *Walden* is Harding's "Five Ways of Looking at *Walden*." Also useful as a general introduction is Linck Johnson's "Revolution and Renewal: The Genres of *Walden*." For teachers, the debate about student responses to *Walden* in the 1956–57 essays by Louis B. Salomon and by Wade C. Thompson is still instructive. Useful especially to those teaching *Walden* for the first time is Harding's brief article "On Teaching *Walden*."

The criticism of *Walden* after the publication of Matthiessen's *The American Renaissance* was dominated by formalist studies of structure, symbolism, and style. Woodlief's bibliography provides a comprehensive list of such studies, but among the best are those given in the next two paragraphs.

Lane's "On the Organic Structure of *Walden*" is still a useful introduction to the structure of *Walden*. John C. Broderick's "The Movement of Thoreau's Prose," Leo Marx's "Thoreau's Excursions," and Tony Tanner's "Thoreau and the Sauntering Eye" all discuss the walking excursion as a controlling structure. Joseph Moldenhauer discusses paradox as a structural device in "Paradox in *Walden*."

Studies of the symbolism of *Walden* abound. Among them, Melvin Lyon's "Walden Pond as a Symbol" is the most comprehensive. Other studies of specific symbols include Broderick's "Imagery in *Walden*" (morning), Moldenhauer's "Images of Circularity in Thoreau's Prose," Albert McLean's "Thoreau's True Meridian" (surveying), Richard Colyer's "Thoreau's Color Symbols," and Rosemary Whitaker's "*A Week* and *Walden*: The River vs. the Pond" (water).

Although Thoreau scholars have been cautious about applying postmodern critical approaches to Thoreau, critics have recently found his paradoxes and ambiguities particularly susceptible to deconstructive and Bakhtinian approaches. The deconstructive approach, which emphasizes Thoreau's inability to reconcile the many contradictions and uncertainties in his writing, is in direct opposition to formalist attempts to demonstrate such reconciliation within individual texts. The Bakhtinian approach also emphasizes the multiple meanings of *Walden* but focuses on Thoreau's stance as an outsider, a subversive critic of the established society.

The landmark deconstructive reading of *Walden* is Walter Benn Michaels's "Walden's False Bottoms," in which Michaels claims that the paradoxes of *Walden* are essentially unresolvable. Joseph Allen Boone responds to Michaels with a more traditional close reading in "Delving and Diving for Truth: Breaking Through to Bottom in Thoreau's *Walden*." For other deconstructive readings, see the essays by Kevin J. H. Dettmar, Henry Golemba, Barbara Johnson, and especially Michael R. Fischer's summary of the problems Thoreau poses for deconstructionists. Bakhtinian approaches can be found in Gilmore's *American Romanticism and the Marketplace*, Malini Schueller's "Carnival Rhetoric and Extra-Vagance in Thoreau's *Walden*," and Joseph Adamson's "The Trials of Thoreau." Reynolds's chapter on Thoreau in *Beneath the American Renaissance* also focuses on his subversive qualities.

Until recently, feminist critics have mostly ignored Thoreau perhaps because he is a pitifully easy target given the scarcity of women in his writing and his frequently negative comments when they do appear. Irene C. Goldman's "Feminism, Deconstruction, and the Universal: A Case Study of *Walden*" provides a first application of a feminist perspective to Thoreau's writing. Other essays that express feminist concerns are Meg McGavran Murray's "Thoreau's Moon Mythology" and Oates's "The Mysterious Mr. Thoreau." Most recently, the premier issue of *ISLE* (*Interdisciplinary Studies in Literature and Environment*) includes four brief feminist critiques of *Walden*, by Leonard Scigaj and Nancy Craig Simmons, by Leigh Kirkland, by Laura Dassow Walls, and by Louise Westling. The Kirkland and Walls essays make a particularly teachable pair, the first chiding Thoreau for not transcending the sexism of his time and the second defending *Walden* as a "feminist manifesto."

Critics frequently discuss specific chapters or even specific passages from *Walden*. Lane's "Thoreau's *Walden*, I, Paragraphs 1–3" and Golemba's "Unreading Thoreau" give detailed attention to the opening pages of *Walden*. Probably the most often written-about passage in *Walden* is the cryptic hound, bay horse, and turtle-dove passage in "Economy" (17). A recent treatment of this passage is Barbara Johnson's "A Hound, a Bay Horse, and a Turtle-Dove: Obscurity in *Walden*." Johnson surveys earlier discussions of the passage, as does Harding in his endnote 44 to *Walden* in *The Variorum* Walden *and "Civil Disobedience."* Another frequently discussed passage is that about the thawing sand in the "deep cut" by the railroad track in "Spring" (304–09). The most detailed readings of this passage are in Gura's *The Wisdom of Words*, Michael Orth's "The Prose Style of Henry Thoreau," and Boudreau's *The Roots of* Walden; but most full discussions of *Walden* necessarily deal with it as central to the meaning of the book.

Other essays focus on specific chapters. Thomas Woodson's "The Two Beginnings of *Walden*" provides an excellent discussion of how "Economy" and "Where I Lived, and What I Lived For" were shaped from Journal passages and lectures. Woodson's "Thoreau on Poverty and Magnanimity" also discusses issues central to "Economy." A *Consumer Reports* article titled "Has Our Living Standard Stalled?" might be useful to teachers of "Economy" for its chart of the relative costs, in minutes, hours, and days of labor, of common items in the 1960s through the 1990s.

For discussions of other chapters, see Paul's "The Wise Silence" ("Sounds"); Judy Schaaf Anhorn's "Thoreau in the Beanfield"; Stuart Woodruff's "Thoreau as Water-Gazer" and Neill R. Joy's "Two Possible Analogies for 'The Ponds'" ("The Ponds"); Lawrence Scanlon's "Thoreau's Parable of Baker Farm";

Thomas Blanding's "Walton and *Walden*" and Suzanne Rose's "Following the Trail of Footsteps" ("Brute Neighbors"); Jim Springer Borck and Herbert B. Rothschild's "Meditative Discoveries" ("The Pond in Winter"); and Edward J. Rose's "'A World of Full and Fair Proportions'" ("Conclusion").

Another facet of *Walden* that interests critics is Thoreau's humor, for discussions of which see especially Raymond Adams's "Thoreau's Mock-Heroics," M. Thomas Inge's "Thoreau's Humor in *Walden*," and Edward L. Galligan's "The Comedian at Walden Pond." A useful book-length study is J. Golden Taylor's *Neighbor Thoreau's Critical Humor*. See also the comments on Thoreau in Jesse Bier's *The Rise and Fall of American Humor*. Because so much of Thoreau's humor involves puns, many of the works listed above in the paragraphs on Thoreau's interest in language theory are also pertinent. See especially West's "Scatology and Eschatology."

Given the frequency with which essays on *Walden* appear, many teachers will find it convenient to consult the various collections of critical essays that have been published over the years. The most readily available, in chronological order, are the following: Lane's *Aproaches to* Walden (1961), Richard Ruland's *Twentieth Century Interpretations of* Walden (1968), Moldenhauer's *The Merrill Studies in* Walden (1971), Harold Bloom's *Modern Critical Views of* Walden (1987), Myerson's *Critical Essays on Henry David Thoreau's* Walden (1988), Rossi's updated Norton Critical Edition Walden *and "Civil Disobedience"* (1992), and Robert Sayre's *New Essays on* Walden (1992). All these collections are useful, although Bloom's takes a decidedly negative appproach to Thoreau and contains an erroneous chronology. The most comprehensive are Lane's and Myerson's; the ones most in tune with postmodern critical views are those by Rossi and by Sayre.

Critical Commentary on "Civil Disobedience" and Other Works

With "Civil Disobedience," teachers will first need to get straight the facts of Thoreau's incarceration. One account is in Harding's *Days*; for evidence that Thoreau's arrest was illegal, see also Harding's "Was It Legal? Thoreau in Jail."

The publication history of "Civil Disobedience," especially its title, has been much debated since Wendell Glick's decision to use "Resistance to Civil Government" as the title in the 1973 Princeton edition of the reform papers. For the teacher the best tactic is probably to start at the most recent end of the controversy, with Fritz Oehlschlaeger's "Another Look at the Text and Title of Thoreau's 'Civil Disobedience,'" because Oehlschlaeger chronicles the swings of the debate as well as discusses its significance.

The idea of passive resistance that Thoreau espouses in "Civil Disobedience" has always inspired strong controversy. To spark such discussion in students, two negative views are surefire, Lewis Van Dusen's "Civil Disobedience: Destroyer of Democracy" and Alfred Kazin's "Thoreau and American Power." See also the essays by Eulau and Buranelli previously mentioned. The most carefully argued defense of Thoreau's political views is John Aldrich Christie's "Thoreau on Civil Disobedience." William Herr in "Thoreau: A Civil Disobedient?" draws a distinction between Thoreau as conscientious objector and as civil disobedient, which might stir class discussion, as might Drinnon's consideration, in "Thoreau's Politics of the Upright Man," of whether Thoreau should be considered an anarchist.

Other helpful essays on "Civil Disobedience" are Wendell Glick's " 'Civil Disobedience': Thoreau's Attack on Relativism," Michael Erlich's "Thoreau's 'Civil Disobedience': Strategy for Reform," and Barry Wood's "Thoreau's Narrative Art in 'Civil Disobedience.' " See also the books and essays listed above in the paragraphs on Thoreau's politics.

It has recently become clear that "Civil Disobedience" is best studied in relation to Thoreau's other reform essays, especially those on John Brown. For discussion of the John Brown essays, see the books and essays listed above on Thoreau's interest in abolition, especially Meyer's "Thoreau's Rescue of John Brown from History." But see also Robert C. Albrecht's "Thoreau and His Audience: 'A Plea for Captain John Brown,' " Lane's "Thoreau's Autumnal Archetypal Hero," and, for a comparison of Thoreau's view of John Brown with Melville's, Woodson's "Thoreau on Poverty and Magnanimity."

A Week on the Concord and Merrimack Rivers, though probably taught rarely in its entirety, is essential for upper-level seminars on Thoreau and exceptionally helpful for comparison with Walden, if only through brief excerpts. The essential work on A Week is Linck Johnson's Thoreau's Complex Weave: The Writing of A Week on the Concord and Merrimack Rivers, which provides the text of Thoreau's first draft and a comprehensive discussion of how Thoreau wrote the book. The best early essays about A Week are those by Carl Hovde on how Thoreau used his Journal as well as other literary materials in writing the book and by Jonathan Bishop on Thoreau's interest in the sacred. Among the most helpful of more recent essays are those by Fink on Thoreau's changing personae, Radaker on the relation between A Week and luminist painting, H. Daniel Peck on Thoreau's concern with memory, and Marvin Fisher on the relations among Thoreau's interests in anthropology, ecology, and theology.

The Maine Woods is usually taught in its entirety only in seminars on Thoreau, but excerpts from its three essays appear in most collections of Thoreau's works and in some anthologies of nature writing. The best source of factual background on Thoreau's three trips to the Maine woods is J. Parker Huber's The Wildest Country: A Guide to Thoreau's Maine, which provides itineraries, maps, and pictures of the people and places mentioned in Thoreau's book. The essay from The Maine Woods most frequently taught is "Ktaadn," his account of climbing Maine's highest mountain. For background on Thoreau's interest in mountain climbing, see *Thoreau in the Mountains*, a collection edited by William Howarth. "Ktaadn" has been the source of perhaps the most heated controversy in Thoreau criticism, on the question of whether Thoreau's encounter with the wilderness on Mount Katahdin undermined or confirmed his transcendentalism. Summaries of this controversy can be found in Jonathan Fairbanks's "Thoreau: Speaker for Wildness" and Schneider's chapter on *The Maine Woods* in his *Henry David Thoreau*. The majority view seems to be that Thoreau did to some extent question his transcendentalism as a result of climbing Katahdin. A well-argued dissenting view is Ronald Hoag's "The Mark on the Wilderness," which also contains a summary of earlier views.

Discussions of other portions of *The Maine Woods* usually focus on Thoreau's account in "Chesuncook" of the killing of a moose or on his interest in Indians, particularly his two Indian guides, Joe Aitteon in "Chesuncook" and Joe Polis in "The Allegash and East Branch." For the former topic, see Thomas L. Altherr's essay on Thoreau's attitude toward hunting; for Thoreau's interest in Indians, see the works cited above in the paragraphs on minority and ethnic groups. The last two *Maine Woods* essays also contain frequent scientific observations of nature, and there has been some controversy over the accuracy of Thoreau's scientific methods. Those interested in that controversy as it pertains to *The Maine Woods* should see the essays by Eckstorm and by Sherwood cited above in the paragraphs on nature.

Of Thoreau's nature essays, the most frequently anthologized and taught is "Walking." A not quite seamless joining of Thoreau's thoughts on two of his favorite topics, the art of sauntering and the importance of wilderness, "Walking" is the next best thing to *Walden* for introducing students to his views of nature. To place "Walking" in the context of Thoreau's other nature essays, see Sattelmeyer's introduction to his edition of *The Natural History Essays*. There are not many essays devoted specifically to "Walking," but among the few before 1980 are those by Garber and David L. James. More recent essays are those by Kenneth V. Egan, Lorrie Smith, and Rossi. The last two focus on the essay's relation to British Romanticism.

There has been increasing interest in Thoreau's Journal, both as background for his published works and as a work having literary merit of its own. Two recent books are devoted entirely to the Journal. The first, Howarth's *The Book of Concord*, focuses on how the Journal expresses Thoreau's interest in Concord as a microcosm of the world and as a literary metaphor. The second, Sharon Cameron's *Writing Nature*, provides a deconstructive close reading of a number of passages to demonstrate Thoreau's use of the Journal as an end in itself, not just as a testing ground for material to be included later in published books and essays. The most recent studies are the fine sections on the Journal in Joan Burbick's book and in Peck's. The length of the Journal makes it difficult to handle in an essay format, but there are nonetheless several good recent essays: Rossi's "Roots, Leaves, and Method," which deals with Thoreau's use of the natural sciences in the Journal; Peck's "Killing Time / Keeping Time," which explores the Journal as a means of confronting the problem of time and mutability; and Slovic's chapter on the Journal in his *Seeking Awareness*, which views the Journal as Thoreau's way of exploring his mental processes.

Thoreau has been the subject of a number of collections of reprinted essays throughout the years. The following is a selection of the most useful, listed in chronological order by publication date: *Thoreau: A Century of Criticism* (Harding, 1954), *Thoreau: A Collection of Critical Essays* (Paul, 1962), *Thoreau in Our Season* (Hicks, 1966), *The Recognition of Henry David Thoreau* (Glick, 1969), *Henry David Thoreau: A Profile* (Harding, 1971), and *Modern Critical Views of Henry David Thoreau* (Bloom, 1987). *Heaven Is under Our Feet* (Henley and Marsh, 1991), a collection of original brief tributes to Thoreau by various entertainers, public figures, authors, and scholars, may catch the interest of students because of the star power of some of the contributors, such as Jack Nicholson, Whoopi Goldberg, Jimmy Carter, and Ted Kennedy.

Visual and Sound Resources

Because one of Thoreau's main themes is the importance of truly seeing and because his imagination is so intensely visual, it is especially appropriate to use visual resources in teaching his works. Several books provide abundant pictorial supplements. See Milton Meltzer and Walter Harding's *A Thoreau Profile* for photographs, maps, newspaper clippings, and miscellaneous items on Thoreau; Philip Van Doren Stern's *The Annotated* Walden for miscellaneous pictures and photographs; Robert F. Stowell's *A Thoreau Gazeteer* for maps and other visual representations of places Thoreau visited; and Huber's *The Wildest Country* for maps and pictures of places Thoreau visited in Maine. Herbert Gleason's *Thoreau Country*, a book of photographs, can also help students envision Thoreau's environment. Photographers whose works provide analogues to Thoreau's vision are Eliot Porter and Ansel Adams.

The visual art of Thoreau's own time can help students understand the attitudes toward nature that were then current. Of particular interest are the paintings of the Hudson River school, especially Thomas Cole, and of the luminists. For discussions of these painters, accompanied by prints of their paintings, see the books by Novak and Wilmerding listed above in the paragraphs on Thoreau's views of nature. See also John K. Howat's *The Hudson River and Its Painters*. Thoreau was much interested in the illustrated guides to landscape written by the British writer William Gilpin. The paintings of John James Audubon can provide analogues to Thoreau's views of wildlife. For Thoreau's influence on twentieth-century landscape art, see Francine Amy Koslow and

Walter Harding's *Henry David Thoreau as a Source of Artistic Inspiration*. Two videotapes that can supplement discussion of Thoreau's view of landscape are Kenneth Clark's *The Romantic Rebellion* (from the PBS television series) and *The Hudson River and Its Painters* (available in the Metropolitan Museum of Art's Home Video Collection).

An increasing number of videotapes provide an introduction to Thoreau's works or a dramatization of his life. Some show scenes of Walden Pond with voice-over readings from Thoreau's works. One such videotape is from the PBS series *The Naturalists*, but it has not been reshown or advertised for sale in recent years. Other voice-over productions are *Thoreau's Walden: A Video Portrait* (Photovision, 7 Minola Rd., Lexington, MA 02173) and *Thoreau's Walden Pond* (Educational Video, 1401 19th St., Huntsville, TX 77340; this company has a similar videotape titled *Thoreau's Cape Cod*). Some instructors have found helpful the Encyclopedia Britannica's rental videotape *Talking with Thoreau: Twentieth-Century Conversations*. A recent dramatization of Thoreau is by David Barto, who does impersonations of the author at Walden Pond in the summer months. His videotape is *History of Myself at Walden: Henry David Thoreau* (Videocom, 502 Sprague St., Dedham, MA 02026). Although the effectiveness of Barto's in-person performance is not conveyed particularly well by this videotape, it may still be a useful introduction for students; it includes a list of study questions. There is a background videotape, *Concord, Massachusetts*, on the literary and historical sites of Concord; it is available through the Thoreau Lyceum (156 Belknap St., Concord, MA 01742). The Lyceum sells various slides of Walden Pond and some of the other videotapes listed above. The *Thoreau Society Bulletin* reports that Ronald Pesha, of the Department of Broadcasting, Adirondack Community College, Glens Falls, NY 12801, is currently compiling a bibliography of Thoreau-related videotapes.

Sound recordings for teaching Thoreau are also available. The Caedmon Company has recorded readings of both *Walden* and "Civil Disobedience." Audiotape readings of selections from *Walden* are among the most popular purchases for use by commuters while driving to and from work. One such audiotape is *Thoreau and Emerson: Nature and Spirit*, which contains brief portions of works by both writers read by Howard Mumford Jones, Kenneth S. Lynn, and Russ Barnett (Audio Prose Library, PO Box 842, Columbia, MO 65205).

Thoreau has inspired composers of both serious and popular music. The most well known is the "Thoreau" movement of Charles Ives's "Concord Sonata"; but students may find it difficult because, as one survey respondent quipped, "It doesn't have a beat; you can't dance to it." Thomas Oboe Lee has recently composed *That Mountain*, based on passages from Thoreau. The world-premier performance in honor of Walter Harding was in 1991, but at this writing the piece has not yet been recorded. Popular songs that provide points of departure for discussion are Linda Ronstadt and the Stone Ponies' "Different Drum" and James Taylor's "Walking Man" (the walking man is a reference to Thoreau).

Popular movies, too, can provide discussion openers, although they almost always oversimplify Thoreau's ideas. Three recent movies that contain obvious Thoreauvian themes are *Amazing Grace and Chuck* (civil disobedience), *Dead Poets Society* (the power and dangers of individualism), and *Awakenings* (psychological and spiritual renewal), but imaginative instructors can surely find many others. There are several scripts extant for plays about Thoreau, the most well known of which is Jerome Lawrence and Robert Lee's *The Night Thoreau Spent in Jail*.

The simplest visual aid used by the respondents to my survey is an object from nature—a plant, a rock, a leaf, an insect. Students are asked to observe the object daily and record their responses to it in a journal, an exercise that helps them approximate Thoreau's methods. The keeping of journals on walks in the woods, canoe trips, or overnight camping trips, or even in the classroom as a response to reading Thoreau, is also an obvious but effective way of helping students understand him.

Note: Throughout this volume references to Thoreau's works are to the standard Princeton University Press edition unless otherwise indicated. For some volumes of the Journal and other works not yet published by Princeton, the previously standard 1906 Walden edition is cited. The standard version of "Civil Disobedience" appears as "Resistance to Civil Government" in the Princeton edition of *Reform Papers* (63–90).

Part Two

APPROACHES

Introduction

One of the most difficult challenges in teaching Thoreau is to overcome students' misconception that he was a uniquely isolated figure retreating from the turmoil of his time. The essays in the first section, "Thoreau and *Walden*: Contexts," address this challenge by putting Thoreau and instructors' methods of teaching him in literary and cultural context: Linck C. Johnson discusses Thoreau's relation to the American Renaissance, Frederick Garber his relation to British and European Romanticism (especially Wordsworth, Coleridge, and Goethe), T. S. McMillin his relation to transcendentalism, and William Howarth his relation to environmental writing.

Both Garber and Howarth are interested in Thoreau's search for a location, a home, in which to root his life—a search college students should also find pertinent. The placing of this theme in two different (though related) intellectual and literary traditions should suggest pedagogical strategies. McMillin's emphasis on transcendental questioning has interesting connections to the idea of multiplistic thinking in the essays by Henry Golemba and Richard J. Schneider that follow. Readers may wish to compare Johnson's approach with Deborah Meem's use of cultural context in the next section and Howarth's approach with those of David M. Robinson and David G. Fuller in subsequent sections.

The first five essays in the second section, "Teaching *Walden*: Pedagogical and Critical Strategies," focus on both the options for teachers and the problems for students that *Walden* presents. Richard Lebeaux begins by laying before us a wealth of pedagogical options with which teachers can approach *Walden*, while Richard Dillman's reader-response study raises the question of how teachers can best deal with student preconceptions and expectations about Thoreau. Robert Franciosi and Frank J. McGill present student-centered perspectives: Franciosi shows the various and powerful effects that reading *Walden* can have on students, and McGill contrasts the effects that reading *Walden* had on him as an undergraduate student, as a high school teacher, and as a graduate student. Michael D. West's essay presents one strategy for making *Walden* more accessible through humor.

The essays by Stanley S. Blair, Scott Slovic, Annette M. Woodlief, and Deborah T. Meem discuss ways to teach *Walden* at different levels, from freshman to upper-level courses. Woodlief's essay includes some provocative and practical suggestions for a hi-tech computerized approach. Meem's essay should be read in conjunction with Johnson's essay, from the preceding section, and with

Leonard Neufeldt's, which follows hers, because it suggests further classroom application of those writers' cultural approaches to Thoreau. Leonard Neufeldt and Henry Golemba conclude with essays on how recent critical theories can affect our teaching of *Walden*, the former focusing on new historicism and the latter on deconstruction. Golemba's approach bears comparison with McMillin's essay in the preceding section and Schneider's essay in the following section.

In the third section, "Teaching Thoreau's Other Works," essays are arranged in approximate chronological order according to publication dates of the writings being discussed.

Stephen Adams's essay on *A Week on the Concord and Merrimack Rivers* suggests this early work as a text not only for understanding Thoreau but also for exposing students to genre theory. Michael Meyer and Laraine Fergenson approach "Civil Disobedience" from two very different angles: Meyer offers a revision of the usual views of Thoreau's ideas on politics and social reform, and Fergenson proposes methods for presenting Thoreau's best-known essay as a rhetorical model for composition students.

Schneider's essay compares *Walden* with excerpts from Thoreau's later works, an approach that, I suggest, can have interesting implications for the students' cognitive development (compare this idea with the approaches of McMillin and of Golemba in earlier sections). David M. Robinson's essay argues the importance of "Walking" to an understanding both of Thoreau and of current ecological theory. Robinson's essay could be read profitably in conjunction with Howarth's above and David Fuller's in the next section. Daniel Peck concludes the section with a provocative argument for teaching Thoreau's Journal both for its relation to *Walden* and, despite the difficulties of its length, for its own sake.

The titles in this section might suggest a neglect of *The Maine Woods*, but approaches to that book are included to varying extents in the Garber and Howarth essays, in Schneider's essay, and in the Fuller essay.

As a schoolmaster, Thoreau liked to take his students out of the classroom for field trips, and he himself insisted on being "extra vagant," on going beyond the usual bounds. So it seems appropriate that the three essays in the last section, "Thoreau beyond the Conventional Classroom," remind us of how going beyond the usual bounds pedagogically can put Thoreau to creative use and open up his texts to new audiences.

David Fuller reports on student responses to Thoreau taught in a wilderness environment (the Boundary Waters of Minnesota), suggesting a way to expose students practically to some of the "ecological tensions" described in David Robinson's essay in the previous section. Wesley Mott shows how Thoreau can be put to work in support of community projects. Although Mott's location is at an institution that might seem unique, being near Walden Pond and emphasizing engineering, the practical approach he describes has interesting implications for teaching Thoreau anywhere. Finally, Thoreau addresses *Walden* to students but does not specify their age, and he emphasizes throughout his writings the importance of "negative knowledge," the ongoing search for knowledge throughout a lifetime. From that perspective, what better audience is there for his works than senior citizens still eager to learn? Gordon Boudreau reports on the rewards, both for the students and for the teachers, of teaching Thoreau in Elderhostels.

Walden and the Construction
of the American Renaissance

Linck C. Johnson

Of the American "classics," *Walden* is one of the most securely canonical. In addition to being available in innumerable editions, it is frequently reprinted in its entirety in anthologies of American literature, where it takes its place with texts like Franklin's *Autobiography*, *The Scarlet Letter*, and the *Adventures of Huckleberry Finn*, the sheer bulk of which seems to proclaim their special status. Moreover, Thoreau's *Walden* clearly asserts its connections to those and other "classic" texts. Disciple of Emerson, friend of Hawthorne, and admirer of Whitman, Thoreau shared with his closest contemporaries some central concerns and anxieties: interrelated questions about the nature of perception, the relation of the individual to the community, the consequences of rapid social change, and the status of the writer in a society in which authorship was still a suspect vocation, at least for men. Partly as a result of those shared concerns, *Walden* is frequently taught in relation to other familiar works of the antebellum period, from Emerson's *Nature* and essays like "Self-Reliance" through the novels and stories of Hawthorne, Poe, and Melville to Whitman's "Song of Myself." In fact, the constellation of texts amid which *Walden* is most usually studied is probably not far different from the one mapped more than fifty years ago in F. O. Matthiessen's *American Renaissance*.

As tempting and useful as that approach to *Walden* is, it has inherent dangers and limitations. First, it tends to reaffirm a kind of monolithic conception of antebellum literature and culture, giving implicit support to certain treasured stereotypes, especially the common view that America's "best" writers were ignored or undervalued in their time. Second, it establishes as natural and universal a set of critical standards that may make it difficult for students to understand and appreciate works by less celebrated writers of the period. Finally, reading *Walden* in relation to other familiar "classics" obscures its equally close connections to popular writings of the antebellum period, especially works by women and African Americans. Critics of attempts to expand the canon and thereby to reconstruct American literary history often suggest that such efforts are inspired by social and political concerns having nothing to do with either literature or literary study. Yet surely one goal of literary study should be to help students understand that the term *literature*, in the sense of creative or imaginative works of enduring aesthetic value, emerged only in the nineteenth century; certainly that historical development informed Thoreau's commentary on books, "the oldest and the best," in the chapter "Reading" in *Walden* (102).[1] Moreover, one need not reject the critical standards that promote the teaching of "classics" to grasp the importance of approaching those texts in their fullest historical context, which for *Walden* is more varied and complex—and finally far more interesting—than the literary culture usually evoked by the phrase "the American Renaissance." Venturing beyond the established canon to explore other writings of the antebellum period therefore not only makes available for study a large body of works that are interesting and significant in their own right but also offers new perspectives on acknowledged masterpieces like *Walden*.

Although publishers have not been particularly venturesome in this area, there are now suitable teaching editions of several works that provide rich insights into *Walden*, antebellum society and culture, and our own construction of that era. The economic forces, social concerns, and cultural values that so powerfully shaped Thoreau's book are revealed in different but no less compelling ways by the most popular books of the period, novels written by, primarily for, and usually about women. Any one of the blockbuster novels of the early 1850s—Susan Warner's *The Wide, Wide World* (1850), Harriet Beecher Stowe's *Uncle Tom's Cabin* (1851), or Maria Susanna Cummins's *The Lamplighter* (1854)—might usefully be paired with *Walden* (1854). But hard-pressed teachers daunted by the length of those novels can turn to a much shorter and, I think, even more apposite work, *Ruth Hall* (1855), an autobiographical novel by Fanny Fern (Sarah Payson Willis Parton), the first woman newspaper columnist in the United States.

Another formidable figure whose writings I believe should be taught alongside *Walden* is Frederick Douglass, the abolitionist lecturer, editor, and author of *Narrative of the Life of Frederick Douglass, An American Slave* (1845) and its revised version, *My Bondage and My Freedom* (1855). Douglass, unlike Fanny Fern, is fast becoming a canonical writer, aided by the groundbreaking work of scholars in African American studies, some excellent paperback editions of both the *Narrative* and *My Bondage and My Freedom*, and, no doubt, the brevity of the *Narrative*, which has begun to appear in standard anthologies of American literature. The growing interest in Douglass's works also underscores one of the ironies of American literary history: that such slave narratives, which constituted the first truly indigenous genre produced in the United States, were ignored by twentieth-century critics, who identified the native characteristics of "classic" texts like *Walden* as signs of the birth of our national literature during a period thereafter called "the American Renaissance."[2]

The biographical similarities between Thoreau and Douglass make a comparison of their divergent narratives all the more interesting and instructive. Born only a year apart—Thoreau in 1817, and Douglass in 1818, though he never learned the exact date and was uncertain even about the year—the two men embarked on their careers at roughly the same time. Thoreau delivered his first lecture in 1838, the year after his graduation from Harvard, and under the tutelage of Emerson he published his first essay two years later, in the first issue of the Boston *Dial*. For Douglass, 1838 meant delivery from slavery; soon after his escape, he began to speak at abolitionist meetings, and in August 1841 he gave his first speech to a predominantly white audience at an antislavery convention in Nantucket. There he met William Lloyd Garrison, the editor of the *Liberator*, an abolitionist newspaper published in Boston. Garrison shaped Douglass's early career much as Emerson shaped Thoreau's. During the years 1841–44, Douglass traveled as a lecturer for the Massachusetts Anti-Slavery Society, of which Garrison was president, while Thoreau primarily wrote for and helped Emerson edit the *Dial*. The year 1844 marked a turning point for both Douglass, who began to write an account of his experiences as a slave, and Thoreau, who began to gather material for his first book, *A Week on the Concord and Merrimack Rivers*. Douglass's *Narrative* was published in the spring of 1845, by which time Thoreau was preparing to move to Walden Pond, where he wrote *A Week* and began *Walden*. Like the *Narrative*, which was based on Douglass's earlier lectures, the first version of *Walden* was an outgrowth of a lecture Thoreau delivered early in 1847, "A History of Myself," though he radically revised and expanded the book during the following seven years. Similarly, Douglass wrote a greatly enlarged version of the *Narrative*, which was published as *My Bondage and My Freedom* the year after the publication of *Walden*.

Although both Thoreau and Douglass were profoundly concerned with issues of freedom and bondage, they addressed those issues in radically different ways. For Douglass, of course, bondage meant slavery, the "peculiar institution" of the South. In his *Narrative* he therefore tended to play down the fact that the North did not represent true freedom, since he was there confronted by both racism and the possibility that he could be returned to slavery if his true identity became known. In fact, after the publication of the *Narrative* he was obliged to sail to England. Douglass was not legally emancipated until his English friends raised the money for him to purchase his freedom in 1846. In *My Bondage and My Freedom* he devoted greater attention to the barriers he encountered after his escape from slavery, including efforts by abolitionists like Garrison to make him toe the party line. Nonetheless, Douglass

divided his book into two parts—"Life as a Slave" and "Life as a Freeman"—
and he was understandably reluctant to alienate his primary audience by emphasizing the more subtle forms of bondage escaped slaves confronted in the
North. By contrast, Thoreau in *Walden* was far less concerned with external
barriers to freedom, north or south, than with what he viewed as self-enslave-
ment, a product of American materialism and the market economy. Although
vigorously opposed to slavery, which he attacked in "Resistance to Civil Government" (1849), now better known as "Civil Disobedience," and in "Slavery
in Massachusetts" (1854), Thoreau at the opening of *Walden* seemed to deny
the primacy of the abolitionist cause, declaring:

> I sometimes wonder that we can be so frivolous, I may almost say, as to
> attend to the gross but somewhat foreign form of servitude called Negro
> Slavery, there are so many keen and subtle masters that enslave both
> north and south. It is hard to have a southern overseer; it is worse to have
> a northern one; but worst of all when you are the slave-driver of yourself.
> (7)

As that provocative statement suggests, Thoreau was free of the burdens assumed by Douglass and other writers of slave narratives, the conventions of
which were shaped by their polemical purpose as well as by the expectations of
their white audience. Suggesting some parallels between the *Narrative* and
Walden, which may be read as "a white version of a slave narrative," Michael
Meyer also indicates a crucial difference between the two works. "Douglass's
purpose is to convince his mostly white readers that he is really no different
from them," Meyer observes; "Thoreau attempts to alert his readers to the possibility that they can be like him" (Introduction 26, 28). Consequently, whereas
Thoreau sought to remove his readers from the world they inhabited, Douglass
sought to establish his qualifications to enter their world, the values of which
he firmly embraced. In the course of his *Narrative*, Douglass carefully charted
the ways in which he had attained literacy, embraced Christianity, and learned
a trade, all of which prepared him for his escape to the North, where he swiftly
married and found a job, thus assuming "the duties and responsibilities of a life
of freedom" (146). (In *My Bondage and My Freedom* he revised that sentence
to read "the rights, responsibilities, and duties of a freeman" [341], an indica-
tion perhaps of how difficult he had earlier found it to assert his "rights" and
his status as "a freeman," both of which Thoreau took for granted.) In effect,
Douglass affirmed precisely the values of northern culture—domesticity, religion, and the Protestant work ethic—that Thoreau so vigorously challenged in
Walden.

Similarly, although both Douglass and Thoreau established an opposition between nature and culture, they offered dramatically different accounts of that
conflict. As H. Bruce Franklin points out, Douglass in his *Narrative* treated in unconventional terms one of the most conventional themes in antebellum literature,

the movement from the country to the city: "The city to him represents consciousness and the possibility of freedom; the country represents brutalization
and the certainty of slavery" (Franklin 13).[3] For Douglass, nature was symbolized by the world of the plantation, not an Eden but an infernal realm in which
the slave was relegated to the status of brute and beast of burden. "By far the
larger part of the slaves know as little of their ages as horses know of theirs,"
Douglass remarked at the opening of his *Narrative*. "They seldom come nearer
to [their birthdays] than planting-time, harvest-time, cherry-time, spring-time,
or fall-time" (47). That passage, an example of Douglass's pervasive use of animal imagery in the early chapters of his *Narrative*, offers an ironic commentary on the writings of a number of his white contemporaries, from section 32
to "Song of Myself," where Whitman mused, "I think I could turn and live with
animals," to the chapter in *Walden* where Thoreau proclaimed his closeness to
his "brute neighbors."[4] Douglass considered freedom an escape from the state
of nature, in which a slave was trapped in the endless cycle of seasonal labor
on the plantation, while Thoreau built those seasonal patterns into the very
structure of *Walden*.

Unlike Douglass, whose place in white society remained problematic even
after his escape from slavery, Thoreau could easily withdraw from the community because his place in society was assured. In *Walden; or, Life in the Woods*,
as he originally titled the book, Thoreau depicted his removal to Walden Pond
as an act of self-liberation. In sharp contrast, Douglass dramatized a similar removal as a cruel act of confinement. In one of the few extracts from the *Narrative* he quoted verbatim in *My Bondage and My Freedom*, Douglass offered
an account of his aged and infirm grandmother's expulsion from her home by
her new owners, who "took her to the woods, built her a little hut, put up a little mud-chimney, and then made her welcome to the privilege of supporting
herself there in perfect loneliness." Underscoring the horror of her isolation,
he continued: "The hearth is desolate. The children, the unconscious children,
who once sang and danced in her presence, are gone. . . . Instead of the voices
of her children, she hears by day the moans of the dove, and by night the
screams of the hideous owl" (*Narrative* 92–93; *Bondage* 180–81). Living in his
own hut in the woods, Thoreau flatly denied that he was ever lonely. More significant, whereas Douglass used the doleful sounds in nature to emphasize the
"gloom" of his grandmother's situation, Thoreau celebrated them in "Sounds,"
where he remarked the "deficiency of domestic sounds" in his world, ironically
observing that there was "neither the churn, nor the spinning wheel, nor even
the singing of the kettle, nor the hissing of the urn, nor children crying, to comfort one" (127).

Thoreau thus acknowledged that *Walden* "is not a novel, with its domestic
sounds" (Cavell 20).[5] Indeed, his account of "housekeeping" at Walden Pond
was designed for a purpose and written for an audience different from those of
the popular domestic novels of the 1850s. In the preface to *Rose Clark* (1856),
for example, Fanny Fern urged that her "unpretending story" be read by a

family gathered around a cozy hearth on a cold winter night. "For such an hour, for such an audience, was it written," she added. "Should any *dictionary on legs* rap inopportunely at the door for admittance, send him away to the groaning shelves of some musty library, where 'literature' lies embalmed, with its stony eyes, fleshless joints, and ossified heart, in faultless preservation" (Baym, *Women's Fiction* 32–33). As his diatribe against the novel in "Reading" suggests, Thoreau was precisely the kind of intrusive literary man she had in mind. His book was written not for "such an hour" but for the ages, since he obviously designed *Walden* to become the kind of timeless "classic" it is now widely considered to be, in sharp contrast to the productions of what he dismissively called "the modern cheap and fertile press" (*Walden* 100). He affirmed ideals of art and artisanship against the emerging modes of capitalist book production, with its standardized commodities, a mechanical process that in Thoreau's view transformed both authors and their readers into "machines" (104–05). For him reading was not an aspect of domestic culture but a fundamental element of self-culture, "a noble exercise, and one that will task the reader more than any exercise which the customs of the day esteem" (101).

Just as many antebellum health reformers attributed the physical debility of Americans to their poor diet and lack of proper exercise, Thoreau attributed their intellectual decline to a diet of "easy reading," especially the "provender" provided by popular novelists (105). With that implicit explanation of the commercial failure of his writings, Thoreau also offered posterity a convenient rationale to dismiss all but a handful of "classic" texts from the 1850s. But one need only read Fanny Fern's first novel, *Ruth Hall: A Domestic Tale of the Present Time*, to discover that popular books and the literary marketplace were more complex than Thoreau suggested in "Reading." Certainly *Ruth Hall* exemplified "easy reading" in its appeal to the broad audience Fern had gained through her writings for mass-market periodicals like the *Olive Branch*, one of the family newspapers Thoreau denigrated (109). In another respect, however, Fern's writings were just as challenging as *Walden*. She frequently spoke out on the plight of women and on other social issues, and she bravely defended *Leaves of Grass*, which most critics had branded coarse and indecent. For different reasons, conservative critics were almost equally shocked by *Ruth Hall*, a roman à clef in which she satirized her pious in-laws and members of her family, especially her brother, the popular writer Nathaniel P. Willis. In fact, the novel is worth reading today if only to relish the ways in which Fern subverted the stereotype of the submissive and self-effacing "female writer" of the antebellum period, offering instead a kind of Franklinesque account of her rise from poverty and obscurity to wealth and status.[6]

Ruth Hall is worth reading for other reasons as well, and it is particularly rewarding when studied in relation to *Walden*. The narrative structure of *Ruth Hall*, for example, challenged both the cherished assumptions of antebellum society and the alternative values affirmed in *Walden*. In contrast to many sentimental novels—stories, as Thoreau contemptuously summarized them, of

"Zebulon and Sephronia, and how they loved as none had ever loved before, and neither did the course of their true love run smooth" (105)—*Ruth Hall* begins with its protagonist's marriage. Soon after that event, Ruth and her husband move to a seemingly withdrawn and secure world, a country cottage that is a domestic equivalent of Thoreau's cabin at Walden Pond. From the beginning, however, Ruth's bucolic world is threatened by her meddling in-laws, who are akin to the most intrusive figures Thoreau depicted in "Visitors," the "ministers who spoke of God as if they enjoyed a monopoly of the subject" as well as the "uneasy housekeepers who pried into [his] cupboard and bed when [he] was out" (153). More crucial, whereas in *Walden* nature is associated with renewal and rebirth, the death of Ruth's first child is a powerful memento mori, like the famous motto "Et in Arcadia ego" ("Even in Arcadia am I"). The sudden death of her husband is still more traumatic, for it strikes at both the domestic harmony and the economic security of her world, offering a vivid reminder of how completely the relative ease of her country life depended on his wearisome work at a countinghouse in the city. With his death, Ruth thus confronts a problem that preoccupied Thoreau throughout his life: how to earn a living.

Ruth's dilemma reveals the limitations of Thoreau's social vision and the inadequacy of the solutions he offered in *Walden*. Like most of his contemporaries, Thoreau evidently did not consider that a woman might need to earn a living. Once Ruth loses the support of her husband, she is rejected by both his family and her own. She is consequently forced to move from the country to the city, in which setting *Ruth Hall* opens out to depict a far darker social reality than that glimpsed in *Walden*. Thoreau initially addressed the condition of his "townsmen," the laborers, farmers, and shopkeepers whose "lives of quiet desperation" he dissected in "Economy." Fern depicted the considerably more desperate plight of immigrants in urban slums, especially women driven to prostitution. As a reminder of social injustice and an illustration of the confinement of civilized life, Thoreau in "The Village" gives an account of his arrest and brief incarceration. In a much more harrowing chapter in Fern's novel, Ruth visits an "insane hospital," where her perfectly sane friend Mrs. Leon has died, abandoned by her husband, and where she hears a chained woman screaming for her child, who was carried off by that woman's husband. "She went to law about the child, and the law, you see, as it generally is, was on the man's side," the matron matter-of-factly remarks (111). Few writers of the day so squarely faced the hard facts of life for women, who had little security within marriage and few opportunities outside it. I "earned my living by the labor of my hands only," Thoreau bragged (3); but the only such labor available to Ruth Hall is "the needle trades," as they were called, work that pays too little to support her two children. Failing to find a job as a teacher, one of the few occupations open to women, Ruth finally tries her hand at writing.

Nothing so clearly distinguishes Fern from Thoreau as their conflicting views of authorship. For Thoreau writing, at least as he defined it in *Walden*, was less a profession than a vocation, a high spiritual calling. In a parable of his literary career in "Economy," he compared his earlier efforts to an Indian's unsuccessful attempts to sell baskets in Concord. "I too had woven a kind of basket of a delicate texture, but I had not made it worth any one's while to buy them," he observed, alluding to the commercial failure of *A Week*, which he had published at his own expense in 1849. He continued:

> Yet not the less, in my case, did I think it worth my while to weave them, and instead of studying how to make it worth men's while to buy my baskets, I studied rather how to avoid the necessity of selling them. The life which men praise and regard as successful is but one kind. Why should we exaggerate any one kind at the expense of the others?   (19)

Thoreau's Olympian posture was shaped by both his bitter experiences in the literary marketplace and his ideal of a work of art untainted by commercial considerations. At the end of *Walden*, he thus offered another parable, the fable of "an artist in the City of Kouroo," whose absolute dedication to his craft freed him and his work from time and the ravages of history. "The material was pure, and his art was pure," Thoreau concluded; "how could the result be other than wonderful?" (326–27).

Thoreau's lofty conception of "pure" and timeless art was very much a product of his time. His genteel disdain for the literary marketplace and his apparent indifference to commercial success were certainly far more respectable attitudes than the one assumed by Fern, a "Bedouin authoress" who wrote for "the sake of profit," as one outraged reviewer put it (A. D. Wood 4). Fern was in fact remarkably open about the economic considerations that spurred her labors and shaped her writings. Although she attributed Ruth's professional success to her sensitivity to the problems of her audience, especially of the poor and downtrodden, that success is measured not only by letters from grateful readers, several of which are included in the novel, but also by the growing amounts of money she can and does command for her writings. In contrast to the artist of Kouroo, whose finished work expanded before his eyes into "the fairest of all the creations of Brahma" (327), in the penultimate chapter of Fern's novel Ruth is presented with a very different reward for her labors, a certificate for one hundred shares of "Capital Stock of the Seton Bank" (209). Ironically, that certificate, a facsimile of which is boldly printed in the text, is made out to "Mrs. Ruth Hall," when it is actually a potent symbol of her independence and self-possession.

No less than Douglass's narratives and *Walden*, *Ruth Hall* is at once an account and the triumphant result of an effort to repossess or to reposition the self. As Douglass sought to break free of the bondage imposed on him by slavery in the South and by his race in the North and as Thoreau struggled against the entrepreneurial ideal of manhood spawned by the emergence of a market economy, so Fern fought the restrictions imposed by contemporary ideals of true womanhood.[7] Indeed, that Ruth Hall writes for money and assumes the role of head of the family was as unconventional as—and proved much more threatening to contemporary reviewers than—Thoreau's apparent rejection of the claims of professional success and domesticity, both of which were considered the proper aims for educated white males. Thoreau offered a vision of freedom through self-culture to men "so occupied with the factitious cares and superfluously coarse labors of life that its finer fruits cannot be plucked by them" (6). Fern insisted that women would be free only when they embraced a life of labor. "When you can, achieve financial independence," she urged women. "Freedom from subjection may be gotten by the fruits of your own labors, and by your own efforts you can learn to conquer yourselves" (F. B. Adams 23). Thoreau's stance, however, was far more combative and unyielding than that adopted by either Fern or Douglass. At the opening of *Walden*, for example, he seemed to give his audience no quarter, demanding an unconditional surrender of its values and beliefs. In contrast, Douglass challenged racial stereotypes by affirming his solidarity with his white readers, whose fundamental values he embraced and whose genteel language he adopted, especially in *My Bondage and My Freedom*. Similarly, despite her challenge to conventional wifely and motherly roles, Fern did not mount a frontal attack on them: as she emphasized in *Ruth Hall*, her protagonist is forced to work by the death of her husband, and her concern for money is a result only of her need to support her children. In effect, she becomes a self-reliant individual by necessity and only in the service of traditional familial values.

Ruth Hall and Douglass's narratives were far more popular than *Walden*. One way to approach those books—that is, to discuss the relations among them as well as their connections to both antebellum and our own culture—is to ask students to give reasons for the difference in popularity. In that context, students might be asked to read Hawthorne's outburst against the "d----d mob of scribbling women," especially since he sharply distinguished between Cummins's *The Lamplighter*, the most popular of all women's novels of the period, and *Ruth Hall*. "The woman writes as if the devil was in her," he approvingly observed of Fern, adding that when women "throw off the restraints of decency, and come before the public stark naked, as it were—then their books are sure to possess character and value" (*Letters* 304, 308). Read in the light of Thoreau's animadversions on clothing, which for middle-class women was particularly restrictive and concealing in the 1850s, Hawthorne's comment raises some fundamental questions about the relations among class, social convention, and literary expression. Why, for example, did Sara Payson Willis Parton appear before the public as Fanny Fern while her brother, Nathaniel P. Willis, published under his own name? Since *Ruth Hall* is closely based on the actual events of her life, why did she cast it as a novel in the third person instead of constructing a first-person narrative along the lines of *My Bondage and My Freedom* or *Walden*? Why did the title page of *Walden* display a sketch of Thoreau's cabin, built from the boards of "the shanty of James Collins, an Irishman who worked on the Fitchburg Railroad" (43), while in the portrait used as the frontispiece of *My Bondage and My Freedom* Douglass is arrayed in the impeccable garb of a middle-class gentleman? In short, why were issues of marginality so central to the writings of the antebellum period?

The commercial success of *Ruth Hall* and Douglass's narratives also raises questions about the literary marketplace and the social role of writing, in both the antebellum period and our own time. Students might, for example, be asked to consider why, if given a choice, many of them would prefer to read *Ruth Hall* or one of Douglass's narratives than to read *Walden*. The teachers might explain their own preference for reading (or at least for teaching) books like *Walden*, which is now required reading in a sense that differs from what Thoreau had in mind when he urged his audience to "read the best books first," the well-known advice given in his first and least-read book (*A Week* 96). In discussing *Walden*, we need to alert students to the ways in which his conception of *culture*—a term he used to signify both a process, as in self-culture, and the artistic fruits of that process—has at once vitalized and restricted scholars and teachers, who until relatively recently have toed the firm line Thoreau drew between literature and popular writing. Similarly, in teaching Douglass and Fern, we need to explore the reasons their works have generated increasing interest and attention; we need to acknowledge that literary traditions are not fixed but contingent, not bequests from the past but constructs in and of the present. Indeed, teaching *Walden*, one of Douglass's narratives, and *Ruth Hall* as a group not only offers a revealing glimpse of society and culture in antebellum America but also illustrates the ways in which our conception of the American Renaissance has been shaped by the changing social conditions and evolving cultural concerns of twentieth-century America.

NOTES

[1] Discussion of the terms Thoreau employs in the chapter "Reading," including *art* and *culture* as well as *literature*, is greatly enhanced if students are asked to read about the evolution of those terms in Raymond Williams (40–43, 87–93, 183–88).

[2] An excellent recent study of the origins and development of the slave narrative is William Andrews, *To Tell a Free Story*.

[3] Observing that "the white academic establishment still pretends that Frederick Douglass does not exist as a literary artist," Franklin states that his chapter on the *Narrative* was in part intended "to show that individual early Afro-American works of literature merit the kind of close attention we usually reserve for works of the canon" (7).

[4] For illuminating discussions of the role of animal imagery in the *Narrative*, see Houston Baker (75–76), and Franklin (7–22).

[5] For a discussion of Thoreau's challenge to the emerging ideology of domesticity, and of *Walden* as a parodic response to books like Catharine Beecher's *Treatise on Domestic Economy* (1841), see L. C. Johnson, "Revolution."

[6] In the introduction to *Ruth Hall*, Joyce Warren offers a brief account of its writing and reception, as well as an interesting analysis of what she rightly calls the

"revolutionary" aspects of the novel. Warren's edition also includes a substantial selection of Fern's newspaper writings, including the 1856 review of *Leaves of Grass* (274–77).

[7]For a stimulating discussion of the entrepreneurial ideal of manhood, as well as of the interplay among race, class, and gender in various texts of the period, see David Leverenz, especially his superb chapter on *My Bondage and My Freedom*, "Frederick Douglass's Self-Refashioning" (108–34).

Thoreau and Anglo-European Romanticism

Frederick Garber

To ponder the question of teaching Thoreau's relation to Romanticism is to ask, Which Romanticism? therefore, Which authors? To ponder such a question is also to ask, What does that relation mean not only in Thoreau's writing but also in our establishing who he is, what he is as a human person? We need to ask these questions because the Anglo-European Romanticism that made its way to America did so in several forms and from several locations. One hub was Emerson's momentous visit abroad in 1833, when he met Landor in Italy and Carlyle, Coleridge, and Wordsworth in England. In listing these authors, we name significant influences, but we also need to specify the broad Germanic strain that came largely from Goethe (especially through Carlyle's translations) and the Rousseauesque influence, much of which was indirect but potent all the same. Simply to suggest these names is to invoke a variety of views that will not always sit comfortably together: there is much in Wordsworth not to be found in Goethe's *Werther*, while the High Church motives of Coleridge find nothing comparable in any aspect of Rousseau. Thus we should emphasize to students that the Anglo-European Romanticism that came to America presented no monolith. But students should also realize that certain elements in these authors (and in others like Byron, Shelley, and Keats, who are less relevant to our purpose) held a special attraction for the Americans who read them. It is to those elements that I will give special attention.

Consider, first, organicism. Nature is seen not in terms of eighteenth-century mechanism—imaged most lastingly in the person of a Great Watchmaker who set the universe running and stepped gracefully aside—but as a living, dynamic entity, self-sufficient and self-contained. For Goethe as for Wordsworth, nature, taken as a whole, was as instinct with life as any plant or human being. Indeed, the image of the plant replaced that of the machine, not only for the element of life that resided in the plant but also for the way each of its aspects contributed to the whole. Nature, further, grew from seeds, pods, germs; grew into maturity, died, and then grew again in a radical cyclicality that was a fascinating aspect of every organicism. It fascinated largely because the fact that human beings did the same made possible an inexhaustible series of analogies, made possible the structure of texts such as *Walden*, which builds much of its argument from echoing versions of organic cyclicality.

Still, we have to be cautious about unrestricted acceptance of correspondential claims. If most Romanticisms forge versions of those claims, most also contain ironies that are equally endemic and make necessary qualifications. Wordsworth begins *The Prelude* with a version of analogy: a gentle breeze fans his cheek, a breeze that seems "half-conscious of the joy [it] brings" to him from out of nature (line 4). The breeze is an emissary, a messenger, a wind with a mission. Several lines later it grows analogous (perhaps that is part of its mission), becoming a "correspondent breeze" (35), corresponding to the creative energy within him. A defining text of Anglo-European Romanticism, *The Prelude* begins with the argument for analogy emergent in most readings of organic nature. Yet as it continues, the poem starts to undermine (never fully but always tellingly) the very analogies it had so openly proclaimed. The poem shows that if nature enfolds, it can also rebuff, that fracture can coexist with claims of unity. It is as though the beginning of the text posits analogy to seek to undo it, as though the positing and undoing make a counterpart (counterpoint) narrative to the narrative that tells of this poet's acquisition of prowess. Perhaps the counterpart narrative is part of what the poet learns, a point that would not be lost on the writer of *Walden*. (Thoreau was writing *Walden* when *The Prelude* was published, in July 1850, and he owned a copy of Wordsworth's epic.) *The Prelude* is in part a cautionary tale, earlier versions of which Wordsworth had sketched in poems Americans knew and quoted, especially "Tintern Abbey" and the Immortality Ode. If Thoreau learned some of those cautions from Wordsworth's great earlier lyrics, the epic would extend what the earlier works had proclaimed, would confirm Thoreau's intuitions, his own study of prowess, the shapes and terms and cautions of his own autobiography.

Consider next the question of human personality, its place in the Romantic version of organic nature. The analogies of self and nature pervading Anglo-European Romanticism worked for the Americans too; yet as the example of *The Prelude* shows, the analogies have to be taken with considerable caution, and many Romantics did so. We must distinguish carefully between claim and actuality, between what some profess is there and what their texts show is there. Few of the major authors in America or abroad accepted such likening without some qualification, implicit or otherwise, without a counterpart stress on the otherness of nature, its separateness from us. The self-sufficiency so admired in organic nature turned out sometimes to contain a disconcerting aloofness—as it did, for example, in Shelley's "Ode to the West Wind," or as it did when Thoreau climbed to the top of Maine's Mount Katahdin and found a pure nature that would have nothing to do with him. Still, the element of difference came not only from nature's otherness but from our own otherness as well, a condition that is also suggested in Wordsworth. Emerson put the point bluntly at the beginning of *Nature*, which, in 1836, defined much of the tone and dialogue for subsequent American speculations on nature. "The universe," he said, "is composed of Nature and the Soul." Nature is "all that is separate from us, all which philosophy distinguishes as the NOT ME" (*Works* 1: 8). If that distinction comes from German Romantic philosophy (it is based on Fichte's Ich–Nicht Ich), it can be found in various forms throughout Romantic writings. It appears in authors like Blake, whom the Americans hardly knew, and in aspects of Wordsworth, who commanded Romanticism in its British and American forms. One has, then, not only the likening in organic nature but the differentiation in the Emersonian self, that self's sense of separateness from the nature in which it works.

Such tidy, binary packaging of diametrical opposites tells only part of the tale. No neat bifurcation of ME and NOT ME stands up to a detailed reading of Emerson or Thoreau. Thoreau knew too much about his own relations to nature to accept either-or when experience called for both-and. The nature that emerged from Anglo-European Romanticism never settled for a single categorical image or for any one kind of use; nor did it settle for exclusive alternatives and the compulsion to choose between them. Emerson and Thoreau saw and practiced that refusal to choose. Analogy, Emerson knew, is based on aspects of likeness; yet Emerson, the greatest American exponent of analogy, began *Nature* with an argument for nature as radically other. Thoreau put his refusal of neat bifurcation in all sorts of ways, as he did, for example, when he wrote about his trips in *The Maine Woods*. When he saw local Indians on those excursions, he could speak, as he sometimes did, of "the red face of man" (e.g., 79), that is, one category of the genus human being. Yet at other times on those trips he would argue something quite different, that even the most "civilized" Indian, a figure like Joe Polis, the guide of Thoreau's group, could speak more intimately to the muskrats than he could to these visitors from Concord (206–07). The Indian was like the visitors and yet very much unlike them, radically akin and radically different, not only me but simultaneously not me. Joe Polis was in some ways as foreign to the visitors as they were to that place. The Concordians could only gaze as the Indian spoke to the muskrats, as he engaged himself in their world and showed himself to be quite comfortably at home within it.

The questions I have been pursuing about the place of the human being in the context of organic nature appear with particular force in this passage. It shows plainly how the Romantic version of the encounter of nature and the self must deal with the problem Thoreau and others faced often, what Thoreau and Goethe spoke of as the difficulty of being at home in the world. At this point we can recognize some of the reasons for Goethe's broad popularity in America, not the Goethe of *Werther* or *Faust* (largely alien to such as Thoreau) but Goethe the scientist as well as the writer of *Wilhelm Meister* and the *Italian Journey*. As much as anyone of his time, Goethe suggested the interrelations of organic nature and the self's place within it. Goethe was one of the age's supreme organicists, his work doing much to support the doctrines of correspondence that went with organicism, especially in its Romantic phases. Goethe's theory of plants argued for the leaf as the fundamental model of the objects and workings of nature. The interdependence of parts that characterizes the leaf, based on the system of veins that transport vitality, was not only the basis but also the symbol for the dynamic self-sufficiency that defined organicism. To paraphrase Baudelaire, nature is a forest of analogies and correspondences. A structure true for one aspect is true for others as well, each element thus a potential synecdoche for the whole. Nature is a system of echoes that is never merely abstract but instinct with the life that pervades organic wholes. Consider, then, the scene of the sandbank in *Walden* ("Spring,"

304–09), its language, texture, and arguments profoundly Goethean, the rivulets in the sand running like veins in the leaf, the life that is emergent speaking for all organic life. Consider as well Thoreau's frequent comment that the various elements of nature "answer" to each other. That too is Goethean in its stress on natural mirroring.

Other aspects of Goethe affected Thoreau so closely that he echoed them several times, concerned with their implications for his own local conditions, for who he was in his world. Those aspects came, in particular, from Goethe's record of his journey to Italy. One of the earliest entries in Thoreau's Journal (15 Nov. 1837) is a translation from the *Italian Journey*. After he enters Trent, Goethe speaks of the beautiful evening and how he feels "once more at home in the world, and not as an alien—an exile" (*Journal 1* 11). Two days later Thoreau speaks of an experience of his own and echoes Goethe's words: "the smothered breathings of awakening day . . . come they to me, and I am at home in the world" (13). Goethe was more than a source and model for organic thinking: he was also a model for being at home in the world. A passage in the "Thursday" chapter of *A Week on the Concord and Merrimack Rivers* substantiates that point with extended remarks on Goethe, in which words of at-homeness take on more elaborate life. But the influence does not stop there. We gain a further sense of what Goethe meant to Thoreau from the linking of that passage to the one immediately following, a passage that describes Thoreau's journey down the river. Goethe's organicism echoes in Thoreau's description of the way all things flow together in a vital and unified whole: "[A]ll things seemed with us to flow; the shore itself, and the distant cliffs, were dissolved by the undiluted air" (331). At-homeness and organicism, at-homeness *in* organicism: that potent combination is what Goethe was coming to mean to this American reader, what Anglo-European Romanticism was speaking (not always with confidence) through Goethe and Wordsworth and the Coleridge of "Dejection." Such issues turn up in Shelley, whom Thoreau hardly noticed, and also in Carlyle, whom he noticed extensively. What appears early in the Journal and in the later part of *A Week* began Thoreau's local version of some of the deeper issues emergent in most Romanticisms, especially questions dealing with at-homeness in the world. He worried those questions at every point in his work. Consider again the Indian and the muskrats. Was organic mirroring sufficient to make one at home in the world? How far did that mirroring go? The Indian's at-homeness in the world of the muskrat was something the guests from Concord could observe but never share.

There was still more to ponder in Goethe, especially the kind of selfhood he showed at work in nature. If Thoreau was not an Indian, he was not Goethe either and did not want to be. In the later part of *A Week* he praised Goethe's precision in rendering objects and events but regretted Goethe's inadequacies in getting beyond such facts into a sense of the sublime, or—as Thoreau would put it elsewhere—in making facts blossom into truths. What he was concluding from Goethe he concluded in similar ways from Wordsworth, Coleridge, and Carlyle and could also have got from Keats and certainly from Byron. The splendid richness of Goethe's organicism, his rich sense of the question of at-homeness in the world, needed and did not have an equivalent richness of self. One could see the same problem in Carlyle's *Sartor Resartus*. Thoreau would find it in Coleridge's "Dejection," singling out that poem for comment on the title page of *Walden*. Every Romanticism sought a richness of correspondence in self places and home places, what we are and where we live, what we are *as* where we live. Self places and home places should "answer" each other in perfect organic analogy, but for Goethe they did not. That Thoreau paid so much attention to this deficiency in Goethe shows that he turned to his recent forebears for models of self as well as of thought.

At many points in his writing Thoreau showed that the problem of answering was not only his to work out but America's as well. This former colony had to establish the sense and contours of its own Romanticism, which meant that it had to define an American version of nature and the self's at-homeness within it. As early as his undergraduate days at Harvard College, Thoreau understood that this was the American nation's problem. In April 1836, six months before the publication of Emerson's *Nature*, he wrote a student paper entitled "Advantages and Disadvantages of Foreign Influence on American Literature" (*Early Essays*). "The nations of the old world have each a literature peculiarly its own," Thoreau said. We of New England, however, though "we whistle . . . our national tune," have not yet established the character of the literature we will offer. Perhaps because, in terms of our literature, we are still "but colonies," we tend to be blind to native merit, affecting "a servile adoration of imported genius." Our writers are too often "prone to sing of skylarks and nightingales, perched on hedges, to the neglect of the homely robin-redbreast, and the straggling rail-fences of their own native land" (38, 39, 40–41). The echoes of Shelley's skylark and Keats's nightingale are put with civility. Later, however, Thoreau was rarely as gentle as this, especially when he discussed American nature and its difference from European nature. What Thoreau in several places called America's "unexplored wildness" found no counterpart in European conditions. That point had been made long and often by some of the earliest explorers (Thoreau liked to quote them at length). It came to be crucial to an American understanding of the local interplay of self places and home places. If Americans had no long civil history of the European sort, they had an ancient natural history still visible throughout the land. Many of America's antiquities had never ceased to be wild in a way no European could finally comprehend.

American writers thus needed to develop a language that spoke the idiom of American wildness. No imported voice, even the commanding sounds of Wordsworth, could utter the needs of a nature as organic as any in Europe but with tonalities and components no nature in Europe could match. Thoreau said so in his Journal for 1841:

Day and night—mountain and wood are visible from the wilderness as well as the village— They have their primeval aspects—sterner savager—than any poet has sung. It is only the white man's poetry—we want the Indian's report. Wordsworth is too tame for the Chippeway.

(*Journal 1* 321)

Wordsworth became Thoreau's paradigm of Europe's deficiencies because he was Thoreau's paradigm of Anglo-European Romanticism. But whatever Thoreau thought of Wordsworth's inadequacies, he quoted him more extensively than he did any other European author in the Journal of 1841, where he spoke of Wordsworth's tameness. To challenge Wordsworth was to argue the need for a home brew stronger than any America's Old World forebears knew how to produce, a natural brew of the sort Thoreau would find in the Maine woods. For the rest of this essay I look at several of his texts, doing as Thoreau did, thinking of Wordsworth as an instrument for the making of an American voice.

It may be best to think of Wordsworth as a counterinstrument, as Thoreau did in his first published essay, "Natural History of Massachusetts." Emerson had commissioned the essay for the *Dial*, asking for a review of a newly published report on Massachusetts flora and fauna. What he got was an acknowledgment of recent cultural history and a sly declaration of cultural independence—a substantial echo of Wordsworth turned into New World conditions, into American sights and sounds. The text with which Thoreau begins his writing career begins with an allusion designed to locate him precisely (in what could be called a scene of self-locating). He begins the first paragraph with "books of natural history make the most cheerful winter reading," then lists New World landscapes from Florida to Labrador, and ends the survey by saying that he owes "an accession of health to these reminiscences of luxuriant nature" (*Excursions* 37). That last point is a plain echo of Wordsworth's "Tintern Abbey." Thoreau could depend on the *Dial*'s readers to hear and interpret the echo and to understand the politics that made the echo work. This grounding firmly established, he quotes one of his own poems, its mode that of "Tintern Abbey": "I have remembered when the winter came . . . How in the shimmering noon of summer past. . . ." And those introductions lead into local specificities. "Tinturn Abbey" established a mode of Romanticism that culminated in *The Prelude* and has continued not only deep into the twentieth century (the work of Wallace Stevens leans heavily on it) but also into contemporary poetry that deals with the mind's possession of externalities. None of the current rethinkings of Romanticism has disputed the age's grounding in the encounter of consciousness and nature, though critics have elaborated on and debated the contents of that grounding, the stability of the elements of consciousness and nature, their shifting relations to each other and to themselves, the relative power of each. "Tintern Abbey" makes a fit occasion for such debate. It ponders memory and desire, departure and a return to that which is not quite the same, irreparable loss and what Wordsworth claims, not always convincingly, to be measurable gain. It is as much about self in history as it is about self in nature, as much about memory as it is about immediacy, about different modes of remembering and different modes of nature (none of these issues is separate; each is linked with all the others). Thoreau continues the confrontation of consciousness and nature that defines much of the basis for Anglo-European Romanticism, and he invites us to read his essay in terms his predecessors established. He redefines the confrontation for local circumstances, begins what will become a principal guiding agon that pervades his major work and culminates in *Walden*.

"Natural History of Massachusetts" offered not only an homage to Wordsworth but also a claim for recognition. It was brash in a way Thoreau would eventually tame, though no more brash than Joseph Turner's donation of certain of his paintings to the British nation with the proviso that they be placed next to the Claudes, with which he wished his work to be compared. I have called Wordsworth a counterinstrument. I could call him a contrary instrument, part of a politics in which we need to posit the other in order to posit ourselves. The beginning of Thoreau's first essay is not only a manifesto but also a canny exercise in the politics of allusion.

The essay as a whole is in addition an anthology of Romantic themes of the time, echoes that, heard along with the sounds of "Tintern Abbey," suggest several directions Thoreau would later take. "In society you will not find health, but in nature. . . . Society is always diseased, and the best is the most so" (39); that is the Rousseauism that by 1842 was long since simplified, hackneyed. "The doctrines of despair, of spiritual or political tyranny or servitude, were never taught by such as shared the serenity of nature" (39); that is the Wordsworth of "Expostulation and Reply" and "The Tables Turned," put into the pitch of Thoreau's extravagance. "There is no scent in [society] so wholesome as that of the pines, nor any fragrance so penetrating and restorative as the life-everlasting in high pastures" (39); that last point is emblem making, coming out of an old tradition that authors like Blake knew and that Emerson and Thoreau revitalized into current American speech. Whatever their claims for virgin lands, Americans had to speak—to learn to speak their way out of—the sounds of acquired discourse, the rhetoric of others.

Such speaking, such learning can be followed throughout Thoreau, not just through his earlier work. There is a very important sense in which Thoreau, as he studies the American landscape, keeps testing himself in terms of "Tintern Abbey" and related texts (he need not have read "Tintern Abbey" to find the Romantic mode to use as a model for his own writing). What he so openly put as a challenge at the beginning of his first essay became an ongoing project whose limits he never found, whose contours he could never exhaust. Testing a generic Anglo-European Romanticism in terms of a local organic nature so different in kind turned out to reveal much about the tester and the thing tested: either the "Tintern Abbey" mode would prove insufficient or it would show that it had dimensions that could be expanded to encompass Thoreau's America. Both possibilities were given expression throughout Thoreau's career. The question of insufficiency appears at a number of points, for example, the ascent of Mount Saddleback described in the "Tuesday" chapter of *A Week* and the ascent of Mount Katahdin recorded in *The Maine Woods*. The revealing of new dimensions appears later, in *Walden*, which one can see as a compromise between the Romanticism of poems in the mode of "Tintern Abbey" and the various alternatives Thoreau came to find in a lifetime of landscape walking.

Thoreau's two mountain ascents should be compared with the climb up Mount Snowdon described at the end of Wordsworth's *Prelude*. The three present an extraordinary series of feats and defeats of consciousness, testings of the power of mind against the world, allegories of the arduous confrontation with physical nature. In each account, what the climber finds at the top of the mountain shows a different result from that confrontation. Thoreau ascends Saddleback on a gray and grim day, but when he reaches the top, out above the gloom, he sees a brilliant sun shining down on a cover of clouds that hides the murky earth and looks just like a sea, the tops of the mountains jutting up like islands. He too turns murky and gloomy as he sees that, as he is now, he can only get so far on his way to the source of things, halfway in an ascent whose extent he can envision but has no power to realize. The heavy-handed emblem making of "Natural History of Massachusetts" turns taut, subtle, grim in this allegory of a prowess too painfully limited. "Ktaadn" delivers an even fuller defeat to the mind in confrontation with a nature that is only physical, a nature that is mother and matter but estranged from us at a height where we are intrusive only and literally powerless. Consider then the ascent of Mount Snowdon in *The Prelude*. At the top is the sea of clouds Thoreau saw on Saddleback, again with a luminary that lights up the sea. This time it is the moon, endemic Romantic symbol of the potent imagination. Wordsworth takes the scene as an emblem of the triumph of mind, which shines down on the world and orders the scene into images. The claims of Anglo-European Romanticism were rarely so dramatically put as in the scene on Mount Snowdon. (Whether those claims hold up, whether the scene undoes itself, whether *The Prelude* contains a major strain of self-subversion are issues that ought to be pondered in a reading of the text.) Though Thoreau makes similar claims elsewhere in his work, in these crucial mountain scenes he cannot do so, overwhelmed as he is by a nature that has him struggling up a mountain only to meet his limitations. The confidence in mind claimed at the top of Snowdon finds no comparable faith on Saddleback or Katahdin.

There is more confidence in *Walden*, but it is qualified by what Thoreau learned on the mountains, by what they showed of his need and inability to adapt the desires and claims of some admired predecessors. Thoreau gets that issue going by putting on his title page a reference to Coleridge's "Dejection": "I do not propose to write an ode to dejection, but to brag as lustily as chanticleer in the morning, standing on his roost, if only to wake my neighbors up."

That locks the issues of *Walden* into the arguments of Romantic forebears, tells the reader to read in terms of precisely those arguments as a way into the book. "Dejection" probes a falling off from the "Tintern Abbey" mode, considers what happens when the mode goes wrong, when the mind grows insufficient and the radical relations through which the mind reads the world lose their intensity, burning out. Coleridge does as his colleagues do, works on questions of correspondence: the analogy of the creative breeze with which *The Prelude* was to begin collapses because the speaker cannot respond in kind. *Walden* also works with basic analogies, preeminent among them being that in which the rhythms of organic nature profess to tell us something about the rhythms of the human spirit. Thoreau accepts the organicism he saw in Goethe and others, accepts it finally to undo several elements of the basic analogy between our workings and those of nature. One has to read *Walden* partly against the grain of organic claims. One has to read it as qualifying (though never fully rejecting) the previous half-century's analogies of self and nature, qualifying them precisely because of the partial but crucial difference, so patent up on the mountains, between the human and the natural. At the center of this autobiography, in the chapter "Higher Laws," comes a pained, discomforting view of the natural wildness within ourselves, a component of the human that, here at least, Thoreau vehemently rejects in favor of the claims of spirit. That is why *Walden* ends not with the recurrence of natural cycles but with an opening out of spirit that both fractures those cycles and problematizes the claims of fundamental likeness between human beings and organic nature. Spirit does not whirl around in cycles as human bodies must do (Wordsworth showed this whirling in "A Slumber Did My Spirit Seal") but breaks out of their hold into a wonderfully promising dawn. In his rejection of Coleridge's ode, Thoreau repudiates a major claim of his strong but inadequate forebears. Virgin land can be scary as well as exhilarating. It can challenge in ways that will not support the professions of poems like "Tintern Abbey" or the failure to meet those professions in poems like "Dejection." Goethe's analogy of the plant cannot account for all the conditions *Walden* claims for the human being. "Dejection" shows one type of failure: we cannot live up to the fundamental analogies of self and nature. *Walden* shows another failure, this time not in us but in nature's limitations. The prized analogy claimed by the writers Thoreau so admired had to be refurbished for a transcendental Romanticism that had its own claims to make.

"Extra Vagant" Education: Teaching *Walden* in the Context of Transcendentalism

T. S. McMillin

> Modern education has not dealt with these deeper
> questions of life and being.
>
> —Amos Bronson Alcott

> I mean that they should not *play* life, or *study* it merely,
> while the community supports them at this expensive
> game, but earnestly *live* it from beginning to end.
>
> —Thoreau

The Problem

Octavius Brooks Frothingham, in his well-regarded account of American transcendentalism (written while many of its participants and sympathizers yet walked the earth), warned, "It was once the fashion—and still in some quarters it is the fashion—to laugh at Transcendentalism as an incomprehensible folly, and to call Transcendentalists visionaries" (xxvi). Teaching transcendentalism today no doubt entails discussing what was, and would even now be, deemed folly: dreamy Alcott as an avatar of Orpheus; Jones Very's mad messianism; Emerson as a behatted, spindly-legged, transparent eyeball. Indeed, if transcendentalism is remembered at all, it is precisely as visionary folly, middle-class escapism, or a benign rejoinder to Unitarianism. In its best light, transcendentalism is depicted by scholars as a momentary flourishing of the literary arts in mid-nineteenth-century New England, most useful pedagogically for its historical value, for the reaches of its influence. Neither a denial of nor a capitulation to such versions, the present essay suggests that transcendentalism is more than these definitions and that it is this excess, this extravagance, that makes it a vitally important contribution to "modern education."

As Philip Gura and Joel Myerson observed, "From the 1830s on, the abiding difficulty in discussing the American Transcendental movement has been that of definition, a problem augmented by the posture of the Transcendentalists themselves" (xi). Deciding just what transcendentalism *was* is, as Alexander Kern noted,

> difficult to do because it was a developing movement, not a static philosophy, and because the Transcendentalists were, as separate thinkers, hardly logical system-builders, while, as a group, they were radical individualists who often disagreed with each other, however much alike they may have appeared to their opponents. For these reasons no completely successful definition of Transcendentalism has ever been worked out. (248)

Kern described what developed into and continues as a struggle between two approaches to the problem of transcendentalism. One approach seeks to define the indefinite movement as "the latest form of infidelity" (Norton), as "a distinct philosophical system" (Frothingham 136), as "one of the many instances of the widespread religious ferment which took place in America during the first half of the nineteenth century" (Buell, *Transcendentalism* 4), as "a literary and historical artifact" (Gura and Myerson xxi). The other approach resists such attempts at definition. A fellow traveler of the movement, Cyrus Augustus Bartol, insisted that "the Transcendentalist at least is belied and put in jail by the definition which is so neat at the expense of truth" (qtd. in Frothingham 342). Accordingly (and perhaps maddeningly), Emerson offered what we might think of as "indefinitions" of transcendentalism; an example appears in his "indefinitive" essay "The Transcendentalists," in which he characterizes the movement as "the Saturnalia or excess of faith" (*Works* 1: 206).

Hence while one side of the problem may wish to conclude, with a certain sense of finitude, that there was such a thing as a definable transcendentalist movement with an identifiable "heyday [that] lasted for a little more than ten years, from 1836 to the collapse of Brook Farm in 1847" (Hochfield, "Transcendentalism" 154), the other side will push the consideration that "[c]ontrary to many popular accounts, Transcendentalism did not cease to exist after the national trauma of the 1860s . . ." (Gura and Myerson xxiv). Sympathetic with the transcendentalists' aversion to conventional and institutional definitions yet hoping to offer a useful context in which to approach transcendentalism, I provisionally define the movement as a rather diverse, vaguely bordered set of ways of thinking, arising in the 1830s and concerned with provoking new relations between human beings and the world (or, more transcendentally, the universe). Furthermore, the movement's methods for achieving these new relations involve especial attention to vision (or the way one sees the world), to participation (or one's responsibilities in and to the world), and to movement itself (allowing oneself to be "unsettled," as Emerson puts it in his essay "Circles" [*Works* 2: 189])—hence the interest in excess (going beyond), extravagance (wandering beyond), and "extra vagant education."

As this essay's epigraphs suggest, the transcendentalists may be said to have taken education seriously. Nearly all those who wore the transcendental mantle were either teachers or preachers at some point in their careers, and they lectured on, conversed on, edited, or published their versions of education, enculturation, and the "upbuilding" of men and women. "What they were calling for, in effect, was the *liberation* of mankind" from "that mass of forms and conventions and institutions by which men were held captive . . ." (Hochfield, "Transcendentalism" 143–44). Their strategic preferences varied. Emerson was an excellent and inspiring (if often incomprehensible) lecturer. Alcott favored conversation, stating that "[t]he lecture is too formal. It is, beside, presuming. Man doth not meet his fellow on equal terms . . ." (Buell, *Transcendentalism* 81). Thoreau, however, was most effective as a writer. A not

always compelling lecturer, at times an altogether too combative conversation-
alist, and a professional teacher for only a brief period, he nevertheless suggested in his writings a devotion to a form of education one might call
transcendental or "extra vagant." It is in the light of this approach to education
that I suggest *Walden* itself be taught.

What, however, is "extra vagant" education? I have lifted the term from the
conclusion of *Walden*, in which the writer says:

> I fear chiefly lest my expression may not be *extra- vagant* enough, may
> not wander far enough beyond the narrow limits of my daily experience,
> so as to be adequate to the truth of which I have been convinced. *Extra
> vagance!* it depends on how you are yarded.   (324)

His expression is, as he notes at the book's commencement, a wake-up call
"more particularly addressed to poor students" (4). The call is designed to
rouse them, to bid them rise and wander beyond their limits, there to examine
the narrowness of their experiences. The writer's call to extravagance resembles both Alcott's belief in education as a drawing forth or bringing out and
Emerson's claim, in his Divinity School address, that education must be a
"provocation," or a calling forth (*Works* 1: 80). One might wish to insist, with
Frothingham, that such calling forth meant tapping into the spirit. According
to the historian, Alcott's "mission was to educate—to draw out souls, whether
of children or adults. . . . The process of education was spiritual, therefore, to
entice the indwelling deity forth by sympathy" (Frothingham 261). The spiritual, however, was not the only salient characteristic of transcendentalism and
its modes of refining education. To teach *Walden* in the context of transcendentalism, one must look into what is meant by teaching, by *Walden*, and by
transcendentalism.

Responses

> Now I think of it, I should have told them at once that I
> was a transcendentalist. That would have been the
> shortest way of telling them that they would not
> understand my explanations.
>
> —Thoreau

My seemingly excursive introduction should convey the sense that to teach
Walden in the context of transcendentalism, one must open up the meaning of
that movement to critical scrutiny by both teachers and students. It is in keeping with the spirit of the movement that instead of relying on previous definitions of transcendentalism, we who are involved in this most (or most post-)
modern of educations be invited to reconstruct the context in which we approach Thoreau's text. Thus the introductory excursus is a curricularly necessary

beginning, one that invites students and teachers to think about what transcendentalism means (or could mean).

Once the question of transcendentalism is opened, there are many possible avenues by which one can proceed, avenues contingent in part on the context of the class itself. If *Walden* is to be read in a survey of nineteenth-century American literature or a more advanced examination of American Romanticism, a brief historical perspective will suffice to provide students with an idea of the economic and political, philosophical and literary conditions informing the writing of *Walden*. A course devoted to a thorough investigation of transcendentalism, however, would establish a more complete transcendentalist context. Readings from Kant's *Critique of Pure Reason* and other German texts (Frothingham is helpful for those in need of an overview on this front), some background of French interpretations (see George Ripley's edited volumes of *Foreign Standard Literature* for the contemporaneously influential works of Victor Cousin et al.), selected prose of Coleridge and Carlyle, some of Wordsworth's poems (e.g., "Intimations of Immortality")—such works, depending on time and inclinations, provide a crucial view of the complexity of transcendentalism or, more accurately, of the sundry transcendentalisms that North Americans inherited and to which they responded.

Perry Miller's *The Transcendentalists: An Anthology* and Emerson's essays further demonstrate the difficulties of defining the movement. Particularly Emerson's writing makes clear (so to speak) why those difficulties are meaningful, what the stakes are in critiquing oversimplified versions of transcendentalism, and why it is necessary that we essay to arrive at our own ideas of its significance. Having thus prepared the way for a reading of *Walden* in the context of transcendentalism, we are better prepared to see the changes that Thoreau's interpretations bring to the movement, the particular moves he makes both within and away from what scholars have come to characterize as transcendental. Hence we as readers are ourselves more mobile, more apt to be moved by the writer's promptings, more likely to participate in his questions, more capable of responding to his provocations: all of which are "responsibilities" cultivated in Thoreau's transcendentally constructed home away from home.

How one guides students through the text of *Walden* will no doubt depend on how one gets them to the text. The course I have been surveying prepares for a discussion of Thoreau's work as a historically situated work but also outfits students for a philosophically responsible saunter through the text. *Philosophically* here does not refer to a specific disciplinary methodology. "To be a philosopher," *Walden* asserts, "is not merely to have subtle thoughts, nor even to found a school. . . . It is," rather, "to solve some of the problems of life, not only theoretically, but practically" (14–15). *Responsible* connotes both being able to respond (to the world around one) and acknowledging one's obligation to respond philosophically, as it were, or at least thoughtfully—hence the responsibilities described in the preceding paragraph.

Saunter (as Thoreau defines the word in his essay "Walking") has to do with a particular way of moving through the world, a way of moving that is not unconnected to philosophy and responsibility and that requires a devoted attention to the environment through which one moves and of which one is part. "In my walks I would fain return to my senses," Thoreau remarks. "What business have I in the woods, if I am thinking of something out of the woods?" (*Excursions* 259).

The writer's philosophically responsible saunters through the world, his journeys to and from Walden, are the best metaphorical directions for reading and teaching *Walden* transcendentally. (And Stanley Cavell's *The Senses of Walden* provides a provocative gloss to these directions.) Thoreau's "extra- vagant" describes an important aspect of the efforts made by many transcendentalists to rethink the world through the interrelated actions of motion, vision, and participation. Motion involves transcending the static or accepted ways of construing the world, involves moving beyond prejudice:

> But alert and healthy natures remember that the sun rose clear. It is never too late to give up our prejudices. No way of thinking or doing, however ancient, can be trusted without proof. . . . Old deeds for old people, and new deeds for new.   (*Walden* 8)

Movement qua movement (and particularly movement away from an established site) matters more than destination, just as, in the parable from the opening chapter, "Economy," getting to Fitchburg in a hurry, by rail, is portrayed as more expensive (i.e., less economical) than going to Fitchburg deliberately, by walking. Perhaps the latter movement transcends the former by giving us time to think, which can also be a moving experience: "With thinking we may be beside ourselves in a sane sense" (134). Going beside ourselves is thus a way of losing ourselves, which makes possible the finding out who we are through observing what we have become: "Not till we are lost, in other words, not till we have lost the world, do we begin to find ourselves, and realize where we are and the infinite extent of our relations" (171).

Transcending, as the word's root indicates, therefore depends on movement. In moving, one must be thoughtful, deliberate, and, after brief periods of rest, ready to move on. The writer moves to Walden for reasons that do not include quitting the world; he departs under similar circumstances.

> I went to the woods because I wished to live deliberately, to front only the essential facts of life, and see if I could not learn what it had to teach, and not, when I came to die, discover that I had not lived.   (90–91)

> I left the woods for as good a reason as I went there. Perhaps it seemed to me that I had several more lives to live, and could not spare any more time for that one.   (323)

Teaching *Walden* in the context of transcendentalism thus involves encouraging students to experiment with moving through the text in ways similar to those in which the writer moves through his own texts. ("Books must be read as deliberately and reservedly as they were written" [101].) This approach, in turn, involves participating in the transcendental movement of *Walden*. Moving deliberately, unhurriedly, "philosophically," we become better readers—indeed, transcendental movement as it is expressed in *Walden* is arguably necessary for us to truly see.

Accordingly, a failure to move (and especially to move extravagantly) has serious consequences for the ability to see. "The result is dulness of sight, a stagnation of the vital circulations, and a general deliquium and sloughing off of all the intellectual faculties" (105). Awaking, arising, and moving on are imperative if one is to shake off the sleep of the habitual, the routinized, the established (or firmly placed). "By closing the eyes and slumbering, and consenting to be deceived by shows, men establish and confirm their daily life of routine and habit every where, which still is built on purely illusory foundations" (96). The writer of *Walden* would have us open our eyes and look around, if only to better read the text that is before us. The reading lessons professed in the text afford a description of an integral element of Thoreau's extravagance: "[W]e must laboriously seek the meaning of each word and line, conjecturing a larger sense than common use permits out of what wisdom and valor and generosity we have" (100). Careful and laborious attention to textual detail, conjecture that moves beyond the common use—such is transcendental reading. To teach *Walden* in a transcendentalist light therefore necessitates both a thorough discussion of the practice of reading and the practice of that practice.

In the classroom, such a discussion might occur around the passage cited immediately above. What does it mean to "laboriously seek the meaning," as Thoreau suggests? Does it mean that meaning is not simply there, on the page, waiting to fall before our eyes and be received as truth? Does meaning hide? Perhaps meaning is something that is made, and made with a great deal of labor. But by whom or what? Can we describe the process of the making of meaning? Does it really necessitate pondering over "each word and line"? If so, how can such a practice be enacted by students who must meet countless other institutional demands? At what price do we withhold participation from this making of meaning? And what about conjecture—what is it? What is the nature of the "larger sense" at which we are to arrive, and why does "common use" preclude that hoped-for arrival? Can we wander far enough beyond the limits of our daily experience to better discern the meanings to be made out of our "wisdom and valor and generosity"? And how? Such questions—and again, *Walden* is very much an invitation to students and teachers to participate in the raising and addressing of questions, a call for us to see just how we are yarded—belong to the practices of transcendental reading.

In Conclusion

Reading is, of course, not an end in itself; to the contrary, it is but a crucial aspect of the transcendental call to movement, vision, and participation:

> What is a course of history, or philosophy, or poetry, no matter how well selected, or the best society, or the most admirable routine of life, compared with the discipline of looking always at what is to be seen? Will you be a reader, a student merely, or a seer? Read your fate, see what is before you, and walk on into futurity. (111)

Read, see, walk. How can these injunctions be taught? The simple answer is by reading, seeing, walking; that is, by doing. My suggestion is thus that to teach Thoreau's *Walden* in the context of transcendentalism, we must teach transcendentally—not from the outside, observing a lifeless object, but from the inside, moving extra-vagantly within the bounds of transcendentalism, trying those bounds. This method means nothing more and nothing less than moving with students deliberately through the text of *Walden*, reading it with considerable care, seeing the infinite extent of its and our relations; participating in its questions, our questions; becoming responsible to its words, and for our words; conjecturing a larger sense than common use permits.

All those comments might seem to suggest that *Walden* requires an entire semester—and, of course, it does. In the absence of such luxury, it is better to move deliberately through sections that raise questions more pertinent to the course of which *Walden* is a part. I have painfully and who knows at what peril elided chapters 10–15 ("Baker Farm" through "Winter Animals," excepting "Higher Laws") and can report that even students the most interested in or captivated by the text forgave me (and most read the missing chapters on their own). Pursuing a study of transcendentalism from the inside, we engage one another with the issues raised by that movement while moving ourselves, in the course of a semester, between lectures, small-group conversations, and writing assignments that vary from shorter epistolary experiments to journal writing to the composition of formal essays. This movement allows students to slow down, to ponder, to discuss, while encouraging them to wander beyond the narrow limits of their daily experience, to keep the texts of transcendentalism, as well as their own minds, open.

Buell reminds us that Thoreau, in his sixteen-page interpretation of Emerson's "The Sphinx," was "forced to conclude that 'all commentaries must be finite, but a text is infinite'" (*Transcendentalism* 183). Definitions, in transcendentalism, become indefinite; conclusions become inconclusive—"around every circle another can be drawn" (Emerson, *Works* 2: 179). Consequently, we cannot properly close the book on these texts or on that movement. To engage *Walden* on its own transcendental terms, we must prepare students for participation in the arduous excavation of the book's foundations; we must encourage them in their explorations of its extra-vagances; we must converse with their deliberations and their provisional interpretations. We can neither flinch when confronted with "these deeper questions of life and being" nor shun our responsibilities to texts that provoke and educe. Do we run the risk of moralizing? Do we run the risk of neglecting the historical importance, the literary value of *Walden*? Perhaps. If, however, we neglect the educational extra-vagance of *Walden*, if we ignore the questions of living and being, if we fail to invite students to consider these questions actively and responsibly, participating in new definitions, do we not, as the writer of *Walden* observes (153), sit as many risks as we run?

"Where I Lived":
The Environs of *Walden*

William Howarth

> Both place and time were changed, and I dwelt nearer to
> those parts of the universe and to those eras in history
> which had most attracted me. Where I lived was as far
> off as many a region viewed nightly by astronomers.
>
> —Thoreau

In teaching *Walden*, I ask my students to see how the book maps a land both near and far, where the waters of New England mingle with the Ganges. The scene that inspired this "home-cosmography" (320) also lay far from Concord: on the highest peak in Maine. During August 1846 Thoreau tried to scale Mount Katahdin, until the mountain resisted his plans. On his upward climb he often lost the trail, and heavy storms barred him from reaching the summit. His descent led to more discovery, for the slope that his map called "Burnt Lands" was in fact a lush young forest, thickly strewn with blueberries. As he later wrote in "Ktaadn" (1848), the wild autonomy of this place haunted him:

> It is difficult to conceive of a region uninhabited by man. We habitually presume his presence and influence everywhere. . . . Here was no man's garden, but the unhandselled globe. It was not lawn, nor pasture, nor mead, nor woodland, nor lea, nor arable, nor waste-land. It was the fresh and natural surface of the planet Earth, as it was made forever and ever . . . Talk of mysteries!—Think of our life in nature,—daily to be shown matter, to come in contact with it,—rocks, trees, wind on our cheeks! the *solid* earth! the *actual* world! the *common sense! Contact! Contact! Who* are we? *where* are we? (*Maine Woods* 70–71)

This early passage, rhapsodic yet trained on forest succession, marks Thoreau's turn toward the empiricism that sustained his later work in literary ecology and environmental history. On Katahdin he discovered the inadequacy of maps and plans in the face of wilderness, a primeval world that dwarfed civilized effort. His prior life had passed in town and country, amid pastoral lands that obscured the solid "mysteries" of actuality. To think of nature was easy enough, yet what did nature think or need of humanity? Katahdin gave no answer, but it raised two central questions: Who are we? Where are we? At home Thoreau began to connect those questions by composing *Walden*, the story that relates just where and why he lived.

Teaching *Walden* is an enormous challenge, because the text enacts mystery and prophecy while cloaked in everyday garb. Its hero moves to a woods to ponder the universe, then finds his vision in "the long lost bottom" of a glacial pond (285). To know ourselves, Thoreau urges, we must awake to a true sense of place, our position in a material world. The "where" we live also defines who we are and what we live for, whether at home or counting cats in Zanzibar (322). He also describes time as a place, a spatial dimension that has weight and shape yet many elusive forms:

> In any weather, at any hour of the day or night, I have been anxious to improve the nick of time, and notch it on my stick too; to stand on the meeting of two eternities, the past and future, which is precisely the present moment; to toe that line.   (*Walden* 17)

Figures of geometry—line, parabola, angle, arc—often recur in Thoreau's prose after 1847, when he began to work as a land surveyor. From the perspective of a philosopher, surveying was a highly problematic trade. As a surveyor he could freely tramp Concord's woods and fields, yet his task was to fix locations and draw boundaries, using rational calculus to convert land into property. Drawing a chart was thus no innocent pastime, for the lot lines of someone's "place" also established that owner in a social hierarchy. Surveys staked claims and struck attitudes; they also bent their creator's personal talent toward larger communal designs.

After 1848 Thoreau sought to apply his "genius for mensuration" (*Excursions* 2) to founding a metaphysics on material landscape. He read extensively in geography and natural history, and most of his writings focus on the paradox of New England, a region of poor economic value but rich biological diversity. *Walden* examines the cool, temperate climate and its four distinct seasons; *The Maine Woods* and *Cape Cod* explore the glacial antipodes, rocky upland and sandy coast; and still other books describe the inland waters and forests. He constantly studied the "where" of his country, to grasp both its history and destiny. As he wrote in "Walking," "to what end does the world go on, and why was America discovered?" (*Excursions* 183).

In pursuing his ideas about land, Thoreau replaced the old mind-matter dualism of Western thought with an elastic monism in which reality is the environs, or full surroundings, of conscious life. The sources of his vision were varied and eclectic. Raised in a Unitarian family, he knew Eastern religions and transcendentalism, yet in time rejected their supraspatial ideas. The observation and experimentation of science attracted him, but Thoreau was never a strict logical positivist. A practical man, skilled at carpentry and gardening, he stubbornly clung to his common-sense mysticism. His mind embraced European Romanticism as well as the animism of Native Americans. Ultimately he saw reality as both fact and idea: hence he called time a line to toe and life a spiritual way through actual places.

Any teacher of *Walden* knows that readers often balk at crossing its rough and difficult ground. At a literal level the book describes "real" scenes and characters, yet always through highly refractive language. Each sentence uses the locative signals that linguists call deixis—at, in, upon, front, back, above, below, under, within—to position firmly the most fanciful ideas. This style generates many parables and riddles, the enigmas Thoreau calls necessary to his methods:

> You will pardon some obscurities, for there are more secrets in my trade than in most men's, and yet not voluntarily kept, but inseparable from its very nature. I would gladly tell all that I know about it, and never paint "No Admittance" on my gate.   (*Walden* 17)

His obscurity arises from writing so concretely, yet aspiring to attain "the language which all things and events speak without metaphor" (111). At times that goal eludes him, as when he calls oral and written language our "mother" and "father" tongues, with the feminine side "almost brutish" and the masculine "reserved and select" (101). This analogy is sexist and also atypical, for elsewhere Thoreau describes language as a single natural force, like the "sand foliage" at the railroad cut (306–09).

Facing the tangle of words and ideas in *Walden*, the teacher finds little help in previous critics, who tend to fumble works that are sui generis. Thoreau's advocates see *Walden* as a defiant manifesto, which urges us to drop out and seek our private arcadia. His detractors say *Walden* is a bitter diatribe, written by a hermit who was a misanthrope and bad economist. Both views are literal and reductive; both concur in the view that *Walden* is antisocial. As Thoreau dryly observes, stirring his mélange of memoir, jeremiad, and spiritual odyssey, "It is not all books that are as dull as their readers" (107). Although his focus on landscape often suggests to some that *Walden* is "nature writing," that terrain—as Robert Finch and John Elder admit—"is vast and only partially mapped" (17), and *Walden* seems quite particular about its domain. The "scenery of Walden" (*Walden* 175) is not a backdrop but the very foreground of Thoreau's purpose.

Students trained in science may ask if *Walden* is a work of natural history. Thomas Lyon traces that prose tradition from Carolus Linnaeus, whose *Systema Naturae* (1735) created taxonomy, the naming and categorizing of species. Linnaeus shaped such early naturalists as Gilbert White and William Bartram, but Thoreau pushed beyond them to absorb the dynamic ideas of modern geology and biology, as expressed by Charles Lyell, Louis Agassiz, and Charles Darwin. Inspired by evolutionary theory, Thoreau spent years studying plant succession and distribution, yet he published little of that work before his death, in 1862. Surviving manuscripts indicate that he saw how interspecies relations affect reproduction; his original discovery was later confirmed by Gregor Mendel's theory of genetics (1866) and Ernst Haeckel's coinage "ecology" (1869)

This melding of science and philosophy distinguishes Thoreau from the early naturalists, while the range of his ideas links him to the movement now called environmentalism. The word *environment* means surroundings and enfolds the old nature-culture dichotomy into a biocentric union. In *The Maine Woods* Thoreau wrote that he and a pine tree might one day go to the same heaven, a bit of heresy that anticipates the ecological concept of nature as a self-sustaining aggregate, containing diverse yet related organisms and conditions. Thoreau anticipated ecology by exploring and analyzing Concord, which he saw as both an actual landscape and the ideal of common ground, a place of natural community.

Among American writers Thoreau is what biologists call a type specimen, the original that establishes a species' name and description. Difficult to classify by conventional terms, he raises new categories of definition. In *Walden* Thoreau attacks the waste of natural resources and calls for greater thrift and simplicity, anticipating today's global call for low-impact, sustainable economies. His essay "Walking" urges the preservation of wilderness for its cultural value, an idea often cited now to protect endangered species and habitats. Famed also for his antislavery stands, Thoreau has become a prime mentor to many literary successors, from John Muir and Mary Austin to Annie Dillard and Barry Lopez. When Aldo Leopold based *A Sand County Almanac* (1949) on a year in rural Wisconsin, he paid homage to Thoreau. By connecting landscape to the seasonal cycle, *Walden* offers environmental writers a prototype in both form and content.

I often warn my students that *Walden* may task their patience. Its tone is at first harshly didactic, but then it matures and moderates through the seasons. To convey this calendar cycle, Thoreau compresses two years of life into one "for convenience" (84). In his study of the *Walden* papers, J. Lyndon Shanley found that the multiple drafts (1847–54) have a consistent plan: first a discourse on economy, then the circle of a fabled year. That design gives the story its rhythmic cycle, as time turns on a fixed place, once in "Economy" and again on a wider circuit. The effect resembles music, an overture followed by movements. Winter first appears in one passage on ice cutters (75), but later the season provides a long interlude, the months of confinement that induce Thoreau to survey Walden Pond.

The annual cycle also has its daily rounds, which bring "a fresh prospect every hour" (112) and repeat the circle of time. Thoreau shapes the day into "an epitome of the year" (301) and a mirror of history. Morning "brings back the heroic ages" of early Greece (88), while evening leads toward future dreams, glimpsed as he drifts at night, his mind led "to vast and cosmogonal themes in other spheres" (175). The passage of time gives *Walden* its evolving pace, as Thoreau turns from a voice of "quiet desperation" (8) into a seasoned observer, ready to leave the woods and become "a sojourner in civilized life again" (3).

This adaptive course also governs Thoreau's places, the landscapes that form an environs in *Walden*. At first his place references are general; then they grow more defined and related, as in an ecosystem. Or he uses induction to link facts and ideas, turning opposites—large and small, near and far—into constituents, until a local scene acquires global scale. Walden is a freshwater pond, yet also a mountain tarn, a holy stream, a mirror of heaven. If New England seems a hard, mean country, then "our vision does not penetrate the surface of things. We think that that *is* which *appears* to be" (96). By that symbolic logic the pond lies both here and there, near and far: "It is as much Asia or Africa as New England. I have, as it were, my own sun and moon and stars, and a little world all to myself" (130).

Students may see this rhetoric as egocentric, but Thoreau's purpose is in fact expansive. His notion of "a little world all to myself" accords with J. B. Jackson's idea of vernacular landscape, the everyday places that cultures too often dismiss as local, rural, or provincial. Thoreau argues that Walden may echo thoughts of great range and depth, for a pond also has those dimensions. That is why his township is a sufficient realm to survey, for it comprises in one place and name a common ground of harmony: "I have travelled a good deal in Concord" (4).

To travel in Concord, students may examine maps or pictures of its landscape. A map will verify that Thoreau is no hermit, since his house at Walden lies a mile and a half from town, a short walk by road or railway track. This proximity brings traffic his way, as townsfolk often stop at Walden to fish, hunt, or pick berries. He welcomes such visitors, heaping scorn only on neighbors who live "imprisoned rather than housed" (34) and never escape their confinement: "It is time that villages were universities . . . Cannot students be boarded here and get a liberal education under the skies of Concord?" (109). Even so, "The Village" reports his visits to town "every day or two" for news, gossip, and errands. Given that society, Concord, "taken in homœopathic doses, [is] really as refreshing" as the woods (167).

His alternative to town or pond might have been a country farm, for Thoreau spent several months in 1844 hunting for tenant land. *Walden* gives a jocular account of that failed bargain: "But I retained the landscape, and I have since annually carried off what it yielded without a wheelbarrow" (82). This radical notion of value affects his later story of visiting Baker Farm, where he urges its "shiftless" Irish tenant, John Field, to give up hard labor and a gross diet. The advice seems callous, given Thoreau's privileges, but his main advantage over Field is locational. While fishing, Field has no luck, even after changing places, because he ignores his surroundings, "thinking to live by some derivative old country mode in this primitive new country,—to catch perch with shiners" (208).

Students who know forest ecology will see why Thoreau finds suitable environs at Walden Pond. Receding glaciers left the region dotted with knobby hills and deep lakes, known as drumlins and kettles, and this undulant terrain provides both good vistas and well-drained soil. Add a cool, moist climate, and the earth produces mixed woodland, a biome that supports diverse species. Within easy reach Thoreau has pitch pines for shelter, oaks for fuel, and hickories for food. Lining his footpath to the pond are berry bushes so laden with fruit that they break their "tender limbs" (114). He never gets lost in these woods, not even walking at night on faint paths, though many of his visitors do, wandering half the night in rain and mud near their destinations.

This passage deserves a close reading, for it sums up Thoreau's environmental vision. In tracking his lost visitors, he identifies with them, opening into broader thoughts on place and orientation. The moment recalls his epiphany on Katahdin, when confusion and surprise challenged his habits. Losing one's way leads to revelation: "[N]ot till we are completely lost, or turned around . . . do we appreciate the vastness and strangeness of Nature." The turning spins us around, into dark woods and then new light: "[N]ot till we have lost the world, do we begin to find ourselves, and realize where we are and the infinite extent of our relations" (171). Rejecting the denials of Jesus, who offers everlasting life to all who relinquish home and family (Matt. 19.29), Thoreau celebrates the binding force of relations. His book is a narrative, related to readers; it bonds with neighbors and friends, who give him words and tropes; and it incarnates the ecology of Walden, where natural relations sustain all life.

His house embodies that congruity, for he builds it with native and recycled materials, gathering stones from the pond and lumber from a used shanty. An abandoned woodchuck burrow suggests the location of his cellar, dug into a sandy, south-facing slope well below the frost line. Sunlight and air spill into his home; he scrubs its floor with pond water and sand. In fall he plasters the walls and erects a chimney, concocting mortar from burnt clamshells. At the fireplace he burns driftwood or waste wood, and moles creep into the cellar below, partaking of warmth and a few potatoes. His house is no intrusion at Walden but a place adapted to its site and function, "as open and manifest as a bird's nest" (244).

Equally well located is his crop field, Thoreau's major source of food. For this site he moves up the slope to a sunny clearing and plants two and a half acres with hardy vegetables: beans, potatoes, peas, corn, and turnips. His hoe often unearths Indian relics, a sign of early planters, and though the sandy, graveled soil is "lean and effete" (155), his harvest yields over thirty bushels, enough for food and a modest profit. In his second year he reduces the plot of beans, to increase their meaning to him, and sees this ground as a boundary, "the connecting link between wild and cultivated fields" (158), where he may cross lines: "It was no longer beans that I hoed, nor I that hoed beans" (159). The act of bending his mind to land proves suitable, "if only for the sake of tropes and expression, to serve a parable-maker one day" (162). What he serves is cultivation: stirring the earth, he waits for sun and rain "with a corresponding trust and magnanimity" (166).

Learning his relation to place and time brings Thoreau into kinship with his *amicus locus*, the scenery of Walden Pond (175). The pond answers his inner need "to transact some private business" (19), for it has hidden as well as apparent attributes. Constantly he watches the pond's variable surface, sleek and smooth, with ghostly mist rising, or lashed with waves from a strong wind. These shifting moods reflect his own, yet the pond's lower depths may contain "a hard bottom and rocks in place, which we can call *reality*" (98), like the mysterious actuality he saw in Maine. The two planes, surface and depth, become his means of charting both literal and figurative dimensions. Thoreau's task is not just to personify Walden, as he does with analogies to lips, eyes, and brows (180–86), but also to see it as alien, beyond his power to understand.

The passages that merit close discussion in class all trace Thoreau's shift from surface views of Walden to what lies below. His guides are creatures who know the depths, from fish who tug at lines to the loon who plays "a pretty game" of hide-and-seek, always evading capture by heading to the widest and deepest water (235). He seizes an advantage in winter, when the pond surface freezes to ice, for then it supports his weight and allows him to study the bottom at leisure, "like a picture behind a glass." The ice itself draws his interest, and from patient observation he infers cause and effect: small bubbles of air rise from the bottom, freeze at the surface, and in spring become lenses that magnify the sun (246, 248).

The same inductive process leads him out on the ice "to recover the long lost bottom of Walden Pond." Using a surveyor's tools of compass, chain, and sounding line, he records a depth of 102 feet. Perhaps "this pond was made deep and pure for a symbol," but in drawing a chart he finds a startling new insight: that bottom and surface show a "remarkable coincidence," the lines of greatest length and width intersecting at the point of greatest depth (285, 287, 289). This formula reveals that all dimensions coincide, if we know how to read them. The truth learned at one point applies elsewhere, perhaps anywhere; even in ethics and psychology. That was the question he heard in Maine, a question "which I had been endeavoring in vain to answer in my sleep, as what—how—when—where?" (282), and the answer was clear: awake to the here and now.

After this encounter, Thoreau may return to Concord, the place for preparing his "simple and sincere account" (3). If his desire is "to speak somewhere *without* bounds," he also accepts those limits, since "[f]or the most part, we are not where we are, but in a false position" (324, 327). Repeatedly he seeks an honest post, through acts of civil decency. He shelters a runaway slave, helps lost visitors, recalls outcasts who once lived nearby; and his cordiality extends to nature. "Why do precisely these objects which we behold make a world?" (225). Because we share a place and time: "Shall I not have intelligence with the earth? Am I not partly leaves and vegetable mould myself?" (138). That may be the most enduring truth he imparts in *Walden*, that the earth teaches us not how but where to live.

The Many Paths to and from *Walden*

Richard Lebeaux

"It is remarkable," Thoreau wrote in *Walden*, "how easily and insensibly we fall into a particular route, and make a beaten track for ourselves. I had not lived there a week before my feet wore a path from my door to the pond-side" (323). Though, as educators know, it is always possible to "make a beaten track" by teaching the same material more or less the same way each time, I have found *Walden* to be a work that resists tendencies toward stagnation. Partly I have not worn one path because I am by nature a pluralist and by training a practitioner of interdisciplinary approaches. Partly I have been prevented from falling into one "particular route" because I have taught *Walden* in several different contexts and have had to adapt my teaching to the context, whether it be in freshman writing courses with an emphasis on American culture; in primarily (but not exclusively) undergraduate courses like New England Writers: How Is a Life to Be Lived? and New England Writers: Literature and Life; in American literature survey courses at the community college and college levels; in upper-level and graduate courses on the American Renaissance and on the transcendentalists; or in a seminar on Thoreau. *Walden*, moreover, is a book that does not easily lend itself to closure, to any one reductive interpretation. Finally, my teaching of the book has had to take into account how students have changed with the times and zeitgeist.

It has often been helpful to consider not only the paths that can be taken to or into *Walden*—the various approaches that lead to a richer understanding and appreciation of the book itself—but also the many paths that lead from, are generated by, *Walden*—the ways in which responding to what is written and how it was written lead constructively to student reflection, discussion, and writing.

Walden is such a rich and challenging book that reading it can prove an over-whelming experience for many, from freshmen to advanced students. Thus I seek to prepare all my students for the experience. I encourage them not to get discouraged and to be patient: while the work can have a powerful effect on many at first reading, evoking intense, passionate responses and even changing people's lives, it is initially neither a quick read nor an easily digestible one. One need not understand every statement or allusion Thoreau makes. I stress that one can revise one's reading of *Walden*—in the light of further experience and knowledge, class discussion, and rereading—just as one can revise one's writing. The book frequently grows on and with a reader, not just in the course of a semester or year but over a lifetime. In this context, I would mention Erik Erikson's conception of human development and the life cycle, one approach I have used to understand Thoreau and *Walden*.

The book is a sort of time-release capsule. My own experience of it has changed and evolved over the years. Thoreau advocated continuing education in *Walden*, and the book itself must be considered part of the syllabus for such an education. While telling students not to be frustrated or intimidated by their first encounter with the book (or at least to understand better their frustra-tion)—giving them permission not to comprehend or digest everything—I also try to challenge them, invoking Thoreau's assertion that reading is a "noble in-tellectual exercise" and that "we have to stand on tiptoe to read and devote our most alert and wakeful hours to [it]" (104).

Another path I have found helpful leading both into and away from *Walden* is to stress how the book was written. I explain that Thoreau went to Walden Pond a week before his twenty-eighth birthday and wrote the first draft of *Walden* while at the pond but that by the time the book was published (after several drafts and revisions), he was eight years older—and more seasoned and weathered by his experience and writing in the intervening years. I bring in my imposing two-volume Dover edition of the fourteen-volume Journal, J. Lyndon Shanley's *The Making of Walden* (which includes the first draft), and Ronald Clapper's "The Development of *Walden*: A Genetic Text," and I show how de-liberately, persistently, and craftily Thoreau worked over *Walden*. Stephen Adams and Donald Ross's *Revising Mythologies: The Composition of Thoreau's Major Works* has also proved helpful. In my writing courses (and in other courses where I deal with Thoreau), I emphasize how important both reading and writing are as process, not just product, and how crucial it is to think of writing in terms of composing several drafts. Books like Carl Bode's edition of *The Selected Journals of Henry D. Thoreau* can be used, alongside *Walden*, to reveal something of the author's composing process. For writing students in particular, such text comparison illustrates how journal writing generates ideas, insights, expression, and often a more polished style. Thoreau's example also underscores the humanness of the writing process. Though one can't deny his gifts as a writer, a finished work like *Walden* did not spring full-grown from his forehead. Both perspiration and inspiration were necessary ingredients, and this realization helps take the mystique (if not the mystery) out of the creative process. Of course, Thoreau's vividness, wit, and rhetorical strategies also serve as fine models for writers, both novice and advanced.

In a recent seminar on Thoreau, I stressed the ongoing composition of *Walden* in the context of the author's life and other writings. Thus the early portions of *Walden* primarily associated with Shanley's first draft were shown to date from the 1845–47 period at the pond. Making use of Clapper's "Development" and Adams and Ross's *Revising Mythologies*, I assigned other chapters of *Walden* somewhat later in the course, to reflect the chronology and stages of their composition during the 1849–54 period and their relations to Thoreau's life and to such works as the Journal, "Chesuncook," parts of *Cape Cod*, and his letter to H. G. O. Blake, "Chastity and Sensuality." Also assigned in the course were chapters from my book *Thoreau's Seasons*, which seeks to trace and understand the evolution of *Walden* in the context of Thoreau's life, psychology, writing, and artistic development. Such an approach dramatizes the extent to which *Walden* did not simply describe the Walden experience itself but also emerged crucially from the experience, writing, and artistic growth of the years between his departure from Walden and his composing of the final draft of the book.

One perspective or hypothesis set forth in *Thoreau's Seasons*, which I introduce particularly to advanced students, is that *Walden* might more aptly be subtitled "Life in the Words" than "Life in the Woods," that the author was primarily a creator of a persona that must be distinguished from the historical Thoreau and of a world (or woods) of words that must be distinguished from the real experience of living at the pond. Thus *Walden* cannot be taken strictly as autobiography. I try to explain how the persona of *Walden* emerged from Thoreau's psychological needs and life context.

On every student level I attempt to instill a sense of the process of analogy, emphasizing Thoreau's belief in the correspondence between nature and human experience. Indeed, as one way of introducing transcendentalism, Thoreau, and *Walden*—a way that has generated much student enthusiasm—I have sometimes brought to class (particularly in the autumn) leaves and photographs of leaves of varying colors and shapes. I encourage the students to examine the leaves carefully, to consider the life cycle of leaves, and reflect on how they may serve as metaphors or analogies for human truths. As we ponder what the autumn leaves tell us about human maturity, aging, mortality, and possible immortality, I invite students also to note the structural similarities among leaves—the veins, the branchings out, the river-and-tributary qualities. Such an activity helps bring home the process of analogizing and seeking correspondences, which was central to Thoreau. I quote Emerson's statements from *Nature*: "Particular natural facts are symbols of particular spiritual facts" and "Nature is the symbol of spirit" (*Works* 1: 17). I quote a passage or two from Thoreau, such as his observation in "Autumnal Tints" about how the leaves "teach us how to die" (*Excursions* 241). I refer to the connection

Thoreau made between ice crystallization and leaves (I may bring in pictures of ice crystals and ask my students to scrutinize them for comparisons with the leaves), and then I discuss the "Spring" chapter in *Walden*, in which Thoreau observes the thawing clay, or "sand foliage" (306); declares that "there is nothing inorganic" (308); and suggests (as Robert Richardson also points out in *Henry David Thoreau: A Life of the Mind*) how the leaf reflects a universal organic pattern and law of growth—a truth that was crucial to Thoreau (304–09). I have, in fact, begun to explore with students the extent to which the lessons of the leaves may be a key to understanding Thoreau's art and vision.

I introduce advanced students to the many sources now available for studies of Thoreau and *Walden*, invoking Thoreau's injunction in the book that he "would have each one be very careful to find out and pursue his own way" (71). I demonstrate how this book, which calls on others to simplify, has both engendered an enormous body of varied interpretations and is itself highly complex and sophisticated in content, form, imagery, and rhetorical strategies. I encourage students to see the writer and book in many contexts and from a wide spectrum of critical approaches. I try to get advanced students to trust their responses; to see what works, is meaningful, or makes sense for them and not to be intimidated or overwhelmed by the wealth of scholarly writing. I present my views on Thoreau and *Walden* as articulated in *Young Man Thoreau* and *Thoreau's Seasons*, but I certainly do not push students to accept these views, even though some prefer a more authoritarian or doctrinaire stance. There is, then, ample room for eclectic and pluralistic inquiry, controversy, and new departures in my advanced classes.

For all my students, I give a biographical introduction to *Walden* (as well as a literary historical one), part of which stresses that the myth of Thoreau as a man living alone in the wilderness, far from civilization, is just that, a myth. I will read to them, say, from Walter Harding's *The Days of Henry Thoreau*, the description of Thoreau's life while at the pond, and we will consider how Thoreau got to Walden—his search for purity and independence, for a moratorium, a satisfying identity, and a commitment. The facts often evoke disillusionment or disappointment in students who have either accepted the myth from previous exposure or are quick to accept, need to accept fully, the persona and life that Thoreau projects in *Walden*. Sometimes I have to defend Thoreau, especially from charges of hypocrisy. I share my belief that the facts humanize him for me, make him a more interesting, complex, accessible figure, who had to struggle and whose achievements were hard-won. Also, I appreciate fully the power of Thoreau's language and art and the power of the audience's desire or need to believe in the myth and persona. Bringing to the fore the historical Thoreau also dramatizes the distinctions between life and art and leads readers to inquire into the dynamics, the creative and psychological processes, by which life is translated and transmuted into art. And I argue that the book stands on its own as a work of art and is not delegitimized by the divergencies between the historical Thoreau and the persona of *Walden*. The force of the word to inspire and instruct is, I emphasize, embodied in such classics as *Walden*.

It should come as no surprise that *Walden* was in some ways easier to teach and met with a generally more receptive audience in the 1960s and early 1970s than now. Recent students—especially those who are not majoring in the liberal arts—are often put off or threatened by such chapters of *Walden* as "Economy." Many see themselves striving for the very economic security and material rewards that Thoreau criticizes so sharply there. I sometimes discover myself defending Thoreau's ideas about success and material wealth to angry or uneasy students who see Thoreau challenging their premises, values, and goals. (In the early 1970s, however, I often had to play devil's advocate against Thoreau, since more students then seemed to accept what he wrote.) Such a dynamic has led to many heated but fruitful discussions and essays. I seek to supply some historical perspective (as Michael Meyer does so well in *Several More Lives to Live*) on the people of my generation who in the 1960s were generally attracted to Thoreau's ideas. Yet I add that if they were transplanted into the 1980s or later, they would probably feel just as threatened. I say that I understand why many students tend to be career-oriented and relatively conservative or apathetic today: the economy has led them, legitimately, to be concerned about their economic future, and they feel they must commit themselves early to particular (and lucrative and secure) careers. At the same time, I explain that reading *Walden* can be a liberating and consciousness-raising experience, can suggest alternatives they may not have considered (or allowed themselves to consider), can give them perspective, or at least reduce the fear, sense of entrapment, and push toward premature commitment many students feel. I add that, even if they are not ready to accept what Thoreau is saying now, there may be a time later in their academic or nonacademic lives when *Walden*'s lessons make more sense and provide them with the insight and courage to make changes or to remain true to principles they might otherwise discard. Even if many undergraduates are not prepared to accept the possibility that they may face "quiet desperation" in their lives (and some students *do* find themselves articulating desperation), that they may be prematurely committing themselves to careers, they may come back to *Walden* for refreshment, encouragement, and validation in future years. Many students still do champion Thoreau and find in *Walden* a philosophy that speaks to some of their deepest yearnings and idealism. The give-and-take in class, as well as Thoreau's own dramatic, emphatic, often purposefully exaggerated "extra vagant" pronouncements in *Walden*, tend to generate excellent topics and papers. I make it clear that students need not agree with me or Thoreau in their discussion and writing; thus they learn to stand up to, talk back to, and question authority (both the teacher and the "great writer") in ways that Thoreau would approve of.

I try to present a differentiated point of view on Thoreau, indicating that I question or feel uncomfortable about much in *Walden* (some concerns the students often raise themselves): the argument that philanthropy is "greatly overrated" by humankind; the apparent lack of compassion and the arrogance that seem to characterize Thoreau's response to John Field; the discussion of sexuality in "Higher Laws"; the overemphasis on individualism and the relative lack of concern for community and human interdependence; the potential that Thoreau's philosophy has for legitimizing a conservative mentality; and the occasional misanthropy and misogyny in *Walden*. I also point out some of Thoreau's seemingly contradictory statements about "wildness" (sometimes I use handouts or selections from "Ktaadn" and the moose-hunting section in *The Maine Woods*) and suggest that even someone as self-assured as Thoreau had not fully resolved the conflicts in his book or in his life. Furthermore, views that are apparently contradictory may ultimately be complementary, both-and (or yin-yang) instead of either-or. Thus students are encouraged to perceive Thoreau in a more complex light, which leads to more sensitive, less reductive essays on *Walden*, Thoreau, and other topics.

One set of questions that is consistently successful in freshman and survey courses asks students to consider *Walden* and the Walden experience as metaphor or archetype of what Erik Erikson calls a psychosocial moratorium: "'Every person should have a Walden': how would you interpret this statement in a metaphoric sense? Do you have a metaphoric 'Walden'—or have you had a Walden-like experience?" I have received all sorts of responses: students may find their Walden in a favorite natural spot where they can get away from it all; in an activity like walking, jogging, listening to music, or reading; in a close friend or family member; in a special state of mind; in the keeping of a diary; in a small, shabby, but somehow peaceful room in a tenement.

When I teach *Walden* as part of courses like New England Writers: How Is a Life to Be Lived?, I urge students to keep a journal (a practice of many transcendentalists, I stress) in which they can not only respond to *Walden* but also reflect on their lives. This approach almost always works; *Walden*, as difficult as it may sometimes be, impels people to meditate on how they live, how they see the world, how they may change or grow in constructive ways. *Walden* was meant to be provocative, and it still does provoke questions and soul-searching about how a life is to be lived—whether or not students agree with Thoreau's particular perspectives and answers. It contains much wisdom, even if each person ultimately must find his or her own way.

Walden has also served to stimulate some fine creative writing. One of the most memorable student works I ever read was written by a freshman in my first New England Writers class. She created a drama that put Thoreau, Emerson, Hawthorne, and Melville in the same room, to contemplate and discuss among themselves how to deal with a Bartleby-type figure. (Our class trip to see a production of *The Night Thoreau Spent in Jail* may have planted the seeds of her dramatic project.) Another remarkable creative work by a student was a haunting song written as if through Thoreau's eyes and voice and performed on tape by the singer-songwriter.

Though I have taught *Walden* many times, I still believe the paths to and from the book are not exhausted. For example, I developed a seminar, New England Writers: Literature and Life, that, using *Walden* as a starting point and touchstone, considers women's, feminist, and men's Waldens; utopias and dystopias; the interplay between writing and life; and the formulations of particular writers on how a life is, or is not, to be lived. Among the works I have included are Nathaniel Hawthorne's *The Blithedale Romance*, Herman Melville's "The Paradise of Bachelors and the Tartarus of Maids," Edward Bellamy's *Looking Backward*, Mary E. Wilkins Freeman's "A New England Nun," Charlotte Perkins Gilman's "The Yellow Wallpaper," Edith Wharton's *Ethan Frome*, Alice Koller's *An Unknown Woman*, May Sarton's *Journal of a Solitude*, Bernard Malamud's *Dubin's Lives*, and Marge Piercy's *Woman on the Edge of Time*. Of course, many other works could be considered, with and without a New England focus. The connections, comparisons, and contrasts among such works have been exciting and edifying to make.

As should be clear, my enthusiasm for teaching *Walden* in a variety of contexts and putting it to a variety of uses remains strong. The book continues to have "several more lives to live" (323) in the classroom. As far as teaching *Walden* is concerned, I am confident that "[t]here is more day to dawn. The sun is but a morning star" (333).

Reader Responses to *Walden*:
A Study of Undergraduate Reading Patterns

Richard Dillman

Henry David Thoreau's *Walden* is a fascinating book to teach because it elicits a wide variety of responses from undergraduate readers. The responses fall into identifiable patterns and illustrate much about undergraduate reading processes as reflected in the classroom experience. This essay deals with the response patterns that I have observed over the past eight years at Saint Cloud State University, a comprehensive regional university of about fifteen thousand students in central Minnesota.

I have used *Walden* in a variety of classes, including advanced composition, American nonfiction, honors freshman English, American literature, and an advanced course in literary theory. In all cases, I ask students to keep an academic journal of their responses to sections of *Walden*, which I later read and evaluate. The sections range in length from two to three chapters. Some of these responses are specifically solicited by questions such as these for chapters 1 and 2: Why does Thoreau forsake society to live by Walden Pond? Why does Thoreau reject commercialism? I also solicit nondirected responses, which I call open responses since students may choose their own topic. Occasionally, in a course in advanced rhetoric, I ask students to comment on Thoreau's style in ways that enhance their understanding of his uses of language.

During this eight-year period, I have used *Walden* in fifteen different classes with an average enrollment of twenty, for a total of nearly three hundred students and three hundred individual journals. From these journals and the class discussions that they generated, I have identified the various reader-response patterns to *Walden* that are the subject of this paper. The paper is based not on subjective impressions but on written student responses. The journals are my research sample, my database. In them, the students were free, inasmuch as the journal format allowed, to be candid about what they thought of the text. I assured them at the outset of each term that their academic journal was a place where they could respond openly and with as much honesty and integrity as possible. I assured them that I was not treating *Walden* as a literary monument to be worshiped, that I did not want my opinions parroted, and that I would not grade students down for negative or unusual responses to the text. I graded students pass-fail for the quantity of their work—if they did the requisite number of entries—and I gave a letter grade for quality, evaluating whether the entries were relevant to the assigned chapters or topics and whether the entries were developed in more than superficial ways. Moreover, the journal did not count for more than twenty percent of the course grade. Reading the journals was an education in the drama and dynamics of reading and a fascinating study of the interactions among reader, text, and other factors, such as the classroom environment. I also knew each student's major or proposed major and so was able to draw connections between responses to *Walden* and readers' interests and career goals.

Why do such a study of *Walden*? The book is excellent for such a study for several reasons. First, it is of enduring value, being widely read over one hundred years after its initial publication. Second, it deals with themes important to American culture, such as the conflict between individualism and the needs of society, the individual's place in a materialist culture, and our relation to the natural world. And, third, it advocates positions outside conventional American thought, consistently arguing against many of the basic assumptions of American economic life. There are, of course, other reasons. Thoreau's aggressive tone and rhetorical tactics, particularly in "Economy" and "Where I Lived, and What I Lived For," often offend student readers as Thoreau challenges them to question established notions. Moreover, *Walden*, to a large extent a book about identity, is being read by late adolescent undergraduates who are examining their lives and asking basic questions about identity. Another reason for selecting *Walden* for such a study is the book's quirkiness. *Walden* is eccentric, not easily interpreted and categorized. Its shifting rhetorical modes challenge readers, requiring them to be intellectually nimble enough to suspend many of their conventional ideas of prose form and narrative movement as Thoreau moves from argument to dialectic to nature description to poetic representation to philosophical exploration. Students must deal with the question of genre at the level of reader response, wondering if the book is a novel, autobiography, a form of nonfiction, a collection of essays, a collection of polemics, or perhaps, in places, a prose poem. The classifications are problematic and unclear.

One common pattern is that students find the first two chapters of *Walden* far more difficult than the rest of the book. In general, they consider "Economy" and "Where I Lived, and What I Lived For" intense, argumentative, and full of complex ideas and sophisticated rhetorical strategies impossible to understand without a teacher's help. Thoreau often puzzles them with his paradoxes and allusions, while he sometimes insults them with his aphorisms. The syntax and vocabulary often seem archaic to them. For many students, these two chapters are a test, a barrier that indicates how far and how deeply they will read. Those that make it through chapter 2 will usually complete the book with less effort, while those who do not will usually have trouble with the remainder of *Walden*, perhaps assuming that it follows the same pattern. I know several students so alienated by the first two chapters that they were unable to finish the book and thus gain a full appreciation of Thoreau's achievement. Ironically, editors of American literature anthologies commonly select these chapters, which become the only Thoreau writings that general education students ever read.

Such a response to the first two chapters is understandable. Thoreau's stance here is often uncompromising, candid, and, to some readers, brutally direct. His purpose is to wake his neighbors (his readers and listeners). He hammers away at his theme point by point, attacking numerous sacred cows with an arsenal of such devices as aphorism, paradox, and the rhetorical question. His pace is fast, his tone assertive, arrogant. Lines like the following abound: "But lo! men have become the tools of their tools" (37); "The mass of men lead lives of quiet desperation" (8); "I have since learned that trade curses every thing it handles" (70); and "I have learned that the swiftest traveller is he that goes afoot" (53).

Generally students respond much more positively to the remaining sixteen chapters. They conceptualize the book into two parts—the intense two initial chapters and the longer, more poetic, more imagistic ones that follow. They feel that in chapters 3 through 16 Thoreau is less argumentative, more humane, more poetic, and more visual. In this second part, they can slow down, enjoy the woods, and view the fish. Occasionally some students are puzzled by such chapters as "Reading" or "Baker Farm." On the whole Thoreau's nature imagery and his skillful and detailed portrayal of the pond impress students, even those hostile to his message. A common response is, "Thoreau has let up on us—now we can enjoy nature writing."

Among more specific kinds of readers are those that appreciate Thoreau's use of language. About twenty-five percent of my sample fits this category. These students marvel at his sententious sentences (aphorisms, paradoxes, proverbs, etc.), frequently transcribing into their journals sentences they find attractive, as though they were making entries in commonplace books. Members of this group often comment on the quality of Thoreau's images and metaphors, expressing enthusiasm for his use of sensory, concrete language like this: "Time is but the stream I go a-fishing in. I drink at it; but while I drink I see the sandy bottom and detect how shallow it is. Its thin current slides away, but eternity remains" (98).

Another group of readers is alienated by Thoreau's message and aggressively anticommercial tone. These readers—about twenty-five to thirty percent of the sample—tend to claim majors other than English. They feel that Thoreau—with his antimaterialist and anticonformist thrust—attacks their values. The idea of someone educated and seemingly intelligent turning away from comfort and the American dream of economic or political success to live a simple forest life often shocks this type of reader. Class discussions and the majors indicated by students suggest that members of this group tend to be strongly committed to economic success and America's corporate culture. Many are business majors, while others have chosen such fields as political science, criminal justice, and computer science. For many of them, Thoreau's ideas, particularly those in the first two chapters, are difficult to confront emotionally; while the students may understand Thoreau, their ideological and personal career commitments prevent them from reading *Walden* with an open mind. Their common response is simply to reject the book as the work of an eccentric, rebellious loner with an aberrant mind. Such readers often seek to diminish Thoreau's stature as a writer and person by asking questions and making comments like these: Didn't he have a family? How did he get along with women? (The assumption being that he did not.) He must have disliked people. He had to be antisocial. He certainly had a distorted personality. They say that his friends invited him over for dinner and that his mother brought food to him at his cabin. (The point here being that such actions contradict the message of *Walden* and thus discredit the author.) Many of these readers illustrate I. A. Richards's concept of doctrinal interference (14), showing how firmly held ideologies can influence the reading process.

In direct contrast to the group of alienated readers is another group—about ten percent of the sample—that agrees with most of Thoreau's ideas. Because these students agree with Thoreau, they allow him all his excesses and unproved assertions. They tend to share his vision, tending also to take a moralistic view of life. They often see American consumer capitalism as excessive, decadent, or unfair to Third World countries. This group comes from a variety of majors, usually in the humanities and social sciences. Many of these "true believers" are strong environmentalists holding firm commitments to the preservation or restoration of ecological balance in America. While they do not necessarily think we should live in small cabins like Thoreau, they do think we can simplify our lives and reduce the conspicuous waste our culture creates. They strongly agree with Thoreau's criticism of America, seeing it as still valid or even more valid today, but they do not necessarily agree with Thoreau's temporary solution for reducing the complexities of life. His solution may have been viable for him, they argue, but it isn't viable for everyone. These readers illustrate what Kenneth Burke calls identification in *A Rhetoric of Motives* (55). They do not have to be persuaded, since they are fellow travelers with Thoreau. The overlap of their concerns with his leads to a positive response and the quick acceptance of his ideas. It is often difficult for such students to critically evaluate Thoreau's ideas, to see holes in his arguments, or to understand other sides to his positions.

Still others read *Walden* as though it were a religious text or a piece of scripture, seeing the book as a guide to life. These readers seem to feel that virtually any section of *Walden* will yield inspirational pearls of wisdom. They are unable to see the text as words on a page or as having identifiable, rhetorical strategies. They focus on passages in which Thoreau uses devices typical of religious rhetoric and sermons—the aphorism, proverb, paradox, exemplum, parable. Compact statements, like the following, that suggest more than they say, appeal to these readers: "We know but few men, a great many coats and breeches" (22); "[F]or a man is rich in proportion to the number of things which he can afford to let alone" (82); "Our life is frittered away by detail" (91); "The Maker of this earth but patented a leaf" (308); and "Walden was dead and is alive again" (311). These students are drawn to aspects of Thoreau's style that are foregrounded, that stand out as unusual modes of expression. Such language, attractive and unusual, resembling the phrasing associated with the Bible or with Oriental scripture, has a way of staying with readers long after they have finished reading. They are often persuaded by Thoreau's style to the extent that the medium becomes the message. Conciseness, suggestiveness, and parallel phrasing are common to this type of scriptural rhetoric—all factors that help memorization. Those who read *Walden* as a kind of scripture are attracted also to Thoreau's use of parable and exemplum. In "Conclusion," Thoreau tells a parable about a bug that emerges from a table made of apple-tree wood, illustrating the idea of spiritual rebirth and renewal (333).

Other readers (about fifteen percent of the sample) interpret *Walden* willfully, focusing on the passages that suggest what they wish Thoreau to mean. The meanings they extract differ, but two patterns of meaning appear most commonly. One group, which is usually opposed to Thoreau's philosophical stances, tends to see the writer as against all commerce, technology, and free-enterprise activity. Students of this type ignore passages in which Thoreau praises commerce and the current economic system or is at least ambivalent toward them. Such passages do not register with these students, or they are somehow glossed over by them. If asked to substantiate their opinion that Thoreau offers a pessimistic, negative view of American life, they can cite appropriate aphorisms or arguments, but they find doing the opposite, giving evidence of Thoreau's fascination with commerce, difficult. If obliged to do this in a writing assignment over, say, a two-week period, they can perform such a task. But they have difficulty providing that information orally after a first or second reading, though many other readers can point to passages in which Thoreau extols the energy and bravery of commerce, particularly the long section in "Sounds" where he describes a train with its loads of diverse freight as a dynamic, fascinating, and even romantic phenomenon (118–22).

The more common type of willful reader is the true believer in Thoreau's antimaterialist theme. This student understands Thoreau as saying that the way to spiritual and ecological salvation lies in emulating his mode of living; that is, Thoreau is telling us to simplify our lives, return to nature, and reject the amenities offered by modern industrial economies. We should all eschew materialism and retreat to a simpler, spartan, primitive mode of life. Such readers ignore key passages like the following, where Thoreau clearly implies that there are many roads to the truth, that the Walden experience was but one stage in his life, and that he indeed has "several more lives to live":

> Why should we be in such desperate haste to succeed, and in such desperate enterprises? If a man does not keep pace with his companions, perhaps it is because he hears a different drummer. Let him step to the music which he hears, however measured or far away. It is not important that he should mature as soon as an apple-tree or an oak. Shall he turn his spring into summer? If the condition of things which we were made for is not yet, what were any reality which we can substitute?   (326)

> I left the woods for as good a reason as I went there. Perhaps it seemed to me that I had several more lives to live, and could not spare any more time for that one. It is remarkable how easily and insensibly we fall into

a particular route, and make a beaten track for ourselves. I had not lived there a week before my feet wore a path from my door to the pond-side; and though it is five or six years since I trod it, it is still quite distinct. It is true, I fear that others may have fallen into it, and so helped to keep it open.   (323)

Overlooking such passages is not simply an inability to read closely; it is an example of reading selectively, of ignoring passages that contradict firmly held opinions. Thoreau is emphatic about his need to leave *Walden* to pursue other paths. Even for him, the simple life by the pond eventually proved tedious and routine.

Readers' formal expectations also pay a major role in student readings of *Walden*. Since *Walden* is such an unconventional book, elements of numerous genres can be found throughout the book, and selections from *Walden* are often anthologized as examples of different forms: persuasion, polemic, argument, essay, natural history writing, autobiography, narrative, and poetic prose. Students bring different formal expectations to their reading; some approach *Walden* as a novel, some as autobiography, and some as a series of essays. Most students are frustrated until they begin to accept the text on its own terms, evaluating selections as unique pieces of discourse with particular rhetorical strategies and patterns. Disassociating themselves from their expectations allows students to understand Thoreau's use of language in new ways. They often ask questions like these: How are the chapters related? What is the significance of the chapters on the ponds? Why are chapters 1 and 2 so different from the rest of the text? What is Thoreau trying to achieve in "Spring" and "Conclusion," the final two chapters? Is there a sequence to their arrangement? What principle governs the organization of *Walden*? Students who are looking for a novel are quickly disappointed, while those looking for autobiography find only fragments of that form mixed with other forms of discourse. Students reading *Walden* as an essay or collection of essays have the most success, particularly if they see the book as a series of separate but related essays. However, students expecting the rigid essay form as often taught in high school and freshman composition courses—introduction, development (proofs, reasons, examples, etc.), and conclusion—often see Thoreau as violating these rules. He doesn't follow formulas common to many composition handbooks. Student readers, however, search for patterns of unity and coherence as they quickly learn not always to expect linear, sequential development, particularly in the movement between chapters, and as they temporarily suspend their formal expectations. Toward the end of an instructional unit on *Walden*, many become adept at identifying unexpected forms of unity, such as the repetition of images and themes or a pattern that follows the movement of the seasons. Once students complete the book, many can reevaluate a chapter like "Reading" to understand how it helps explain Thoreau's expectations for his readers. At this point, some develop an ability to range forward and backward through the text in search of relations. Student-held technical presuppositions place many in positions where their expectations are not met, but this lack of fulfillment forces them to ask searching questions about the text: If this is supposed to be a collection of essays, why do the chapters not look like essays? Where is the conclusion in each chapter? Why does so much of Thoreau's prose sound like poetry? Where are his thesis statements? Why does he spend so much time presenting detailed balance sheets of his income and expenditures?

Such questions provide excellent springboards to discussion. For example, the material on balance-sheet accounting can lead to a discussion of its role in the text and to a consideration of the subtleties of playing to an audience and the possibility that Thoreau intentionally created the persona of a frugal, practical Yankee.

Some readers bring a feminist perspective to their reading of *Walden*, judging it to be a book written for men because it involves stereotypically male activities like fishing, boating, and camping. They see Thoreau's woodsy emphasis as pitched at men and reflecting male experience. Such a response, however, has been expressed infrequently, and often as many women express enthusiasm for *Walden* as men. Another feminist criticism of Thoreau centers on his attitude toward women in the text, on the absence of women in the Walden experience, and on the author's seeming lack of sexuality. The impetus for this comes primarily from the ascetic, monklike image that Thoreau sometimes projects. Both male and female students may ask questions like these: Did he every marry? Did he have healthy relationships with women? Was he against women? Thoreau's direct condemnation of physical sexuality and sensuality in the chapter "Higher Laws" (220–21) contributes strongly to this impression.

Students clearly respond and interpret *Walden* in varied ways. I have illustrated how readings of *Walden* are influenced by such factors as the reader's psychology, ideology, biases, and reading skills as well as by the text itself and the course environment. I wonder to what extent peer pressure and student attachment to conventional thinking inhibit the expression of enthusiasm for or interest in Thoreau's unconventional ideas. The frequency of readings that suggest minds resistant to unpleasant or inconvenient information is surprising. Too few readers are equipped to focus on evidence within the text. Students also show a readiness to read contemporary politics into *Walden*, seeing Thoreau, for example, as anticapitalist (he was antisocialist as well) or viewing him as one who would have been a 1960s-style counterculture radical or an ally of Greenpeace.

Another pattern appearing throughout my study is the lack of close-reading skills: too many students lack the ability to interpret metaphors, images, and unconventional language, and they are often unwilling to look up the meanings of unfamiliar terms. This deficiency is accompanied by a general lack of familiarity with a wide range of discourse forms and by a tendency to hold rigid ideas about what forms good writing should take. Some of the problems that cause writer's block as identified by Mike Rose (72–76) influence how these students read a complex text like *Walden*. Their narrow understanding of discourse patterns makes reading unfamiliar forms difficult.

A lack of grammatical and rhetorical knowledge also affects how students read *Walden*. Too few are familiar with the periodic sentence in its more elaborate uses or with the cumulative sentence, popularized by Francis and Bonniejean Christensen in their studies of American prose style and in the Christensen rhetoric program. Both types of sentences are common to Thoreau's writing, and some students have difficulty reading and understanding them. Students' responses to Thoreau's sententious forms like paradox or the aphorism also reflect a lack of rhetorical knowledge. We might ask if those who read Thoreau as scripture would be inclined to do so if they were sophisticated about these basic sentence types. My study of responses to *Walden* illustrates a reluctance on the part of students to become active readers who probe, question, and interact constructively with the text.

Teaching Thoreau as a Visionary Thinker

Robert Franciosi

Du musst dein Leben ändern.
(You must change your life.)
—Rainer Maria Rilke

How many a man has dated a new era
in his life from the reading of a book.
—Thoreau

Thoreau's place in the college curriculum remains secure, extending well beyond the bounds of the American literature course. Most undergraduates read
excerpts from *Walden* or "Civil Disobedience"—often in freshman composition texts. Many are likely to possess more information about Thoreau the man
than about nearly any other writer of the American Renaissance. He may be,
as Lawrence Buell suggests, "the closest approximation to a folk hero that
American literary history has ever seen" ("Pilgrimage" 175). Like the water of
Flint's Pond, though, most students' knowledge of Thoreau is "comparatively
shallow, and not remarkably pure" (*Walden* 194). Some may read *The Maine
Woods* in an American literature survey or a course on nature writing; those assigned the Heath anthology may even read "A Plea for Captain John Brown";
but seldom do undergraduates, even English majors, encounter *A Week on the
Concord and Merrimack Rivers* or *Cape Cod*, the Journal or "Life without
Principle." For too many students, Thoreau remains little more than a carica-
ture, an odd hermit who went to live in the woods, a man who spent a night in
jail for not paying his taxes.

When I proposed Thoreau as subject for a course entitled Visionary
Thinkers in the Liberal Studies Program at Grand Valley State University, I
had two goals. First, I wished to introduce the students to the full range of
Thoreau's writings, from the celebratory prose of *A Week* to the darker mus-
ings of *Cape Cod*. Yes, we would read "Civil Disobedience," but we would also
read "Slavery in Massachusetts" and the more radical essays on John Brown.
Selections from the Journal would play an important part in the course, as
would Walter Harding's biography. Second, I particularly wanted to present
Thoreau to the class as a cultural figure, one whose life and work have had
traceable effects on subsequent thinkers, writers, and activists—especially
those of the environmental and civil rights movements. To that end, we would
read a variety of texts that exemplify the cultural work to which "Thoreau" has
been put. His influence on how Americans have confronted environmental issues would be charted in Aldo Leopold's *A Sand County Almanac*, Loren Eiseley's *The Night Country*, and Annie Dillard's *Teaching a Stone to Talk*, as well
as in statements by Greenpeace and the Sierra Club. The movement from text
to social action would be explored through the writings and examples of

Gandhi and Martin Luther King, Jr., but more immediately, and more poignantly, in the experience of the Chinese students in Tiananmen Square. "We've studied the civil rights movement in the United States and Gandhi's movement in India," one student told reporters in a May 1989 *Newsweek* interview, a few weeks before the massacre. "The philosophy of these peaceful demonstrations is also from the American philosopher Thoreau" (qtd. in Manegold and Magida). Just how much the Chinese students knew of Thoreau's writings is hard to say. "The imaginative bond between devotee and writer," Buell suggests, "probably operates less at the level of reading experience than we normally think" ("Pilgrimage" 199). In offering the course Visionary Thinkers: Thoreau, I expected my students to read deeply and to think critically; the bonds they shaped would be their own.

Shortly before the semester's beginning, I was in a colleague's cluttered office describing the course to him. He has read extensively in environmental literature, and I was interested in his response to my syllabus, but the conclusion of our conversation surprised me. With a peering, yet whimsical, gaze, he faced me across the desk and said, "You realize, of course, that any students who read such material, who *genuinely* read it, will be almost obligated to change their lives." The students in my class would prove him right.

The Liberal Studies Program at Grand Valley offers students the opportunity to create a major focused on compelling problems, issues, or themes. While a group of interdisciplinary core courses provides an overarching structure for the major, students are largely responsible for constructing their own programs. Each works in close consultation with a faculty adviser to shape the study plan and to write an essay that explains its underlying rationale—describing not only courses to be taken or independent work to be pursued but also applications to the world beyond the university that he or she might explore through a practicum. Although a small program, with about forty majors, liberal studies attracts students who are self-motivated, creative, even radical, individualists. They remain loyal to an integrative concept of education more closely associated with a liberal arts college than with the university of 13,500 students they attend.

Unlike most eighteen- to twenty-two-year-olds in elite private colleges, however, liberal studies students at Grand Valley are a genuinely diverse group who enliven the classroom with a wide range of experiences. Most have worked or are working; some are returning students pursuing new careers; a few have served in the military; some have children. Indeed, there is no typical liberal studies major. Helen W., for example, one of the best students in the program —perhaps in the university—is in her late sixties. A few years ago she inherited some wooded land in Wisconsin and decided that responsible ownership required her to pursue a self-designed degree in environmental studies, a degree concerned less with applications of science to land use than with the study of what Leopold has termed the land ethic. While taking the Thoreau course, for example, she struggled with a course on the geology of the Great Lakes.

She ultimately dropped the geology course, not so much because it was difficult as because it seemed distant from the circumstances and concerns of her immediate life and from such basic propositions as this stated by Leopold: "A thing is right when it tends to preserve the integrity, stability, and beauty of the biotic community. It is wrong when it tends otherwise" (262). Each semester Helen takes a course or two directly connected to her plan and inevitably does more work than anyone else in the class, often including the instructor. And when each spring the Liberal Studies Program invites a major lecturer to campus, someone who embodies its interdisciplinary approach, she not only registers for the minicourse offered in conjunction with the visit but inevitably challenges the speaker—be it Robert Scholes, Tillie Olsen, Edward Said, or Ken Burns—to justify his or her position.

Other students also brought interesting perspectives to the material. Many were liberal studies majors who had completed The Idea of Nature, a popular course that introduced them to Thoreau's environmentalist writings. Several were leaders of campus activist groups or were contemplating Peace Corps service. The class also included students from departments like English, biology, art, and anthropology.

Such an array of students, I knew, would make for an exciting, though potentially volatile, class. On the day we first discussed "Economy," for example, a woman wealthy enough to spend her summers on faraway Cape Cod testily asked, "Does he expect me to sell my children?" (By semester's end she was actively fighting the commercial development of the woods surrounding her home near Lake Michigan.) Other students that day were offended by what they perceived as Thoreau's arrogance. They had loved the seeming gentleness of A Week and the passionate advocacy for the wild in The Maine Woods, but "Economy" disturbed their idealized sense of Thoreau, and so they came to class armed with quotes from the biography that "proved" he was a hypocrite who exaggerated his isolation and self-reliance. Some purists were bothered by Thoreau's manipulation of journal entries to create the longer texts. Throughout the semester the responses were similarly vigorous: pacifists were shocked by his support of John Brown, feminists objected to criticism that Dillard was writing watered-down Thoreau, environmentalists decided Leopold was a more reliable role model, and libertarians never quite convinced the rest of us that the smoking of marijuana was an important issue of civil government.

If the range of response in the classroom was impressive, even more so was the written work produced in the students' journals and term papers. "How can we have a course on Thoreau," I had asked at the beginning, "without a required journal?" And indeed, for many of the students, the journal was central to their reading of Thoreau and of texts by his intellectual offspring. Yet because students typically question the journal form's usefulness or have difficulty distinguishing it from a diary, I decided to assist and challenge this group from the start by providing them with a strong contemporary model, Sherman Paul's "Thinking with Thoreau." I knew that none of the students possessed

Paul's knowledge or erudition, but the sense of engagement, of attentiveness, was within their grasp, as was his method: "Though it is meditative, it was not premeditated. I wrote it without revision as, in [Charles] Olson's formulation, 'language as the act of the instant' and not 'language as the act of thought about the instant'" (18). Only a few student journals managed to balance Paul's kind of spontaneity with careful thought, but those that did were stunning successes, the results more impressive than in any of my classes before or since.

Although I expected that some students would initially balk at keeping a journal, I knew that even more would later challenge the idea of writing an "academic" term paper for a Thoreau course. In their notions of what constitutes acceptable college writing, liberal studies students are notoriously liberal. But after much discussion most agreed that the journal's raw materials could naturally yield formal essays and that term papers might also provide the necessary intellectual distance to evaluate, rather than merely celebrate, Thoreau's work. Even so, I offered the class an alternative to the formal paper—they could choose to write a long essay in the manner of Thoreau, as long as it addressed relevant issues raised by their reading of his texts. About half the class opted for the more creative approach.

The variety of responses in the term papers reflected the students' multifaceted and, for most, newly complicated attitudes toward Thoreau. One essay, by a student who had structured his major around peace studies, traced the history of civil disobedience from biblical times to the present and concluded that Thoreau had in fact added little to the concept. Nevertheless, the student wrote, "he is considered by most to be the founder of civil disobedience." Using this apparent contradiction as his entrance into the issue, the author finally argued that Thoreau's skills as a writer in portraying his response to confinement are what shaped the myth of Thoreau as originator and major theorist of civil disobedience. Other essays, though less critical of Thoreau, were equally incisive. A literature student, for example, drew on phenomenology, especially Gaston Bachelard's *Water and Dreams*, to discuss Thoreau's fascination with bodies of water, while a biology major discussed how Thoreau, Leopold, and Eiseley had employed for writerly ends the observational skills so essential to her field.

Helen W. chose to investigate Eiseley's connections to Thoreau, especially in his responses to *Walden*. "Each reader sees *Walden* differently," she wrote, "because the created *Walden* acts like the clear reflecting mirror to the gazer into its waters, able to show him the unique face of his own genius. Each, pulling up out of its depths that which he needs to build himself." She read widely, delving into the journals, letters, and biographies of both men, and concluded, perhaps with the wisdom of a woman in her sixties, that the writing and the life are always inextricably bound: "It is not possible to understand a man by reading only one of his works, or even all of his published ones. You need to take into account the entire journey to understand what his vision is, and grasp the extent to which he enacted it into his life."

Many of the Thoreauvian essays attempted to enact just such meetings of vision and life, though few went beyond predictable jaunts into the local woods. Not surprisingly, those students with strong connections to the earth and to outdoor work produced the better essays. Like Thoreau, the anthropology student knew from her fieldwork that the past, specifically the Native American past, however distant it seems, is "right beneath our feet," its objects to be held in our palms. Indian arrowheads, Thoreau had written in his Journal, "are not fossil bones, but, as it were, fossil thoughts, forever reminding me of the mind that shaped them" (18:91). She responded in much the same spirit: "I tap into such fragments and pour out the past—feelings, actions, belongings, practices, and beliefs thought to be permanently laid to rest." By meditating on such unearthings, she could also confront her own past, specifically the death earlier that year of her mentor in anthropology.

Other efforts in this vein, though less sophisticated, were often personally engaging. A woman who lived with her husband and four children on what used to be orchard land well understood Thoreau's injunction in "Autumnal Tints":

> If, about the last of October, you ascend any hill in the outskirts of our town, and probably of yours, and look over the forest, you may see—well, what I have endeavored to describe. All this you surely *will* see, and much more, if you are prepared to see it,—if you *look* for it.   (260)

She readily admitted her account of the season was "more homespun than intellectual," and her essay on autumn had its problems, yet like blemished apples from old trees, the essential flavor remained. Not a particularly strong student or writer, she nevertheless had understood Thoreau as well as any, confirming for me Buell's statement that "the consequences of canonization should be measured less than scholars normally do in terms of texts (or criticism) engendered than in terms of lives led" ("Pilgrimage" 199).

And then there was David. He was a student of mine from the previous semester, having taken Life Journey, a popular liberal studies course that aligns literary art and developmental psychology. A colleague in the English department designed it, writing a text and even producing a pilot for a companion series of videos to the course. Only late in the semester did I learn that the colleague was David's father. David claimed to have read more books in that course (twelve short ones) than in his four years of high school and two of college. At first I was not sure how to respond. I was then only in my first year at Grand Valley, and I had been labeled by some students (and faculty members) as the professor who assigned too many books. So I was wary.

When David registered for our Thoreau course, he knew none of the texts. His interest in Thoreau per se seemed based mostly on his growing interest in reading. I had read his father's description of a mentor—"an older adult who is experienced in the kind of life we would like to move into and who is willing to be our guide for a while" (Ford 90)—and suspected David might be putting me in that role as a model reader and thinker. My own interest in Thoreau had been fostered by Sherman Paul, so I respected the mentor process, though in introducing this art major to the pleasures of reading, I believed my influence was mostly circumstantial. Still, I knew he was ripe to take Thoreau's words in *Walden* to heart, that the "same questions that disturb and puzzle and confound us have in their turn occurred to all the wise men; not one has been omitted; and each has answered them, according to his ability, by his words and his life" (108).

Yet the words David wrote in response to Thoreau, however genuine, came only with struggle. His journal often displayed flashes of insight—when he turned it in. He clearly had difficulty maintaining a writerly discipline; late in the semester he started missing classes. Given the dynamic and varied abilities of those in the class, I suspected that the problem was intellectual intimidation and that he would drop the course. But one afternoon late in the term I found a rich and lengthy journal in my mailbox, along with a request for a meeting.

However I try to recount that hour in my windowless office, the essence eludes me. We spent some time discussing a possible essay on *Cape Cod*, but the thoughts (and later, the paper itself) were rather shapeless. Mostly we talked about books and reading lists. At one point David said he couldn't stand to look at television—not when Edward Gibbon's work remained to be read! Yet for all the talk of reading, Thoreau was seldom mentioned. Only in the ensuing semester did I understand the full depth of David's encounter with Thoreau—I learned he had withdrawn from school. For Thoreau, the cabin on Walden Pond was "more favorable, not only to thought, but to serious reading, than a university" (99); for David, a small apartment and a respite from formal education served the same purpose.

After two years, he was back in school and even made the dean's list. Whenever his father and I have occasion to talk about David, the "famous Thoreau course" always comes up. I suspect that my colleague views me—positively, I hope—as an important influence on his son, though he has also written that for a young man or woman "sometimes merely knowing about such a person," such a mentor, is sufficient inspiration (Ford 90).

In teaching Thoreau as a visionary thinker, I realized anew the lasting power of the fable with which he concludes *Walden*:

> Every one has heard the story which has gone the rounds of New England, of a strong and beautiful bug which came out of the dry leaf of an old table of apple-tree wood, which had stood in a farmer's kitchen for sixty years . . . from an egg deposited in the living tree many years earlier still, as appeared by counting the annual layers beyond it; which was heard gnawing out for several weeks, hatched perchance by the heat of an urn. (333)

I merely placed the urn on the table of David's education; the heat that enabled his emergence into his "perfect summer life" was from another source.

Reading the Garden:
Excursions into *Walden*

Frank J. McGill

> The critic knows that any understanding of the subtle
> principle of life inherent in a work of art can be
> gained only by direct experience of it, again and
> again. The interpretation of it demands close analysis,
> and plentiful instances from the works themselves.
> —F. O. Matthiessen

Reflecting on my history of reading *Walden* has helped me catch glimpses of what F. O. Matthiessen calls the "subtle principle of life" (xi) not only in Thoreau's works but also in my life as a reader. I was attracted to a graduate literature course called The American Renaissance by my familiarity with, as well as my fondness for, the central works on the syllabus. To widely varying degrees, I had studied *The Scarlet Letter*, *Nature*, *Walden*, "Song of Myself," and *Moby-Dick* before, and I had taught several of them to high school students. I thought that my previous reading of these works would make an examination of them at the graduate level easier, if only marginally so. Because I had at least an inkling of the concerns that much of the course material addressed, I felt that my reading of the material would go smoothly. Any problems, I surmised, would come only after I had "finished" each work. What I did not know—what I could not foresee—was that my trying to read, analyze, and interrelate these intricate works would actually be complicated by my foregoing encounters with them.

To my surprise, then consternation, then fascination, many of the familiar texts seemed different. I had more trouble with them than I had anticipated, for complexity resided in their ostensible simplicity. Neither straightforward nor entirely knowable, these texts, this time around, began to reveal to me their inner workings, which were far more elusive than I had ever realized. It was not a matter of words and phrases not meaning what they literally said. If that were so, I could at least know what they did *not* mean. More problematically, they did express literal meanings but at the same time pointed in several other directions. These texts were more slippery than I had thought.

Among the major works of the American Renaissance, *Walden* in particular compels readers to think about the processes they undergo when they encounter texts. Thoreau concludes that complete knowledge of a text is impossible, but he encourages us to keep working with his text, to reexamine everything—long-held beliefs, recent hypotheses, and deep-seated misgivings—about his writing and about our approaches to it. Having been inspired to undertake such a re-vision by my study of the American Renaissance, I have begun to recognize parallels between the lessons from my readings of *Walden* and the themes of the work itself. This, too, is a quest, my personal attempt to discover how I, as a reader, have progressed through several encounters of *Walden*.

A passage from Richard Brodhead's *Hawthorne, Melville, and the Novel* prompted me to pursue the connection between what and how I was reading: "We must be less concerned with themes themselves than with the way in which themes are won from or immersed in the novel's actuality . . ." (9). Taking "the novel's actuality" to be my experience of reading *Walden* (which I treat as a work of fiction), I saw here a justification for my linking the book's underlying messages to my studies of it as an undergraduate, a high school teacher, and a graduate student. As a result, I came to consider these seemingly separate reading experiences as a continuum. I now realize that I "won" something from Thoreau's narrative in each of my roles, although at the time my reading did not always give me a feeling of success.

Another of my reasons for approaching *Walden* in the light of past readings is the similarity of such an approach to the work itself: just as *Walden* is a personal narrative, so should "Reading the Garden" be. Furthermore, as the book is self-reflective and self-analytical, so will this paper try to be its own subject. My somewhat nontraditional approach approximates, on a much smaller scale, that of Thoreau, whose innovation helped to ensure his renown and ultimate success as a writer. Success for me will be to have satisfied myself by learning from my reconsideration of past readings and from the effort to record what I observe.

Not So Sad As Foolish

> It is no disparagement of young adults to think that they
> *could* not then know enough to set or understand a
> whole life's course. It would be sad if nothing important
> about life were learned along the way.
> —Robert Nozick

When I first read *Walden*, I was a senior English major at Yale. More young than adult, I would hardly have drawn comfort from Robert Nozick's assertion that I was incapable of planning the path my life would take. At that time I was interested in *Walden* less as an influential work of American literature and mythmaking than as two or three classes' worth of reading and lecture material. I read, as assigned, seven of the book's eighteen chapters, but my memories of the quantity of my exposure to *Walden* are almost as vague now as the quality of my reading was suspect then. Even as someone who had already devoted three years of his college education to the study of literature, I approached *Walden* not with the unbridled enthusiasm of a scholar encountering a new work but with the tame resignation of a student facing more work.

Thus I resembled those people Thoreau criticizes in "Economy," who, "through mere ignorance and mistake, are so occupied with the factitious cares and superfluously coarse labors of life that its finer fruits cannot be plucked by them" (6). Certainly *Walden's* finer fruits went largely unnoticed, not to mention unplucked, by me. The immediate concerns of deadlines and grades, those "factitious cares and superfluously coarse labors" of my academic life, prevented me from realizing just how fine those fruits were. I appreciated literature, but not nearly as deeply as possible. Rather, I enjoyed it; I appreciated mainly its ability to entertain me. My "ignorance and mistake" manifested themselves in skipped lectures, hastily written papers, a general need to get through, rather than into, what I was reading. Like most college students, at least those who consider themselves hard workers, I felt unduly burdened by the course requirements and made few truly taxing demands on myself.

Any requirement, though, may seem onerous when imposed from without. Again in "Economy," Thoreau observes, "We are made to exaggerate the importance of what work we do; and yet how much is not done by us!" (11). Here, too, he describes precisely my situation in college: either by my nature as one who needed to reassure himself often of his own achievements or by extrinsic academic (but not intrinsic intellectual) requirements, I was made to exaggerate the importance of my work. The passive construction Thoreau employs ("made to exaggerate") enacts the assertion that we are neither active nor perceptive at these times of self-pity and self-deceit. The one most led astray by my protestations of overwork was I. And yet it was more like play than work. Furthermore, I neither completed all the reading assignments nor learned all I might have from those that I did complete. How much, indeed, was not done by me. Thoreau's diction in the second half of the sentence quoted above also ensures that "how much" encompasses much more than "what work" we point to as justification for our "incessant anxiety and strain" (11). I marvel at how much went undone even after I saw these words; I had not yet truly read them.

For Thoreau, this broad criticism leads us to consider our precise needs as human beings, which, he suggests, we barely meet despite all our supposed hard work, and he laments how poorly we address our loftier need to "become richer than the richest now are, and make our civilization a blessing" (40). That this initial chapter of *Walden* moves from topics of personal concern to universal ones announces Thoreau's design that all readers apply his words to their own lives, that their personal "economies" profit from his example. The chapter's topical blueprint is reflected likewise in its structure: it begins with a brief synopsis of and introduction to Thoreau's experiment, and it ends with a poem, "The Pretensions of Poverty." This broadening parallels Thoreau's thematic movement as he discusses his personal situation, then the individual lives of people in Concord, and finally the collective lives that constitute a society. After remarking that petty concerns often keep an individual from enjoying the finer fruits of life, Thoreau registers society's need for "the flower and fruit of a man" (77). Thus one must improve oneself before one can remedy society's shortfalls. Enrichment begins at home.

After graduating from college, I became a working man and, in some ways, Thoreau's "laboring man" who "has no time to be any thing but a machine" (6) when I took a teaching job in a suburb of Detroit. Four years passed before I read *Walden* again, and again I read only parts of it. Teaching a junior English class, a survey of American literature, renewed my contact with Thoreau and the other major authors of the American Renaissance. Thoreau himself would appreciate the irony of any attempt to "teach" *Walden* in school: "How can he remember well his ignorance—which his growth requires—who has so often to use his knowledge?" (6). Our use of selections from five or six chapters ensured that my second exposure to the book, like my students' first exposure, would be fragmentary at best. Worse yet, I tried to build from these fragments the kind of coherent system that *Walden* calls, and renders, impossible. I made the common teacher's error of relying too heavily on my own interest in and analysis of *Walden* in presenting the work to my classes.

Thoreau argues against just such uniformity and constriction of thought in "The Bean-Field":

> Removing the weeds, putting fresh soil about the bean stems, and encouraging this weed which I had sown, making the yellow soil express its summer thought in bean leaves and blossoms rather than in wormwood and piper and millet grass, making the earth say beans instead of grass,— this was my daily work. (156–57)

Since I knew what *Walden* was "really about," I felt compelled to guide my students to "the truth." I am sure I put my words into their mouths just as Thoreau put his words, beans, into the earth's mouth, which would otherwise have said grass. I killed, however gently, their weedy responses when those responses did not comport with my reading, because I thought I should make their intellectual "yellow soil express its summer thought" in my beans instead of their grass. In so doing, I violated the very ideal that I had set as one of my goals for the year: to get my students to think for themselves and to rely less on me as a mediator. Thoreau's gardening succeeds, as signified on the literal level by his crops and on the intellectual by his meditation on "the true husband-man," at the end of "The Bean-Field," because he surrenders "all claim to the produce" in favor of "results which are not harvested" by him. By not planting the seeds of this broader harvest with "influences more genial" (166) than myself, I likely failed to a large degree in my gardening.

Not content simply to plant seeds, I often weeded, watered, and hoed for forty minutes at a time even while I thought I was letting my students grow as they would. Unsettled by periods of silence, I hurried to fill them instead of finding out what idea might crop up unexpectedly. When creating essay topics on Thoreau and Emerson, I allowed the authors' appealing aphorisms to close off any original avenues of inquiry that my students (or I) might have been able to pursue. For example, one topic required the students to assemble a series of favorite quotations and comment on how they were interrelated. I would have read much more thoughtful essays if I had proscribed direct quotation altogether.

Emerson's warnings in "The American Scholar"—for example, that "[g]enius is always sufficiently the enemy of genius by over-influence" (*Works* 1: 57)—should have provided a sufficient deterrent, especially since we had just studied this essay, but, like my students, I allowed my admiration for these men's boldness of expression to dwarf my powers of thought, synthesis, and composition.

Like Thoreau's self-interested farmer, whose force of habit misleads him to "[regard] the soil as property," I led "the meanest of lives" (165) by appropriating, sometimes at least, the classroom for my personal garden, where my students came to learn the skills I had already acquired. Had I read *Walden* more circumspectly, with an eye to learning it *with* my students instead of teaching it *to* them, I might have been able to unearth for all of us more than the nonconformist aphorisms to which high school students cling (and that they emblazon on their notebooks and lockers) almost uniformly. My desire that my students understand, enjoy, and remember *Walden*—and not be intimidated by its scope or frustrated by its ethereality—prevented me from gaining Martin Bickman's insight into the book:

> One of the better reasons for spending time with *Walden* is to discover the complexities, even contradictions, of Thoreau's own vision instead of mistaking it for the cultural slogans and cartoons. Read the book, not the bumper sticker! (16)

My classes on *Walden*, indeed many of the classes I taught over six years, relied too heavily on the "cultural slogans and cartoons" that I drew out of the literature; their presence, ineluctably growing to predominance, curbed the growth of other ideas in my students' imaginations and in mine. Since I had read *Walden* as a set of static statements instead of as a series of dynamic exhortations, I fashioned my classroom into a compost heap of dead, if sometimes rich, explication when I should have worked at a fertile field dedicated to fruitful inquiry. Having failed to recognize "the inadequacy of the residual statement," I proclaimed, not elicited, ideas. My thoughts approached no "volatile truth" (325).

Volatility has come only now that I have uprooted my life after six stable but increasingly insular years as a teacher. Crossing back to the student side of the lectern, I perceive myself once again as a seeker rather than as a holder of knowledge. My teaching colleagues and I strove (often, because of our misguided strategies, in vain) to lead others toward understanding; my classmates and I have come together to combat our own ignorance. And yet I have not fought my ignorance. Not knowing, as *Walden* often asserts, is not the enemy; not trying to know is. To Thoreau, not seeking truth means not living truly.

Living encompasses for him a wide range of pursuits, all of them active, investigative, and reflexive.

> What a man thinks of himself, that it is which determines, or rather indicates, his fate. (7)

> In the midst of this chopping sea of civilized life, such are the clouds and
> storms and quicksands . . . that a man has to live, if he would not founder
> and go to the bottom and not make his port at all, by dead reckoning, and
> he must be a great calculator indeed who succeeds.   (91)

The first passage exemplifies Thoreau's exhortation that people mold their lives
in their own unique fashion, according to the dictates of their own consciences.
The second fuses a potentially trite metaphor, a human being as a ship on the
sea of life, with the same clear and simple theme of self-reliance. This call for
"dead reckoning" appears where life itself abounds: in this paragraph and the
preceding one the noun *life* and forms of the verb *live* appear twenty times, all
in a chapter whose title ("Where I Lived, and What I Lived For") at once celebrates a wondrous profusion and rues a wearying redundancy. Paradoxically,
the passage is preceded and followed by redundant, yet clear and distinct, en-
treaties for simplicity. Focusing on the means of navigation rather than on the
end, Thoreau infuses the nautical metaphor "dead reckoning" with new vitality and relevance, so that the paradox resolves itself: what we take away (from
life, from the text) depends to a great degree on what we bring to it. What we
think is how we live and read, to oversimplify the first passage above. Thinking
of myself as the teacher, I tried to transmit knowledge; seeing myself as a
student, I try to discover it. In an MLA volume on *Moby-Dick*, Robert F.
Bergstrom shares his classroom realization of the principle of necessary preparation: "The only students who profited by my talking were those few who already had a vague sense of what I would say" (96).

Instead of fearing or fighting my ignorance, I have begun to recognize its
breadth and depth as I make an effort to transform some of it. I first approached *Walden* expecting it to be a book about living in the woods and lov-
ing solitude, and so it was. Next I tried to make it accessible to others by
building coherent schemes from selected parts of it; and, using pieces that fit
nicely together for me, I created an inaccessible monument. This fall I tried
simply to read it, my only expectations being enjoyment and discovery. Both
were met. In fact, I came to see that *Walden* is about these kinds of experiences, and others as well.

Perhaps, needing to re-create both the literal and literary American experiences of questing, I had to come West to uncover these subterranean impulses
in *Walden*. After journeying into the more expansive part of the country and simultaneously away from my Long Island origins, I discovered many of the simple, intricate pleasures of *Walden*. Never before had I read the whole of the
work or considered its subtext as well as the text itself. Turning to a familiar yet
brand-new book in a similarly dual environment, I heard repeatedly the reso-
nances of more recent works of American literature that I had read in my earlier incarnation as a student at Yale. In particular Robert Penn Warren's
"Rumor Verified" echoes Thoreau's assertion that the only reliable compass is
the one we look within ourselves to read:

> But what can you do?
> Perhaps pray to God for strength to face the verification
> That you are simply a man, with a man's dead reckoning,
>   nothing more.   (96)

What we must do, then, is follow the course of our own selves. My renewed study of the self-reflective works of the American Renaissance has resulted in this piece of written self-reflection. By tracing the development of my readings of *Walden*, I track myself.

Reclaiming Thoreau's Humor
for the Classroom

Michael D. West

In most essays on Thoreau, the *I*, or first person, is omitted; in this one, it will be retained. That, in respect to egotism, is probably the main difference. I would not talk so much about how I teach Thoreau if there were anybody else whose approach I knew as well. Unfortunately I am confined to this theme by the narrowness of my pedagogical experience, so I can provide only a simple and sincere account of my own encounters—not always triumphant—with the "poor students" to whom *Walden* is particularly addressed (4).

Teaching an author whom one loves deeply can be frustrating. Was Oscar Wilde thinking of teachers when he wrote that "each man kills the thing he loves"? When the sun sets on yet another of my guided tours of the American Renaissance, why do I sometimes feel that I was successful in teaching Poe, say—an author for whom my sympathy is distinctly limited—whereas I failed to do Thoreau justice? If a taste for Poe is the hallmark of a decidedly primitive stage of reflection, as Henry James claimed, perhaps a taste for Thoreau requires a more sophisticated sense of humor than we academics realize. *Walden* can be read on many levels, of course—as poetic natural history, as an escapist armchair travelogue, as spiritual autobiography. But this book is also a satire—arguably the keenest and most durable ever penned by any American except Twain. In our urbanized society, where nature is not a natural experience, where students looking for rousing adventure can go bungee jumping, and where mystical experiences are purveyed outside schoolyards by neighborhood pushers, the satiric dimension of *Walden* is potentially its most viable.

But only potentially. Recovering *Walden*'s satiric potential for the classroom takes effort. Thoreau's humor is subtle. James Russell Lowell is only the most famous example of a sensitive reader with a robust sense of humor who nonetheless missed it altogether. And the way Thoreau is commonly taught in high schools fosters a purblind approach among those who take another crack at him in college. Ask a class what they know about Thoreau, and something like this composite portrait will emerge:

"Thoreau? Aw, sure, Professor West, we know all about him. He was that sweet, goofy hermit who built a shack beside a pond to study nature. Much beloved of Concord's chipmunks and so forth, just like Walt Disney's Johnny Appleseed. Sort of a weirdo in some ways, evading taxes and women with equal dexterity, but redeemed for all decent Americans by two righteous causes: devotion to the environment and opposition to slavery. Important therefore as a bearded precursor to Martin Luther King, who even remembered to acknowledge his indebtedness. Sentimental, sententious, doggedly high-minded—a lot like our high school English teacher, in fact. But funny? Aw, c'mon, Professor West—you gotta be kidding!"

So the pedagogical golden rule with respect to Thoreau is this: Never assign most of *Walden* to be read before the class discussions devoted to the book. Such an assignment simply guarantees that a majority of "poor students" will make their way through it in the same humorless spirit in which they were taught to approach Thoreau before. Whatever one does after this point to analyze amusing passages comes too late. You can still teach them that they read Thoreau poorly—which is what I contented myself with doing for too many years—but that is not the same thing as teaching them to chuckle over *Walden* while reading it well.

An initial assignment should probably cover no more than "Economy." And before students read that, it might be a good idea to discuss the book's opening paragraphs in class, clarifying the insouciant wit with such questions as these: What biblical catchphrase is stood on its head by Thoreau's claim to be "a sojourner in civilized life again"? How many English teachers who have urged students to avoid the pronoun *I* are among those who "commonly do not remember that it is, after all, always the first person that is speaking"? Just how withering is the satire implied in the casual afterthought, "for if he has lived sincerely, it must have been in a distant land to me"? Does the first person speaking in this paragraph sound "simple and sincere"? or complex and ironic? Is it really a "narrowness of . . . experience" that makes "poor students" reluctant to grasp that wordplay can be both pertinent and impertinent at the same time? Such questions suggest that reading *Walden* sensitively requires a sense of humor both broader and subtler than that encouraged by TV sitcoms.

After alerting students, turn them loose on "Economy" with a mandate to find the most amusing passage in it and defend their choice in class next time. With any luck that should make for lively discussion, allowing the teacher to weigh the claims of such choice comic set pieces as the covert wisecrack in Thoreau's July Fourth housewarming, the mock balance sheet with its ha'pennies and farthings, the deacon's auction with its dried tapeworm, the densely punning meditation on architecture, the great Yankee tirade against the Pyramids, and the wry description of James Collins's family, where stock pity for shanty dwellers is slyly undermined until they come to seem, like their dead cat, the victims of too much effete luxury. This discussion should not only broach the main themes of the book but also raise questions about the many varieties of the ludicrous: comedy, wit, humor, parody, satire, invective, irony, and so on. Generic definitions of this sort can help expand students' constricted sense of humor by breaking down their naive tendency to treat farce as the comic paradigm and to assume that nothing is funny in the absence of a laugh track.

Unlikely to be nominated for the hit parade of Thoreauvian humor is the famous passage (16–18) where he promises that he "will only hint at some of the enterprises which [he has] cherished." As the teacher's choice, it makes a good climax for a first day's discussion because its riddling jokes are typical and so subtle that most will have been missed. Direct attention to the literalization of clichés like notching the nick of time on a stick or hearing "what was in the wind." Draw out the double entendres of being "reporter to a journal, of no very wide circulation" or assisting "the sun materially in his rising" (i.e., participating in the levee of *le roi soleil*). Dwell on the amusing tableau of Thoreau "waiting at evening . . . for the sky to fall, that [he] might catch something, though [he] never caught much"—then explain that this observer was not emulating Chicken-licken but simply playing with words like *nightfall*, so what later dissolved in the sun manna-wise was simply a cold that in a dead metaphor he *caught*. The covert etymological puns require special comment. Students will need help understanding that when Thoreau sunk all his *capital* into an effort to hear "what was in the wind," he meant that he sunk his head (Latin *capit-*) physically into a chilly breeze. Likewise, "watching from the observatory of some cliff or tree, to *telegraph* any new arrival" [emphasis mine] is simply this witty naturalist's way of saying that he recorded what he observed by writing it down (*-graph*) at a distance (*tele-*) in his field notebook. So prepared, some students will finally be ready to recognize the startling dirty joke with which the passage concludes: "I have watered the red huckleberry, the sand cherry and the nettle tree . . . which might have withered else in dry seasons."

Whether or not students eventually decide that this scatological joke should top the chapter's comic hit parade, it torpedoes their stock conception of Thoreau as a goofy nature lover toting water to parched plants in cupped hands. Suckered by his deadpan humor into reading him sentimentally, they are now ready to see the rest of *Walden* as a challenge to their powers as language users. Are they as dumb as Thoreau claims, that is, so dumb they can't recognize a man taking a leak? (It's worth noting that in common parlance the word *dumb* equates stupidity with inarticulacy.) "You will pardon some obscurities, for there are more secrets in my trade than in most men's, and yet not voluntarily kept, but inseparable from its very nature" (17). This sentence suggests that writing is the process of training people's minds to fathom conceptual puzzles. Language derives from concrete roots, and readers must actively make meaning by interpreting abstract words as verbal conundrums.

This line of argument can be profitably developed in the next assignment, which will no doubt include the chapter "Reading." There we learn that "[t]he heroic books . . . will always be in a language dead to degenerate times; and we must laboriously seek the meaning of each word and line, conjecturing a larger sense than common use permits . . ." (100). Students may be tempted to become more heroic readers—or at least less craven ones—with the news that if one defines wordplay broadly enough, *Walden* contains at least five hundred puns or double entendres, many previously noted by David Skwire and by Joseph Moldenhauer ("Rhetoric" 252–409). The ways in which spelling, grammar, and foreign languages were taught in nineteenth-century America fostered a taste for punning, as I've argued elsewhere ("Spellers"), a taste to which this book remains perhaps the chief literary monument.

Unfortunately, learning the extent of Thoreau's wordplay can paralyze students as well as intrigue them. Small Latin and less Greek suffice to catch much of the etymological punning. But with the erosion of high school curricula, few college students nowadays possess even a smattering of Latin. Emphasizing Thoreau's etymological wordplay can make his humor seem forbiddingly remote. Having displaced the classics as perhaps the central humanizing discipline of modern education, English studies have sawed off the limb they were sitting on. In these sad circumstances what is a teacher to do? Compromise, I fear. Pick out some of the best English puns for illustration, show students why dictionaries contain derivations as well as definitions, and preach the necessity of learning other languages to understand one's own. In *Collective Wisdom: A Sourcebook of Lessons for Writing Teachers* I've sketched one possible classroom exercise along these lines. Such tactics should at least link Thoreau's punning style usefully to his thought by suggesting how profoundly his *radical* conservatism depends on a knowledge of roots (Latin *radic-*). But Thoreauvians must face the fact that recovering this aspect of Thoreau's humor will ultimately require an edition of *Walden* annotated in more detail than any existing. And even then, alas, would glossing all the etymological jokes keep them from being glossed over?

To highlight the antic in the mantic persuasively, the teacher needs a strategy for treating Thoreau's verbal horseplay as an outgrowth of larger satiric and comic concerns. So deeply rooted are students' misconceptions of Thoreau as a hermit that it's worth attacking the stereotype head-on. Of the opening chapters of *Walden* perhaps only "Solitude" suggests a reclusive spirit, and the following one, "Visitors," is half again as long. The teacher should call attention to the fact that Thoreau squatted within earshot not only of the railroad but also of the main pike to Boston, asking whether a hermit would pick a site near the grade of a modern interstate where the trucks shift their gears. Then point out the complexity of his attitude toward the railroad in "Sounds," of his conviction that "[c]ommerce is unexpectedly confident and serene, alert, adventurous, and unwearied. It is very natural in its methods withal . . ." (119). Here a little biography is not amiss. Students are always fruitfully surprised to learn that the author who claims that "there are more secrets in [his] trade than in most men's" was a pencil pusher in two senses, not only using them as a writer but also manufacturing and selling them. As chief product engineer for the family pencil factory (which, I suspect, had "No Admittance" painted on its gate to protect trade secrets), Thoreau retreated to the pond from an enterprise so innovative and successful that it spawned a dozen competitors in Concord alone. Such information helps students grasp that Thoreau explores the topic of language in "Reading" and "Sounds" as a practical man trying to engage people in dialogue. It's noteworthy that when he catechizes a "natural" man whom he admires, the woodchopper's native good sense manifests itself with "positive originality" in—lo and behold—"the re-origination of many of the institutions of society" (150)

Once students concede that Thoreau writes out of his preoccupation with society, they are readier to grasp *Walden*'s comic and satiric dimensions. I like to dramatize those aspects by talking about two opposing drives in the book. The vein of expansive, jocular hyperbole, where Thoreau turns himself into a comic hero by bragging like chanticleer "if only to wake [his] neighbors up" (title page), is counterbalanced by the reductive satiric determination to strip away all inessentials, to knock down society's screens, "to drive life into a corner, and reduce it to its lowest terms, and . . . get the whole and genuine meanness of it, and publish its meanness to the world" (91).

If *Walden* is being taught in an American survey or period course, comparison with T. B. Thorpe's "The Big Bear of Arkansas," the raftsmen chapter in *Huckleberry Finn*, or other tall tales helps bring out the humorous note in Thoreau's boasting. The great paragraph on extravagance as *"extra vagance"* furnishes its rationale (324). The extended passage describing Thoreau's labors in his bean field is a smorgasbord of expansive comic devices, seasoned with a dash of satire against the militia. Wielding his hoe as a weapon against the weeds, this Yankee Achilles inflates himself with mock-heroic nonchalance to gargantuan proportions: "It was no longer beans that I hoed, nor I that hoed beans . . ." (159). Communing with savage tribesmen of the past whose relics he unearths, visiting Egypt in his imagination without leaving Concord, this hero sees himself as a kind of agricultural Paul Bunyan. His expansive vision dwarfs the conventional culture of his neighbors. Yet he does not exclude them so much as go them one better, even trying to pick a fight with a woodchuck. His theme song here could be Irving Berlin's "Anything You Can Do, I Can Do Better." When he claims, "I was determined to know beans," such wordplay drily reminds us that though he knows the clichés of society perfectly well, he has a larger perspective on their meanings. Spiraling from drudgery into vision, the passage lets students see that "this was one of the *great* days" only because Thoreau lived the town's holiday as he tried to live every day—that is, as a holy day (161).

This expansive comic incorporation begins to dwindle by the end of the chapter "The Village," which describes the night spent in jail when "men . . . pursue and paw him with their dirty institutions" (171). In the chapter "The Ponds," the paean to nature's purity inspires startling invective against "the unclean and stupid farmer" who gave his name to Flint's Pond (195). "Baker Farm" describes Thoreau's philosophic endeavor to wean the Irishman John Field and his family from their dependence on civilized foodstuffs, clothing, and shelter, a punning jeu d'esprit that not all students find sympathetic. And this ascetic strain culminates in "Higher Laws," where a diatribe against animal diet reveals just how much Thoreau is eager to discard: "The wonder is how they, how you and I, can live this slimy beastly life, eating and drinking" (218). The figure who earlier strove to incorporate all the rest of society seems reluctant here even to ingest enough to keep his own body alive.

Perhaps not until the sandbank passage do the book's reductive and expansive impulses achieve equipoise (304–09). If that passage is made the focus of a writing assignment due at the class when it is taken up, intense discussion of its many meanings is guaranteed. Sensitized to Thoreau's asceticism, some students may ask whether his attack on social shams does not verge on stripping away the body itself as one more false facade. Biographical background about the threat of tuberculosis helps them understand the poignance of the "truly grotesque" moment when Thoreau must confront in the flowing sands "brains or lungs or bowels, and excrements of all kinds" (305). Functioning as an emotional safety valve, the scatological joking is under enormous pressure here. If one ponders the rhetorical question "What is man but a mass of thawing clay?" (307), one might be tempted to answer, "Mother Nature's diarrhea." Comparisons with imagery of horror movies help students grasp how much is at stake in the spooky, kooky vision of the dissolving face where Thoreau willingly shucks all his carefully cultivated individuality in order to flirt with immortality through reabsorption into earth's "great central life" (309).

"If we are really dying, let us hear the rattle in our throats and feel cold in the extremities," *Walden* proclaimed earlier (98). In the sandbank passage, Thoreau peeps into the abyss and shivers deliciously for a moment, but the offal in the Demiurge's charnel house only fills him with "more delight" (304). Audaciously he converts the spectacle of his own impending death to high comedy. Jesting about the links between *labor, lapse,* and *globe,* his playful philology denies the implicit fall of man and insists on his freedom to keep "sporting on this bank" like the Divine Artist (306). The cheerful destructiveness of the Demiurge leads to rebirth, so Thoreau can exult as the body he rather distrusts is sluiced away to make room for higher forms. Students will need some help understanding the fundamentally comic dimensions of rebirth as a literary theme. But comparisons with Aristophanes, the Gospels, the *Divine Comedy,* Shakespeare, *Huckleberry Finn,* and slapstick movies will clarify the archetypal pattern for many. Once students grasp the connection between re-creation and recreation, they can better appreciate why playing with words is the natural stylistic outgrowth of Thoreau's profoundly comic vision. Comedy qualifies his social satire. The railroad, surprisingly enough, suggests how industrialism may yet transcend itself, since the sandbank resembles "the slag of a furnace, showing that Nature is 'in full blast' within" (308–09). Some students may also note how the comic rebirth is in turn qualified by irony. Despite the luxuriant mock foliage brought on by the thaw, the railroad cut seems destined for sandy midsummer sterility.

The last time I taught Thoreau in a course on the American Renaissance, I encouraged this perspective by making the final paper topic deal with Friedrich Schlegel's seminal notion of Romantic irony. Rejecting Kant's claim that pure reason could not characterize the Absolute, as Anne Mellor explains, Schlegel asserted that the famous Kantian antinomies actually demonstrate that the Absolute must be self-contradictory. Like a Heraclitean flux, Schlegel's dynamic Absolute—*die Fülle,* the Abounding Fullness—was simultaneously both itself and something else, since its essence was energetic change. Mirroring the Absolute's self-contradictory nature, irony was thus exalted by Schlegel into the Romantic trope par excellence. Humankind yearns for both coherent order and chaotic freedom, he argued, yearns to become being (i.e., a human individual) and to be becoming (i.e., to lose individuality by merging with the universal, fertile chaos). "Whatever does not annihilate itself," proclaimed Schlegel, "is not free and is worth nothing" (qtd. in Furst 28). Romantic ironists could achieve transcendence through an orgy of self-destructive recreation. They could rely on literary techniques that, like puns, stress the artificial, illusory nature of the artist's achieved order, which is simultaneously created and destroyed. "There are ancient and modern poems which breathe throughout and overall the divine breath of irony," Schlegel insisted. "There lives in them a true transcendental buffoonery. Inwardly, the mood which surveys all and which infinitely elevates itself over everything finite, including its own art, virtue, or generality; outwardly, in the realization of the mimic manner of an ordinary good Italian buffo" (qtd. in Chai 319).

My handout on Romantic irony makes plain that Schlegel's concept embraces the works of many authors in the American Renaissance. Students who choose to write their term papers on Thoreau are thus invited to reinterpret their initial response to the sandbank passage by seeing it as a paradigmatic expression of Romantic irony. Contemplating his own demise with fascination and detachment, Thoreau becomes Schlegel's divine ironist. His lofty comic perspective amounts to ecstasy (literally, *ek-stasis*, a standing outside). In such an ironic high, being and becoming finally merge, according to Schlegel, and the Romantic artist cavorts joyously in the Abounding Fullness.

Surely such attitudes underlie the remarkable description of the hawk that appears over the marsh toward the end of "Spring." From uncertain footing on "quaking," boggy ground, Thoreau watches the hawk as

> it sported with proud reliance in the fields of air; mounting again and again with its strange chuckle, it repeated its free and beautiful fall, turning over and over like a kite, and then recovering from its lofty tumbling, as if it had never set its foot on *terra firma*. It appeared to have no companion in the universe,—sporting there alone,—and to need none but the morning and the ether with which it played.   (316–17)

Mockingly mimicking its own downfall, hinting at kinship with the sickly observer on *terra infirma*, yet denying it, this astonishing bird, with its "strange chuckle," is a vision of ironic transcendence. Chastened by their encounters with Thoreau's wordplay, many students will be ready to accept the hawk as a fit emblem for the triumphant (though faintly perverse) humor of his strange book.

"What Are You Doing Out There?":
Teaching Thoreau to College Freshmen

Stanley S. Blair

In *Walden* Thoreau often contradicts himself to engage his readers inductively, to make them aware of their confusion about themselves so that they may better understand themselves—or, as he puts it, "Not till we are lost, in other words, not till we have lost the world, do we begin to find ourselves, and realize where we are and the infinite extent of our relations" (171). For college freshmen facing not only new physical and social surroundings but also the daunting prospect of adulthood, perhaps the most important thing a teacher can do with *Walden* is to use Thoreau's contradictions as an opportunity for students to create a community among themselves and to build confidence in themselves as adults.

On the first of the eight class days we spend on Thoreau, I begin by setting up an exercise (borrowed from Ann Berthoff) that helps students understand how he learns about himself by closely observing the world around him. Some time before that first meeting, I gather together a variety of organic objects (milkweed pods, green leaves, seashells, crab claws, seed pods, feathers, twigs with leaves attached, and so on), making sure that I have more than enough of them for the students. During the first class, I place the objects on a desk at the front of the room and ask each student to come forward and choose an object that will be his or her own and to observe and take notes on that object for ten uninterrupted minutes each day for about two weeks, or until we discuss "The Village."

After the students have their organic objects, I provide them with a brief biography of Thoreau, pointing out that when he went to Walden Pond, he was uncertain of what to do with his life but certain that he wanted to avoid the rat race. I also raise the issue of Thoreau's continuing influence on us, including the back-to-nature movement, the interest in organic foods and vegetarianism, the growth of environmentalism, and the widespread use of passive resistance. For each of these issues I let students provide some specific examples.

On the second day of class, the reading assignment is "Economy" and "Where I Lived, and What I Lived For." The length and complexity of "Economy" intimidate many freshmen, so I begin by asking if any students had trouble, and then I spend most of the period discussing why Thoreau went to Walden Pond and what he meant by "economy." In "Economy," Thoreau lists "the necessaries of life" as "Food, Shelter, Clothing, and Fuel," which he treats in reverse order (12). For each he sets up (as he suggests on page 12 and says explicitly on page 61) a basic opposition between necessity and luxury. It might be helpful to put the scheme on the board, as in table 1.

Table 1

	Necessity	Luxury
Fuel	_____	_____
Clothing	_____	_____
Shelter	_____	_____
Food	_____	_____

This scheme helps students understand Thoreau's sense of economy. As much as possible, I let them fill in the specifics, which might include the following: First, fuel: the necessity is that we must retain our "vital heat," while the luxury is that we keep ourselves "unnaturally hot" and become dependent on excessive amounts of fuel and heat, for which we must pay (12–14). Second, clothing: the necessity is that we must retain our "vital heat" and "cover nakedness"—and so patches are OK (22)—while the luxury is dressing fashionably and working hard to meet that expense (21–27). Third, shelter: the necessity is a small house we can construct ourselves, while the luxury is to have a big house built for us, requiring us to worry about the quality of construction and to pay for a mortgage and maintenance (27–40). (It is here, on page 40, that many students get lost, because Thoreau now digresses about how to build a shelter: the sections on building the house [40–45] and architecture [45–49] explain how he built his cabin at Walden Pond, while the section on economy [50–58] explains how by growing crops he paid for his building materials.) Fourth, food: the necessity is that we eat, but we can be as self-sufficient as possible and grow much of our own food, thereby avoiding the luxury of having to pay for all of it (59–65). (He goes on to argue that while some basic furniture and kitchen utensils are necessary [65–69], they can be procured or built at little or no expense and ought not to be a physical or financial burden.)

After contrasting "the necessaries of life" with luxuries, Thoreau concludes that to maintain one's life "is not a hardship but a pastime, if we will live simply and wisely" (70). He thinks that our taste for luxuries not only makes us depend on others but also makes us have to work much harder than we need to; luxuries cause us much "trouble and anxiety" and are "hinderances to the elevation of mankind," an elevation that could occur if we were "to solve some of the problems of life, not only theoretically, but practically" (11, 14, 15). In fact, once we secure the necessities of life, we can then be philanthropic, sharing with less fortunate people anything left over. On pages 72–79 he explains that philanthropy, or doing "good" for others, should be "wholly unintended" and is best accomplished by setting a good example. Arguably, Thoreau follows this advice himself in giving *Walden* to his luxury-bound readers.

If there is sufficient time, in "Where I Lived, and What I Lived For" we focus on the famous "I went to the woods" passage (90–91) and the last paragraph of the chapter and discuss Thoreau's motivations and goals.

On the third day of class, the assignment is "The Bean-Field" and "Reading." Through their writing courses in high school or college, students may have

Table 2

Concrete	*Abstract*	*Personality*	*Writing*	*Society*
beans	product	new self	ideas	humanity
hoeing	process	thinking	revision	wake up
bean field	setting	the mind	paper	the world
rows	form	ideas	sentences	communities
hoer	agent	oneself	writer	the speaker

encountered the notion of writing and thinking as organic processes. In "The Bean-Field," Thoreau metaphorizes writing and thinking as the process of bean growing. After he describes in detail how he hoed beans, he asserts, "It was no longer beans that I hoed, nor I that hoed beans" (159). Here he contradicts himself to make a point: he's talking about something more than hoeing beans. What that something more is may be clearer to students if they are first asked to list on the board the concrete details of Thoreau's bean growing and to draw abstractions from those details. Within the framework of abstraction, eventually (I give them time, not the answers) they can start to explore that something more. Table 2 shows how one class did it. This may be an appropriate time to discuss Thoreau's own composition process, using as evidence excerpts from his Journal and from the published version of *Walden*.

After we consider thinking and writing, we move on to "Reading," which suggests how and what to read and, more specifically, how to read *Walden*. Thoreau contends that most people do too much "easy reading" (104) and are poor thinkers; to become better thinkers they must read better books. His athletic metaphor for reading (101) speaks clearly not only to former high school athletes but also to musicians and scholars, who remember hours of practice and agony (teachers shouldn't hesitate to draw on their own personal experience); he says that good readers must endure similar hardship. It may be helpful to ask students how Thoreau's advice about reading applies both to *Walden* and to our contemporary high-tech culture. Given the difficulty of understanding his sense of economy and given the opposite, the utter simplicity of his expense accounts and shopping lists, does he intend *Walden* to be classic literature or a popular self-help book? And how, if at all, does his distinction between "easy" and "difficult" reading apply, for example, to contemporary film? Some students may call Thoreau's notion of reading elitist. Does "easy reading" have merits that he neglects? Is his vision of "noble villages of men" (110) feasible or even desirable?

Since writing and reading are forms of communication between persons in a community, the class turns next to Thoreau's view of and relation to society. On the fourth day, the assignment is "Solitude," "The Village," and "Baker Farm." I begin by asking students to explain his concept of solitude in terms of his relations to society and nature. He begins the chapter "Solitude" by saying he is "a part" of nature, but later he says that he is "not wholly involved" in it (129,

135). He finally clarifies himself through "a few comparisons" with loons and Walden Pond and other things (137) that "convey an idea of [his] situation": Thoreau is never solitary or alone, because nature is all around him (see p. 131). This perception explains why he defines solitude negatively, as having nothing to do with "the miles of space that intervene between a man and his fellows" (135).

Of course, in human society Thoreau is also never alone, because people are all around him. In "Baker Farm" the class focuses on his view of the Field family. After he describes the Fields (in rather unflattering terms), he discusses how the Fields' way of life differs from his own: unlike him but like the greater part of society, the Fields choose not to live simply, and because of their luxurious tastes they must work hard and suffer spiritual impoverishment (204–06)—an echo of what Thoreau said earlier in "Economy" about necessity and luxury. Despite all this, in the last two paragraphs of the chapter he is tempted to live just as the Fields do, "like serfs" (208). But he overcomes this temptation. Thoreau's contradictory impulses are a topic he explores again and again, most notably in "Higher Laws."

Discussing "The Village," the class focuses on the first third of the first paragraph (167), in which Thoreau compares the wildlife in the woods with the human life in the village, thus alluding to the "few comparisons" he made between nature and himself in "Solitude": natural society and human society, he suggests, are not all that different. If this is so, Thoreau is saying, then access to woods and a pond is not necessary, and his Walden experiment can be performed anywhere. Students may find evidence for this idea in the organic-object journals they have been keeping. The end of this class period (or the beginning of the next) is a good time to read aloud excerpts from those journals and to discuss and evaluate the entire exercise. Like Thoreau in *Walden*, the students in their journals generally move from objective description to subjective association, from describing the dimensions and physical characteristics of their objects to telling what those objects remind the students of or where they may have come from, and even to giving them names and personalities. Students are frequently surprised at how quickly their observations cause their objects, initially meaningless, to become meaningful.

After discussing Thoreau's view of human society and how it compares with nature, during the fifth day the class concentrates on his view of nature and how it compares with the spiritual world; the reading assignment is "Higher Laws" and "Brute Neighbors." "Higher Laws" is a prime example of Thoreau's use of contradiction to engage his readers and make a point. Feeling pulled between the spiritual and animal worlds, he says, "I found in myself, and still find, an instinct toward a higher, or, as it is named, spiritual life, as do most men, and another toward a primitive rank and savage one" (210). He discusses his diet as an example of these contradictory impulses. In "Economy" and "The Bean-Field" he led readers to believe that he would become a vegetarian because with such a diet he could grow his own food, and in "Baker Farm" he attacked the Fields' beef eating as a luxury. But in the first few sentences of "Higher Laws" suddenly he wants to devour a woodchuck like a savage. But then, just as suddenly, he changes his mind, saying that "there is something essentially unclean about this diet and all flesh." But he changes once again, talking about eating fried rats. Finally, he discounts the issue of diet altogether, focusing instead on "the appetite with which [the food] is eaten" (214, 217, 218). Why all this flip-flopping about eating? Thoreau's dilemma about whether to be omnivorous or vegetarian is an outer sign of an inner conflict between his animal and spiritual sides. The relation between the two, he says, is inversely proportional: like a balancing scale, if he suppresses his animal side, his spiritual side will rise (219).

Near the beginning of "Brute Neighbors" he asks, "Why has man just these species of animals for his neighbors . . . ?" (225). This is an important question because, as he suggested in "The Village," there is a clear relation between the animals at Walden Pond and the humans in Concord. "Brute Neighbors" is full of descriptions of such creatures as mice, partridges, otters, ants, dogs, cats, loons, and ducks. What's the point? Are the animals symbolic of human beings? Is Thoreau suggesting that human society should function more like nature? If so, why does he mention the ants' fighting? Does he mean that human society already does function like nature?

For the sixth class meeting the assignments are "The Ponds" and "The Pond in Winter." In the preceding class we discussed the conflict between the animal and spiritual sides of Thoreau's personality; now we focus on his spiritual side, symbolized by the pond: "I am thankful that this pond was made deep and pure for a symbol" (287). By analyzing his descriptions of Walden Pond and the other ponds, the students can consider what Walden Pond symbolizes—perhaps his mind, his spiritual side, that which separates him from animals. I try not to help the students too much with their conclusions, presenting them instead with evidence, which might include the following points: Thoreau describes the pond as an eye (176, 186) and as a mirror (188). Is the pond a means by which he sees and learns about himself? He also describes it in terms of the sky (177, 188–89, 283). What is important for him about the sky and why does he relate sky to pond? Thoreau not only measures the pond (178, 285–91) but goes so far as to draw a very accurate map of it (286). Why? Another possible question: Why is he bothered by the false rumor that the pond is bottomless? Finally, Thoreau fishes and observes fishermen (175, 183–84, 283–85). In the context of the pond's figurative meanings and of fishing's figurative meaning ("Time is but the stream I go a-fishing in" [98]), what does it mean for him to go fishing in Walden Pond?

For the seventh class period we examine Thoreau's spiritual rebirth; the readings are "Spring" and "Conclusion." More than in any other class period, I allow the students to discuss passages of their choice. In "Spring" we focus on why the account of his experiment ends in spring and consider what besides the season itself he means by "spring." In "Conclusion" we address the questions of why he left Walden and what he learned from his stay there (323–24). This provides some nice links to earlier class meetings: in "Economy" he learned that poverty is not poverty, in "Solitude" that solitude is not solitude. Throughout "Conclusion" there are many passages that demonstrate Thoreau's spiritual rebirth; students in their reading should turn up a sufficient number for discussion. I also try to move toward some sort of closure by asking them to explain the complex relation between the human, animal, or spiritual individual and the human, animal, or spiritual community; in fact, this topic provides a good transition to the next class meeting, during which the students will discuss "Civil Disobedience."

In the eighth and final class I remind the students that one of the inspirations for the "Civil Disobedience" experience occurred during Thoreau's stay at Walden when he "went to the village to get a shoe from the cobbler's" and was arrested for tax evasion (171); he refused to pay his tax dollars to support a war he regarded as unjust. The class can come to an understanding of civil disobedience by answering several questions about it, such as what exactly it is, who can or should engage in it, and how and why it should be used. These questions lead to others, such as whether civil disobedience is right or wrong and whether or not it actually works (I invoke as test cases the victims of Nazi genocide and of South African apartheid). If chronologically Thoreau's civil disobedience experience is part of his Walden experience, how are the two works related conceptually?

> But the only true America is that country where you are at liberty to pursue such a mode of life as may enable you to do without these [the luxuries of tea, coffee, and meat] and where the state does not endeavor to compel you to sustain the slavery and war and other superfluous expenses which directly or indirectly result from the use of such things.
>
> (205)

Which experience gave rise to which? Is the relation between the two one of theory and practice, or are they perhaps two different practices? I am fond of recounting to the students an apocryphal anecdote about "Civil Disobedience": On seeing Thoreau behind bars, Ralph Waldo Emerson is supposed to have exclaimed, "Henry David, what are you doing in there?" To which Thoreau replied, "Ralph Waldo, what are *you* doing *out there*?"

An approach to Thoreau that combines deductive and inductive strategies, such as the one I have outlined here, may help allay some of the anxieties of graduate students who are considering teaching Thoreau. When I first put Thoreau on my freshmen's reading list, some of my colleagues suggested that I had made a bad choice because Thoreau was difficult to teach and even more difficult for freshmen to understand. But these difficulties have less to do with Thoreau's style or with freshmen's intelligence, I think, than with a model of education that views knowledge as a commodity to be transferred from teacher to students. This model is indeed acknowledged, if not endorsed, by Thoreau when in "Reading" and elsewhere he quotes from and recommends the classics. But in *Walden* and "Civil Disobedience," he reaches his conclusions in a way that suggests a different model of education—one that views knowledge as created through our observation of and interaction with our surroundings. What this model of education requires of teachers is not that they have all the answers but that, like the students, they have questions; the answers can emerge collectively during class discussions. In short, to engage students both deductively and inductively, those who teach Thoreau may sometimes have to do what from their perspective looks like teaching less, exerting less authority in the classroom and going more with the flow. By engaging Thoreau in this manner, students may reach two insights of which Thoreau would approve: that what one really learns one teaches oneself and that such learning has less to do with pride than with humility.

NOTE

I am grateful to Elizabeth Riley Ostrander, a former fellow graduate student at Marquette University who in 1986 asked me to transcribe my teaching notes into the first draft of this essay, and David Elsberg, a former student of mine who suggested some revisions.

Walden and Awakening: Thoreau in a Sophomore American Literature Survey Course

Scott Slovic

Where I Teach, and What I Teach For

When I began teaching at Southwest Texas State University, we did not yet have telephone registration, nor did students simply complete a registration card and indicate the courses they wanted to take. Registration was a zoo that took place four times a year (two long semesters and two month-long summer terms) in the university's athletic center. Faculty members worked the tables. Some 21,000 students, of all complexions and concerns, raced from line to line, hoping to get into one required course after another. Very few freshmen and sophomores actively sought particular courses and instructors—instead, they referred to courses only by number and meeting time.

"What sections of English 2380 do you have open?" they would ask.

"Tuesday and Thursday at 9:00 and 11:00, Monday night from 6:30 to 9:15," someone like me would respond.

In an average semester, six or eight sections of 2380—Masterpieces of American Literature—were offered, and most enrolled between 130 and 150 sophomores, although one mammoth section accommodated nearly 400 and a few "intimate" sections were limited to 75. Students almost never asked for details about the courses before registering, usually glad just to get a space. Occasionally a choice was available—two or three sections still open and at times that fit a student's schedule—and the inevitable questions emerged: Who is the easiest professor? Which section requires the least reading? Are you sure all these courses will satisfy my sophomore literature requirement?

My colleagues and I did our best to keep emotions in check and respond politely: "We're all tough teachers. Go to the bookstore and see which books have been ordered for each section."

That was the industrial university, the institutional vortex of graduation requirements, course numbers, room numbers, student ID numbers, and computerized exams. In this dehumanized context of nameless faces and numbered identities, I tried to bring my students back into contact with certain essential facets of human experience, emphasizing in my large sections of Masterpieces of American Literature the processes and purposes of "waking up" to one's life and one's relations to the external world, human and nonhuman. A colleague— a friend of mine—warned me, shortly after I arrived at Southwest Texas from Brown University five years ago, that lecturing to an auditorium crowded with 150 bored sophomores, many shamelessly sleeping or chattering, was like trying to teach literature to "a field of wheat." But I vowed to myself that the minute I began thinking of my students as wheat I would pack up my books and walk out of the room, seeking another way of being human. To keep myself and my students attuned to our mutual humanity, I relied heavily on Henry Thoreau—indeed, *Walden* served as the touchstone of my course.

Variations on a Theme

What is a masterpiece? Most of my students, I'd wager, did not even know the official, generic title of my course when they registered for English 2380—some even asked why we read only works by American authors. I usually began by offering a loose definition of a masterpiece, describing it as a literary work that depicts or evokes human experience in an essential and enduring way. But then I proceeded to explain that from the many examples of American literature that could fit this definition, I selected a handful of texts that cohered around the psychological theme of awakening, the process by which people become aware of their mental and physical boundaries and activities, their social contexts, and their places in the natural world. Beyond the generic title of the course, I gave it a specific name on the syllabus each term, such as "To Reawaken and Keep Ourselves Awake": American Literature from Thoreau to the Present or American Landscapes and Humanscapes. The title of my last version of the course was Awakenings: An Introduction to American Literature, which took on added meaning in the light of our meeting time—8:00 in the morning. On the first few days of class I actually brought an old alarm clock, which I set to ring sharply at 8:00. Afterward I relied on the literature to wake people up.

Thoreau and Awakening

Thoreau's most explicit discussion of awakening appears in the crucial second chapter of *Walden*, "Where I Lived, and What I Lived For," which I normally discussed, after making other, preliminary remarks, on the first day of class. Here the writer reveals what I think is the essential purpose of both the book itself and his actual two-year, two-month, and two-day experiment at Walden Pond: the process of elevating his attentiveness to the world and to himself. This process requires vigorous intellectual engagement, not merely passive, painless meditation—certainly not the sort of mechanical memorization to which most of my students are accustomed. "The millions are awake enough for physical labor," writes Thoreau;

> but only one in a million is awake enough for effective intellectual exertion, only one in a hundred millions to a poetic or divine life. To be awake is to be alive. I have never yet met a man who was quite awake. How could I have looked him in the face? (90)

"To be awake is to be alive." Thoreau makes his priorities absolutely plain here. For readers whose principal goals in life tend to be pleasure and comfort or perhaps the security of a well-paying job and a stable family, this statement seems strikingly foreign, even subversive. Why should we, too, value awareness more than security? Frequently Thoreau comes across as haughty and condescending—in my classes I have taken to comparing his harsh critiques of contemporary society with other examples of the tradition of American jeremiads, such as Cotton Mather's "A Voice from Heaven" (1719) or Jonathan Edwards's "Sinners in the Hands of an Angry God" (1741). However, Thoreau's main reason for criticizing the intellectual dullness of his contemporaries was to help them—and himself—improve the quality of daily experience. The moments of subtle humility—"How could I have looked him in the face?"—help humanize Thoreau and show him to be a fellow seeker of awakening, not someone writing from a rarefied and unattainable plane of experience.

In this crucial passage of the second chapter, Thoreau goes on to describe the awakening process so rhapsodically—his writing not merely hortatory but celebratory—that even the drowsier students in my English 2380 classroom seemed to open their eyes as I read these lines aloud:

> We must learn to reawaken and keep ourselves awake, not by mechanical aids, but by an infinite expectation of the dawn, which does not forsake us in our soundest sleep. I know of no more encouraging fact than the unquestionable ability of man to elevate his life by a conscious endeavor. . . . To affect the quality of the day, that is the highest of arts. Every man is tasked to make his life, even in its details, worthy of the contemplation of his most elevated and critical hour. . . .
>
> I went to the woods because I wished to live deliberately, to front only the essential facts of life, and see if I could not learn what it had to teach, and not, when I came to die, discover that I had not lived. . . . I wanted to live deep and suck out all the marrow of life, to live so sturdily and Spartan-like as to put to rout all that was not life, to cut a broad swath and shave close, to drive life into a corner, and reduce it to its lowest terms. . . .   (90–91)

I read and analyzed this entire passage, including the material elided here, and I connected many of the issues revealed in it to what I call key Thoreauvian ideas. Imagine the irony of reading this passage from *Walden* to a group of students who had, for the most part, enrolled in my class under duress (sophomore literature requirement) and who struggled to stay awake while reading the book in preparation for my lecture. When I devoted so much time to reading and explaining Thoreau's wake-up call, my goal was to show that Thoreau wants his readers to get the most out of life and not enslave themselves to either their jobs or their philosophies. I devoted most of the rest of my discussion to showing the various strategies Thoreau describes and employs throughout *Walden* for elevating his own consciousness and that of his readers.

Key Thoreauvian Ideas

The first words that I wrote on the board in English 2380 were *rhapsody* and *jeremiad*, and even before we got to *Walden* I normally lectured on the modes of celebration and critique that emerge in early American literature, from John Winthrop to William Bartram. When we began reading *Walden*, I urged my students to look for contrasting passages of rhapsody and jeremiad, and thus I helped them understand the ways in which Thoreau is coaxing and provoking us to achieve intensified awareness. In my book *Seeking Awareness in American Nature Writing: Henry Thoreau, Annie Dillard, Edward Abbey, Wendell Berry, Barry Lopez*, I argue that the main function of Thoreau's personal Journal was to test the Swedenborgian-Emersonian notion of correspondence through constant scrutiny of the rhythms and changes in the natural world and through the effort—often unsuccessful—to match up those rhythms with the author's moods. The rhetorical modes of rhapsody and jeremiad in *Walden* often mirror the discussions of the corresponding states of mind. For instance, in the chapter "Solitude," Thoreau writes rhapsodically of the sense of correspondence ("something kindred to me" [132]) he feels when alone in nature: "Every little pine needle expanded and swelled with sympathy and befriended me" (132). Elsewhere, in the chapter "Reading," feeling alienated from his fellow human beings, Thoreau complains, "The heroic books, even if printed in the character of our mother tongue, will always be in a language dead to degenerate times" (100). Both of these rhetorical modes, one aimed to inspire positive enthusiasm and the other to dash cold water in our faces, contribute to Thoreau's project of awakening.

Next I discussed Thoreau's use of synonymous terms to address the same fundamental psychological issue of consciousness. Assuming that most of my students had struggled through the introductory chapter, "Economy," and wondered why Thoreau constantly digressed from the "economics" of building his house at Walden and earning money from bean farming, I pointed out that "simplicity," "necessity," and "economy" all represent the same basic idea of efficiency, essentiality. And when Thoreau writes that he moved to Walden in order to "live deliberately," he is describing this very condition of self-control and self-consciousness. Indeed, "deliberate," when seen in this context, becomes extraordinarily important. "Let us spend one day as deliberately as Nature, and not be thrown off the track by every nutshell and mosquito's wing that falls on the rails," Thoreau writes, a few pages after speaking of his desire to live deliberately (97). Two paragraphs later he begins the chapter "Reading" with the assertion that "[w]ith a little more deliberation in the choice of their pursuits, all men would perhaps become essentially students and observers . . ." (99). Recognizing patterns like this—the repetition of vocabulary to address closely related issues—is crucial not only to the reading of *Walden* but also to the interpretation of any complex literary work. Once students realize how this approach illuminates *Walden*, they become eager to try it with other texts.

I also explained how Thoreau is constantly engaged in the process of testing perspective, in *Walden* and in other works such as the Journal, the chapter "Ktaadn" in *The Maine Woods*, and "Walking." One of the principal goals of the awakening person is to avoid complacency, mindless habit. Thus, throughout *Walden*, Thoreau shows us what he did to break out of mental ruts—even his eventual departure from the house at Walden ostensibly resulted from a desire to avoid such ruts. "The Ponds" may seem to be primarily a catalog of natural historical information about Walden and other ponds in the Concord area. From a psychological perspective, though, the chapter represents the writer's ceaseless efforts to change and revitalize his view of the world and his understanding of his processes of perception and imagination. For instance, he explains in one lengthy paragraph how Walden Pond changes in appearance when you look at it in different directions, when you view it close up or from a hilltop, when the light changes with the passage of time, and even when "you invert your head" (186). As I read this section to my students, I was always tempted to ask them to stand and view the lecture hall from an inverted perspective. This testing of perspective results in frequent disorientation and confusion, from which a person must scramble back to clarity and familiarity. Near the end of "The Village," Thoreau discusses the value of disorientation explicitly, claiming that

> not till we are completely lost, or turned round,—for a man needs only to be turned round once with his eyes shut in this world to be lost,—do we appreciate the vastness and strangeness of Nature. . . . Not till we are lost, in other words, not till we have lost the world, do we begin to find ourselves, and realize where we are and the infinite extent of our relations.
>
> (171)

We ourselves and our surroundings thus come into relief when we cease to take them for granted. By deliberately disrupting his current perspective on experience, Thoreau seeks to avoid the rut of familiarity.

A closely related idea is Thoreau's inclination to value the local and the immediate as opposed to the exotic or the distant past and future. When he writes on the opening page of the book that he is confined to the theme of his own life "by the narrowness of [his] experience," the irony is not yet clear; only later do we realize that the self may well be cosmos enough for the awakened or awakening person. Likewise, when he writes, "I have travelled a good deal in Concord" (4), the purpose at first seems to be humor and irony, for how can one travel at all in such a small place? Gradually, though, the book's travel motif makes it clear that to be genuinely awake is to experience one's life and one's routine surroundings as if they were strange and exotic. As Thoreau quotes William Habbington early in "Conclusion,"

> Direct your eye sight inward, and you'll find
> A thousand regions in your mind

Yet undiscovered. Travel them, and be
Expert in home-cosmography.   (320)

To the home cosmographer, everything in the world has the potential for
mystery and for meaning. The empirical world is thus closely bound up with
the mystical, spiritual realm. Thoreau was clearly aware how alien and impractical his ideas and his very lifestyle appeared to his fellow townspeople, and he
occasionally writes defensively in his Journal. On 1 July 1852, for instance, he
proclaims (as if to reassure himself), "I am abroad viewing the works of Nature
and not loafing" (*Journal* [1906] 4: 166). Similarly, at the end of a meditative
passage in the *Walden* chapter "Sounds," he writes, "This was sheer idleness to
my fellow-townsmen, no doubt; but if the birds and flowers had tried me by
their standard, I should not have been found wanting" (112).

The Rest of the Course:
Social and Environmental Awakenings

You may have the sense by now that I could easily have devoted the entire semester to pointing out the psychological patterns in *Walden* alone. Actually, although we did take constant note of the Thoreauvian echoes in American
literature after Thoreau, we moved rapidly through nine or ten additional
books during the remainder of the semester. (The precise reading list varied
from term to term—in this way I forced myself to prepare anew for each
course, thus reawakening myself.) Because I was concerned in this class with
exposing my students to as much American literature as possible without destroying their often tenuous budgets, we tended to use the cheapest available
editions of books, such as Houghton Mifflin's Walden *and "Civil Disobedience,"* edited by Sherman Paul.

The details of the Thoreauvian patterns we observed in our other readings
are too numerous and complex for complete explanation here, but I will briefly
try to summarize how some of them demonstrate similar aspects of the awakening process, such as deliberateness, disorientation as a springboard toward
awakening, minutely focused sensory awareness, cosmic consciousness, and
various forms of awakening to the self's relation to society. After *Walden*, we
turned to Walt Whitman's "Song of Myself" and observed in his cosmic em-
brace the opposite of Thoreau's deliberate, controlled approach to awakening.
Emily Dickinson, in her emphasis on selection and limited, focused perception, more closely approximates Thoreau's deliberateness. Then we usually
read either Kate Chopin's *The Awakening*, an example of dawning social consciousness and the process of individuation for late-Victorian American women
in the South, or Jack London's *The Call of the Wild*, which I presented as a narrative study of social Darwinism in the context of a domestic dog becoming

conscious of his inherent "wildness" (for Buck, atavism is a type of awakening). A one-week survey of imagist poetry acquainted students with the Thoreauvian fascination with the process of visual perception in such poets as Ezra Pound, William Carlos Williams, HD, and Wallace Stevens, at least in some of their work. In the following weeks, we often read Ernest Hemingway's *In Our Time* or *For Whom the Bell Tolls*, the latter a study of how having only a short time to live focuses one's attention on the present; Richard Wright's *Native Son*, which forces readers to confront social reality in America through a violently naturalistic narrative; and Aldo Leopold's *A Sand County Almanac*, a Thoreau-like testing of perspective and appreciation of the nearby natural world. Arthur Miller uses political allegory in *The Crucible* to awaken his readers or audience to the horrors of McCarthyism, while Ntozake Shange's *For Colored Girls Who Have Considered Suicide When the Rainbow Is Enuf* and Leslie Marmon Silko's *Ceremony* emphasize pride and self-appreciation as antidotes to despair. Perhaps because I taught so many Hispanic students in my survey of American literature, two of the most popular books I used were Tomas Rivera's *Y no se lo trago la tierra—And the Earth Did Not Devour Him* (Evangelina Vigil-Piñon's translation) and Rudolfo Anaya's *Bless Me, Ultima*, both of which demonstrate through naturalistic detail the Thoreauvian celebration of the nearby and the immediate, creating art out of ordinary life.

I often concluded the course by showing how contemporary nature writers have adopted the Thoreauvian project of promoting awareness of the relation between the self and the natural world. In Edward Abbey's novel *The Monkey Wrench Gang*, for instance, we encountered a provocative conflation of moral issues (development versus preservationism) and pure aesthetics (flamboyant, Nabokovian wordplay), which forced us to think critically about the connection between art and the world. Annie Dillard, whose work usually formed the per-fectly symmetrical conclusion to the course, in nearly all her books demon-strates many of the key Thoreauvian ideas mentioned above; I used *Pilgrim at Tinker Creek*, *Teaching a Stone to Talk*, and *An American Childhood*.

Helping Nonreaders Read Hard Books

Many of my students told me openly that they had never read a complete book before taking my course. Imagine, therefore, how they must have felt as they began slogging through a text as difficult as *Walden*. I tried to reassure these tentative readers by pointing out early on what Thoreau says in his chapter "Reading." I explained that he intended the book to slow us down, to make us struggle with language and ideas. Just as Thoreau himself must have arduously "consecrate[d] morning hours" to the study of ancient Greek and Latin texts even as he wrote *Walden*, he has created a book in which the words "are raised out of the trivialness of the street, to be perpetual suggestions and provoca-tions" (100).

All of us may struggle with the complexity of *Walden*, with its odd mixture of digressiveness and condensed meditation, but then "[b]ooks must be read as deliberately and reservedly as they were written," Thoreau assures us (101). If we struggle, that's only because the author himself struggled "to front . . . the essential facts of life." The sort of "gingerbread" that average readers pick up results, he asserts, in "dulness of sight, a stagnation of the vital circulations, and a general deliquium and sloughing off of all the intellectual faculties" (105). Thus, by forcing our minds to grapple with Thoreau's text, we engage in the active intellectual process of awakening, of coming to know ourselves and the world. "The intellect is a cleaver," Thoreau tells us; "it discerns and rifts its way into the secret of things" (98). As we work our way through *Walden* and the other works in the Thoreauvian tradition of awakening, our minds become cleavers, too.

Sharon Cameron has argued in her book *Writing Nature: Henry Thoreau's Journal* that "to write about nature is to write about how the mind sees nature, and sometimes about how the mind sees itself" (44). This statement not only describes Thoreau's Journal and *Walden* accurately; it also identifies an essential psychological current that we can observe throughout American literature. By seeking this current, students become active, enthusiastic readers of literature in general, not just of *Walden*. Often on course evaluations I receive comments such as "I used to hate reading until I read *Walden* in this course. That book changed my life." Thus do we overcome the "quiet desperation" that pervades industrial societies and industrial universities.

Teaching *Walden* as Transcendental Strip Tease Art

Annette M. Woodlief

Walden consistently arouses strong and conflicting emotional responses in an undergraduate American literature survey. Some students dislike the persona, dismissing him as "all attitude, no sex, and too hard to read" or asking, with some discomfort, "What right does he have to criticize me?" Others become disciples, caught up in Thoreau's rebellious stance or the "nature thing." Neutrality, I have found, more likely indicates failure to read than analytic objectivity. Such intense personal engagement can be daunting for someone trying to teach close reading as well as recognition of literary values and cultural patterns to non-English major sophomores (my students are mostly business, art, and psychology majors).

Thoreau understood and exploited personal encounters between reader and writer, as shown when he addresses his readers' impertinent yet pertinent inquiries at the beginning of *Walden*. An honest teacher can do no less. I begin my course by requiring students to write brief responses to and questions on the assigned pages and to turn them in at the beginning of class. Although these responses are usually undirected, especially in the early weeks when students need to relax and open up, by the time we reach *Walden* I suggest topics for the three or four class meetings devoted to the book. I find that once students have revealed themselves in writing and are assured that it is all right to be "wrong," they are eager to test the validity of their responses in class. And I am eager to lead them to (not just tell about) literary subtleties that most people miss on a hurried first reading.

"Could it be that *Walden* is really the work of a transcendental strip tease artist?" With that initial question, I have my students' attention, perhaps shocked or bewildered, and a punning metaphor to guide us through the book. I ask them to focus on these four words as they read and respond to each of the four divisions of their reading: "Economy"; "Where I Lived, and What I Lived For" and "Reading"; "Sounds" through "The Pond in Winter"; "Spring" and "Conclusion." For the first meeting, I also ask them to define "business," "economy," "civilization," and "making a living" in their own terms as well as in Thoreau's (thus alerting them that there may be differences).

Fresh from a reading of Emerson, they do have some notion of what transcendental means, although in Emerson's abstract and metaphorical terms. They seem relieved to sense a real person, not a distant preacher, in the narrative voice of *Walden*. I find, though, that in spite of their enthusiasm for Emerson's idea of self-reliance, many students ask, "Why is Thoreau so stuck on himself?" Thus they need to understand how Thoreau uses—and transcends—his personal history. His explanation in the second paragraph of *Walden* helps, but we must go further so that the quirky, somewhat cantankerous, and apparently contradictory persona the students have generally constructed for Thoreau will not obscure their perception of his literary artistry. Some understanding of transcendental egotism in both Emerson and Thoreau needs to be negotiated.

Defining the transcendental strategy as a moving from natural facts to embedded intellectual and spiritual truths by assuming a microcosmic perspective, we consider how the real person Thoreau can also be a literary persona embarked on an experiment in living both real and symbolic. When the students present and examine their sets of definitions in the light of passages in "Economy," they begin to understand how the Thoreauvian transcendental approach involves redefining key terms. We also look at details of his experiment, particularly his choice of place and method of building his house. I highlight passages that show Thoreau moving from the specific to the broadly mythic as he reshapes common perceptions and concepts.

For the next meeting we are ready to do our own version of redefining of "strip tease," and we begin by stripping away some of the common associations with the term. References to sex seem notably missing from the book and the persona, an omission students do not want to ignore. (Since its lack does not bother them with other writers we study, their concern shows how seriously and personally they take Thoreau's experiment.) However, awareness of the body as part of nature, even in erotic relation to it, is not absent from *Walden*. Exhibition (some might say exhibitionism) is also an element of the book, though transcendental and consciously (the author presenting himself as a model) rather than sexual. Most important, I want them to see that the book exhibits not so much the actions of a single dancer as a mutually revelatory dance of partners, here the narrator-persona we call Thoreau and the reader of *Walden*. We may join that dance by using our (certainly not his) working metaphor of strip tease art, doing some radical redefining in a Thoreauvian style.

Students generally recognize that Thoreau's stripping is much more like a moulting (though he does it in public view) and consists of a sharp questioning of civilized assumptions about the values of things, beginning with clothes and business in "Economy." A close look at his ideas about wearing clothes (which strikes a central nerve in mall-oriented students) shows just how Thoreau's stripping involves the reader in the process of redefining and "transcendentalizing." The clothes to be shed are accepted opinions, assumptions and traditions, somehow of both Thoreau's time and our own, yet they are not just to be removed but to be replaced on a more natural and rational basis. We discuss how Thoreau provokes his readers to enter their own "moulting season" (which must be "a crisis in our lives" [24]) using himself as model and employing certain literary strategies to encourage them to reconsider whether the values they have adopted (or, more likely, simply assumed) can sustain their inner fires of "vital heat" (13).

During the first two meetings I emphasize Thoreau's use of paradox, humor, and wordplay, and his redefinitions of metaphors, listing examples and passages on a study guide. Students will understand his strategy of rhetorical paradox, for example, by considering how savagery and wildness can be more civilized than the artificial nineteenth-century culture he describes. This assessment prepares them for the extended cost-accounting paradox-metaphor that strikes students close to home: that to get the most life (= time) for the least money, making life a paying proposition, one should take on the "voluntary poverty" (14) of living simply and wisely. We also explore, in key passages, the paradoxical and metaphorical connections between sleeping and waking.

To offset the image of a sour and cranky hermit that many students seem to have, I remind them of Thoreau's humor and wordplay and show how these are crucial to the stripping process. Students, upset that Thoreau seems to be making fun of their values, often fail to see that he is also laughing at himself, even as he is making himself over. His humor, essentially transcendental, is based on seeing the discrepancies between the ideal and the actual as comic and thus correctible. When readers smile at Thoreau's comic-serious description of "a poor immortal soul . . . creeping down the road of life, pushing before it a barn" (5); at an auction of goods including a dried tapeworm and other dusty family heirlooms that would be better suited for a bonfire (67); or at a tongue-in-cheek cost accounting to the half cent, they may recognize truths that can also be painful. Like Thoreau and his neighbors, each reader cherishes illusions that can be quite funny when viewed from the distance that Thoreau establishes, and laughing at illusions is a most effective way of destroying them, of stripping them away.

In "Where I Lived, and What I Lived For," the stripping begins to turn into teasing. By this point, students have noted how much Thoreau has stripped literally—to just enough of the "necessaries" to keep the "vital heat": a bare cabin, which he suggests, half-seriously, half-humorously (he avows he is "far from jesting"), could just as well be a six-foot box (29), a bare diet, and minimal, functional clothing and furniture. He is now unencumbered in his search for reality and a way to make a living. Through word, deed, and pointed humorous images, he has repeatedly criticized and questioned his neighbors and his readers, calling his neighbors "they" and addressing his readers with "you," challenging them to think through their own lives. "Why should we live with such hurry and waste of life?" (93).

Well aware of Thoreau's stings, students often do not easily see the softening of his rhetorical stance, as he teases them to join him in getting to the "bottom" of reality to establish new foundations (97–98), new possibilities for "making a living." They must see how "they" and "you" become "we" to understand how Thoreau recruits them as partners learning how to construct clothes, a house, a world, or even art, starting with a bared self planted in nature (not exiting the stage), dressing in new clothes and ways.

In another sense of teasing—coaxing out the truths embedded in facts—Thoreau postulates in this chapter that one must settle in one place and in the present moment, confronting the facts of one's self and the facts of nature to transform them into facts of the imagination. We look at how Thoreau does this at Walden, as well as at the ways he provokes the reader to settle deeply and start building. Teasing also implies that truths can be revealed only as suggestions, as tantalizing hints rather than as full exposure, that come from the constant reexamination of one's relation to nature. Each transcendental reader must translate these hints in his or her way.

To call this process teasing is not to imply that it is an enterprise to be taken lightly. The stripping to necessaries that precedes teasing, or dressing back up, is strenuous, demanding both psychologically and intellectually. Bared to the essentials, one must then mine deeply in one place, even as Thoreau uses his head as "an organ for burrowing" and seeks that "hard bottom" of reality. Typically, the passage ends with a cutting pun, "and here I will begin to mine," (98), as Thoreau looks for glimpses of truth in "my" experience, which has also rhetorically become the reader's "mine." But perhaps most frustrating for students is that what is found by burrowing is hidden and indirect; their labor will stretch out over many pages, and the payoff will be elusive and tantalizing.

The chapter "Reading" is interpreted, then, as an invitation and guide to a careful, even "athletic," reading of nature and the book to tease out or translate hidden truths, to learn to read both nature and the book "as deliberately and reservedly as they were written" (101). We approach the remaining chapters as a joint and intellectually exercising exploration (involving the reader as partner) of many facts—literal and imaginative—that Thoreau discovers at the pond. For guidance through the lengthy reading, I give students a list of facts and encounters to highlight as they read, such as the description and measurement of the pond; the chasing of the loon and the battle of the ants in "Brute Neighbors"; Thoreau's observations of frogs, owls, and pickerel; and the structuring of the seasons. I ask them to tease out any possible transcendental and symbolic meanings and suggestions they find here and in other passages that catch their attention, keeping in mind that Thoreau often leaves his meanings open and ambiguous, giving readers plenty of room for their own interpretations. I too try to tease and not lecture as we "saunter" through Thoreau's observations, to coax out different meanings.

Students are sometimes frustrated by all the interpretive possibilities, asking, "But what does it really mean?" The metaphor of teasing helps show that the "correspondences" between the self and nature, though rooted in fact, are also open-ended and dynamic, dependent on the vision of the subjective seer, whether Thoreau or each reader. We conclude that Thoreau's rhetorical strategy is not so much to instruct or make disciples as to tease each reader into involvement and participation, to make a transcendental strip tease artist (in our greatly redefined sense) out of each reader.

Artist is the crucial word as we read the two final chapters. We look carefully at how the thawing bank in "Spring" becomes a metaphor for the transcendental art of organic expression (304–09). In other words, to return to our strip tease metaphor, art is viewed not as external ornament but as an integral expression of the vital heat (and we are, in a sense, back to our discussion of clothes). The bank is the "laboratory of the Artist who made the world and me" (306), much as Walden Pond has been Thoreau's laboratory for creating a world; and perhaps the reading of *Walden* has provoked readers also to re-create their world from the inside out. In "Conclusion" we note the many exhortations to explore the new worlds now open to readers who are awake and ready to reconstruct, and students like to point out their favorite passages. We look at how the book culminates in the creating and time-defying act of the artist of Kouroo and in the bug from the apple-tree wood, emerging from the dead layers into a "perfect summer life at last!" (333).

Perhaps the prime pedagogical value of the transcendental strip tease artist metaphor is its flexibility in opening different possible readings. The redefinition of terms and the application of our outrageous pun are best done collectively, since the exercise is one that students can join in enthusiastically. By encouraging their responses to the tentative and double-edged metaphor-thesis, a teacher can demonstrate how Thoreau created a similar, though far more artistic, rhetorical strategy. Students appreciate the novelty of the approach, and a teacher may learn much from the originality of their definitions and readings.

At the end of our study of *Walden* students are often surprised to discover that they understand rhetoric (which I may not have mentioned specifically until this point) as a practical and artistically executed strategy of involving the reader in the text. They are also able to discuss more knowledgeably what art does, what a text might be for both writer and different readers, and how art is related to real life and to rhetoric—issues crucial to their understanding of how to read literature, not just *Walden*.

Postscript

Since I wrote the above essay, this rhetorical "tease" has taken an unexpected but productive turn. The problem with writing on pedagogy is that one's approach may change before the print is dry, for good teaching is always a process, adapted to different classes and new possibilities. So it is with this approach. What remains constant is my belief that students need a rhetorical overview of *Walden*, one that helps them deal with their often bewildering experience as first-time readers and as readers who themselves are a subject of Thoreau's. They also need to explore different interpretive possibilities from that personal base. Unfortunately, with a lecture class of 125 sophomores, much of the dialogue of discovery outlined above became wishful thinking. So with the moral and financial support of a state-funded grant for technology and teaching, I turned to video and the computer as tools to generate discussion.

The first reading assignment on Thoreau in this class, an American literature survey, was the first three chapters of *Walden*. We viewed a fifteen-minute video in which I presented my transcendental strip tease overview. Then we discussed it, just as we would have discussed a video presentation by another professor, elaborating and critiquing the ideas. In two subsequent class meetings we continued to examine the metaphor. In the future, I expect to augment the video part of the class with hypertext links between key related passages projected on the screen and monitors.

However, *Walden* deserves closer and more personalized readings than this format allows. Many students in the class chose to do a hypertext project outside class on "Where I Lived, and What I Lived For" (they had four projects to choose from in the course). This interactive project involved a series of staged readings and writing to model how more experienced readers might deal with such a complex text.

The program I use is *Guide*, an IBM-Windows–based hypertext program that is relatively user-friendly and is available in a number of computer centers on campus, as well as to students with personal computers. Since I had used it for class presentations, students were comfortable with it and ready to use it as a reading tool. The protocol I adapted (and will continue to refine) is loosely based on the reader-oriented theories of Wolfgang Iser, Stanley Fish, David Bleich, Michael Riffaterre, Jonathan Culler, Louise Rosenblatt, and Robert Scholes and influenced especially by the ideas of my colleague Marcel Cornis-Pop, as described in *Hermeneutic Desire and Critical Rewriting*.

The project began with the students writing informally before they had read *Walden* for the class. The purpose of this assignment was to start them thinking about preconceptions that might shape their reading. The questions they responded to were as follows:

1. What do you know about Thoreau? What have you heard? Have you read anything by him before? What were your impressions about him as a person and as a writer?
2. How would you define "living fully"? What might that involve for you? Have you ever considered changing your life drastically to try another way of living besides the usual way?
3. Do you appreciate verbal humor, such as irony, double entendres, riddles, and puns? Or would you prefer that people speak plainly and not play with language?

After reading the first two chapters of *Walden*, they wrote responses to the following prompts about "Where I Lived, and What I Lived For":

1. Describe the overall effect of the chapter on you. Consider why you like or dislike it and whether the text has confirmed or challenged the expectations you described in your pre-reading response notes. Have your ideas been revised in any way?
2. Find your dominant responses; describe the major effect of the chapter on you, your strongest feelings about it.

3. Referring closely to the chapter, especially places you might have underlined, note the effects specific images, sentences, phrases, or words had on you.
4. Focus on difficult or problematic areas of the chapter; ask questions; point out gaps, contradictions, ambiguities, intriguing aspects. Is there anything else you feel you need to know? Are there other questions you would insert in the text?
5. Describe connections with other texts or with personal experiences that this work has triggered in your mind. If you have read more of *Walden* by this time, how would you compare this chapter with the others?

These papers were turned in (for quick, encouraging responses), and the students then began working with the *Guide* hypertext. Embedded in the chapter's text on the computer and available by "clicking" were definitions, notes, open questions, biography, some literary critical issues—in other words, all the kinds of information, ideas, and questions an experienced reader would consider in a close rereading. Some of the finer points about how Thoreau encourages his readers to "strip" and be "teased into thought" were incorporated in this hypertext (particularly puns and wordplay students might otherwise miss). At the bottom of the screen was a word-processing file where the reader typed extensive notes in response to text and hypertext.

After completing this second reading (on which many spent numerous hours), the students wrote a second reading response in the same word-processing file. Although they were encouraged to consider and synthesize all the ideas and patterns they had noted, they were asked to respond particularly to these prompts:

1. Go back and reread your first reading notes [these had been returned]. How have your impressions changed or been confirmed?
2. Explore your responses in the following key areas: to certain words, phrases, metaphors, or ideas; to the form: How is *Walden* different from or like other prose pieces you are familiar with?; to the narrator as a person: Are you offended by or attracted to any aspect of Thoreau's personality? Does he seem sincere?
3. What other kinds of questions or notes would you like to see included in this hypertext version of the chapter? Which ones here open up some ideas for you?
4. What connections would you make to other parts of *Walden*? In particular, what relation do you see between this chapter and its paired chapter, "Economy"?
5. Outline possible directions for analyzing and interpreting the chapter and any other thoughts or comparisons that have occurred to you while reading this material.

After the collection of all their responses and notes, the students were ready to write a final, more formally graded response answering questions designed to make them more self-conscious readers. They were guided by, but not limited to, these prompts:

1.   Look over all three of your previous responses. What have you learned about Thoreau in your readings? about yourself? about nineteenth-century American values? about Thoreau's values that differ from those?
2.   What do you find most distinctive about the chapter—the persona? the author behind him? the stated ideas? the submerged or contradictory ideas? the humor? the puns? Thoreau's call to explore oneself and find realities? anything else?
3.   What themes or patterns of imagery strike you as particularly significant? Why do they seem significant?
4.   How would you answer readers who say *Walden* is autobiography or a sermon, not literature (or vice versa)?
5.   If you had to write a more focused paper, which subject that you have unearthed here would you like to explore?

After the projects were completed and turned in on disk, many of the final responses (names given only if students permitted) were posted online and students were urged to read them to understand the range of possibilities generated from their readings of *Walden*. These readings could be the core of thoughtful e-mail or *Daedalus Interchange* conversations, especially for a class that had breakout computer discussion groups (probably my next direction in this process).

The experience proved to be intense, both personally and textually. Students appreciated the (probably illusory, but nevertheless powerful) elements of discovery and choice and created lengthy, thoughtful, and provocative responses. In a sense, they were recording the strip-and-tease process of their own informed and interactive reading of the second chapter and discovering much about themselves, individually and as a group, as readers. Many spent up to thirty hours on the project, returning repeatedly to discover more as the hypertext notes and questions teased them into thought and response. One student remarked that now she truly understood Thoreau's declaration in "Reading" that reading is a "noble exercise" that "requires a training such as the athletes underwent, the steady intention almost of the whole life to this object" (101).

Interactive hypertext encouraged students to own and explode the text, opening up personal responses linked to numerous interpretive possibilities instead of committing them prematurely to generalizations. Their responses were more creative, thoughtful, and clearly written than in most papers I have ever received in this class. Even better, the discovery process did not end with the project. As their subsequent reading and writing in the course demonstrated, they became more confident and skilled readers of other texts, even on first reading. Perhaps they are not quite the "athletic" readers Thoreau had in mind, but they "exercised" creatively with this technological version of a transcendental strip tease.

The Privileged Protester:
Teaching Thoreau to Two-Year College Students

Deborah T. Meem

Since I began teaching in a two-year college in 1984, I have taught the American literature survey—which includes Thoreau—a number of times. Until this year I used the *Norton Anthology of American Literature* (Baym et al.), supplemented occasionally by additional assignments or handouts. Generally speaking, I bought Norton's "Add diversity and stir" approach to American literature and so interpreted Thoreau in the context of mainstream (white male) writing. This year for the first time I used the *Heath Anthology of American Literature* (Lauter et al.). The Heath, as many readers know, goes far beyond "liberal" anthologies such as the Norton; it turns the American lit paradigm on its head. In this essay I discuss the influence of the Heath paradigm shift on my teaching of Thoreau to two-year college students.

First, by way of background, I teach English in University College, a two-year open-admissions unit on the main campus of the University of Cincinnati. University College has a threefold mission: it offers terminal associate degree programs in various areas, such as Court Reporting or Robotics; it provides most of the developmental work for underprepared University of Cincinnati freshmen; and it prepares students for transfer into the various baccalaureate colleges at the University of Cincinnati. The American literature survey is a sophomore course, taken mostly by students who need to fulfill a literature requirement in order to transfer. In having a four-year degree as a stated goal, these students resemble sophomore students at many universities. But they differ in three ways from the "typical" college sophomore: generally they have had mixed success in high school, perhaps graduating in the lower half of their class or completing a GED or non–college-prep program; a significant portion of them, between one-third and one-half, have taken at least one developmental language arts course at the University of Cincinnati; and many are nontraditional students: students over twenty-five, single parents, or disadvantaged graduates of academically questionable inner-city high schools.

These characteristics have several implications that directly affect my teaching of American literature in general and Thoreau in particular. First of all, students who enter the university with academic deficiencies tend also to have had limited exposure to the kinds of reading and intellectual exercise that are valued at the postsecondary level. They are thus likely to be unfamiliar with the history, philosophy, politics, and literature of nineteenth-century America, including Thoreau. Second, as a result of their lack of reading skill and analytical savvy, my sophomore literature students need more instructional guidance than do their baccalaureate-college counterparts. They especially need help when we come to Thoreau, whose writings are hard even for skilled readers. And, finally, a high percentage of my students reach their sophomore year in college feeling some sense of alienation from the American system and its various social, economic, and educational institutions. Often they see their college experience as a ticket to the kinds of material success from which they and their families have been excluded, and it is a great imaginative challenge for them to achieve sympathetic understanding of Thoreau and his chosen downward mobility.

Before this year, I taught American literature from the "manifest destiny" point of view, that is, envisioning literary history as a more or less seamless progression from East to West, from agriculture to industry, from religion to reason, from Romanticism to realism, and so on. This approach, of course, vastly oversimplifies the American experience, but students grasp it—at least until they reach Thoreau. When they encounter an author who "consistently argues against many of the basic assumptions behind American economic life" (Dillman, "Reader Response" 23), they run into trouble. The "progressive" approach has not prepared them to deal with the complex issues of class, education, and privilege that arise in Thoreau's writing.

The Heath anthology greatly expands over previous anthologies the definition of what constitutes American literature. Naturally, it adds more writing by authors from traditionally underrepresented ethnic and gender groups. But in addition, its editors chose not to base "[their] initial selection on that of previous anthologies or on [their] graduate school training and then supplementing or subtracting according to [their] own principles." Instead they "began with the vast range of the literary output of this country and . . . narrowed from that" (Lauter et al. xxxv). Suddenly my American literature survey opened with Native American traditions rather than with the Pilgrims, and a new course took shape. In this re-visionary (in Adrienne Rich's sense ["When We Dead Awaken"]) American literature experience, we arrive at Thoreau after examining diverse literary "conversations" on three principal subjects: nature, slavery, and the counterculture.

Nature

The first course readings of this rethought American literature survey were Native American origin myths—Winnebago, Pima, Zuni, and Navajo. Although, as the Heath editors remind us (6–7), these myths, in the form that we read them, differ in important ways from those that were spoken and sung by the Native Americans before Columbus, they nevertheless introduce us to a society fundamentally at one with the natural world. This is a world where human beings are not assumed to be superior life forms; in it, animals and plants are "people." Into this world come the explorers, colonizers, and settlers, bringing with them European diseases and a Christian worldview: Christopher Columbus seeing nature only as a source of potential profit or Samuel Purchas seeing Virginia as England's "Virgin-portion from the Creation" after the "unnaturall Naturalls"— that is, the Native Americans—have been pushed aside (Lauter et al. 140). It is from here that we trace the ongoing debate about nature. Is natural America, as William Bradford says, a "hideous and desolate wilderness, full of wild beasts and wild men" whose "lasciviousness" and "profaneness" mirror the basically "corrupt natures" of all people (249, 255, 261)? Or is it, as Thomas Morton says, a prelapsarian paradise where, "guided only by the light of nature, these people leades the more happy and freer life, being voyde of care, which torments the mindes of so many Christians" (215)? Is it true, as Jonathan Edwards suggests, that "natural men," by rejecting the "cultivations of heaven," have "deserved the fiery pit" (584, 588)? Or, as Anne Bradstreet says, are nature's creatures far happier than Puritan man, who is a "lump of wretchedness" (301)? Bradstreet's positive view of nature prefigures Phillis Wheatley's neoclassical paean to the "native grace" of "pleasing Gambia" and "Afric's blissful plain" (1061–62) and Ralph Waldo Emerson's later assertion that "Nature always wears the colors of the spirit" (504). We also recognize Emerson's transcendental egotism whereby "man . . . is placed in the centre of beings, and a ray of relation passes from every other being to him" (1510).

And so we reach Thoreau. Seen in the "nature debate" context, *Walden* made far more sense to my students than ever before in my experience. They recognized the latter-day Puritan in Thoreau, the man all too aware of "shame on account of the inferior and brutish nature to which [he was] allied" (2044; "Higher Laws"). One of my students, Clare, wrote in her journal, for example: "This nature thing really hung them up, didn't it? Bradford thought nature was dirty and 200 years later Thoreau seemed to think the same thing." At the same time, students read of Thoreau's sense of kinship with animals: "I found myself suddenly neighbor to the birds; not by having imprisoned one, but having caged myself near them" (2032; "Where I Lived"). They understood the ideal reality underlying Thoreau's view of nature: "No wonder that the earth expresses itself outwardly in leaves, it so labors with the idea inwardly" (2049; "Spring"). And finally, they saw Thoreau's vision of nature as self-centered in the Emersonian sense: "Be . . . the Mungo Park, the Lewis and Clarke and Frobisher, of your own streams and oceans; explore your own higher latitudes,— . . . be a Columbus to whole new continents and worlds within you, opening new channels, not of trade, but of thought" (2057; "Conclusion"). Another student, Donté, saw a connection between this line of thinking and the Columbus excerpts we had read earlier in the quarter: "Columbus as a metaphor makes me nervous, even though [Thoreau] says 'not of trade.' These explorers were conquerors and entrepreneurs, after all." Mary Catherine, however, liked the self-exploration. "It's what psychology grew out of," she wrote. "Not too long after Thoreau, Freud was 'opening new channels of thought' for a living."

Slavery

In 1852 Harriet Beecher Stowe described slavery as "a monstrous system of injustice that lies at the foundation of all our society" (320). One hundred thirty years later Howard Zinn wrote:

> There is not a country in world history in which racism has been more important, for so long a time, as the United States. . . . So it is more than a purely historical question to ask: How does it start?—and an even more important question: How might it end?   (23)

In line with Stowe and Zinn and a host of others, my revised American literature survey traces slavery—as a lived reality and as an economic and ideological institution—from the first contact between aboriginal Native Americans and European explorers. Indeed, we learn that the American slave trade began with Columbus, who, frustrated at finding neither gold nor spices, carried human booty back to his royal Spanish patrons. We read Phillis Wheatley and Sarah Morton, colonial antislavery writers. We follow the rise of the abolitionist movement, which includes the voices of slaves (Sojourner Truth, Harriet Jacobs, Frederick Douglass) and of white leaders (the Grimké sisters, John Greenleaf Whittier, William Lloyd Garrison). We read *Uncle Tom's Cabin*. In short, we are able to see Thoreau's "Slavery in Massachusetts" and "A Plea for Captain John Brown" as growing out of an established tradition of antislavery literature. Douglass and Stowe, for instance, highlight the hypocrisy of "Christians" who preach "equality under God" yet own slaves (Lauter et al. 1727–30; Stowe 126, 187); Thoreau writes admiringly of John Brown, for whom a fanatical neo-Puritanism eliminated conflict between principle and practice (Lauter et al. 2065; "Plea for John Brown"). One of my students, Leslie, an antiabortion activist, agreed: "Thoreau and John Brown knew that if you give yourself completely there is no hypocrisy. God only asks of us that we put our money where our mouth is. I want to live my life that way." Robert, however, expressed doubt: "The problem here is that John Brown was crazy. I agree he was sincere, but there needs to be a better way to change the world than sincere craziness." We notice, moreover, how Thoreau typically places his own stamp on the tradition. Douglass and Stowe draw their imagery from the death of Jesus, the former expecting a "glorious resurrection, from the tomb of slavery to the heaven of freedom" (Lauter et al. 1708), the latter asserting that "Heaven is better than Kentucky" (Stowe 428). Thoreau, in contrast, abandoned the sacrificial stoic Jesus in favor of the image of an activist Jesus. He described fiery John Brown as possessing an "indignation that . . . cleared the temple" (Lauter et al. 2076; "Plea"). Donté wrote: "African-Americans would have been a lot better off if we had thought like Thoreau did. We wasted a lot of time turning the other cheek when we should have been clearing the temple."

We examine how Thoreau reverses the expected order of most abolitionist rhetoric. Sojourner Truth, for example, works from the particular ("Look at me! Look at my arm!") to the general ("And a'n't I a woman?") (1960). Henry Highland Garnet similarly progresses from individual leaders of slave uprisings—Denmark Vesey, Nat Turner, Joseph Cinque, and others—to the exhortation to all slaves: "Labor for the peace of the human race, and remember that you are *four millions*" (Lauter et al. 1876). But Thoreau invariably works from the general to the specific. In "Slavery in Massachusetts" he begins with Congress, framers of the Fugitive Slave Law, then takes on the Commonwealth of Massachusetts, enforcer of that law, and ends urging right-minded individuals to "recognize a higher law than the Constitution, or the decision of the majority" (Baym et al. 1897). Andrew, a gay student, connected this idea with the recent court case over the passage of Issue 3 in Cincinnati, which denied human rights protection to homosexuals: "That's why we have judges, checks and balances, etc. Thoreau was right. The majority shouldn't ever be allowed to vote rights away. And if the court doesn't find it [the removal of the category 'homosexual' from the Cincinnati Human Rights Ordinance] unconstitutional, then people like ACT UP will be out there." So by viewing Thoreau in the context of contemporary abolitionists, my students can recognize the development of a tradition, one individualist's reshaping of the tradition, and how the tradition figures in their own lives.

Counterculture

Walden is no doubt the most frequently taught of Thoreau's works, but I suspect that many people view Thoreau principally through the "Civil Disobedience" lens, that is, less as a pastoral writer than as a rebel against his society. It was, after all, not *Walden* but "Resistance to Civil Government" that inspired Mohandas Gandhi and Martin Luther King, Jr. Before this year, my students were both attracted and mystified by Thoreau's seemingly perverse rejection of nineteenth-century American progress. In 1989, for instance, a student wrote: "He's got guts, for sure. He wasn't afraid to say what he thought. But he was so negative. He didn't like anything, railroad, telegraph, neighbors, taxes. It's fine not to like slavery and war, but he didn't like progressive things either." Certainly, when American history is seen as the seamless progression I described earlier, Thoreau's nonconformism is decidedly negative, as it appeared to the student writer. But what about an American history that acknowledges the voices of opposition to manifest destiny? Such a history includes the Hopi description of the coming of the Spanish, whom they see not as beneficent God bearers but as breakers of harmony. It includes Cabeza de Vaca, whose experience as a captive of the natives led him to profound disillusionment with "Christians," that is, his own greedy and violent people. It includes Washington Irving and his anti-Franklinian counterhero Rip Van Winkle. It includes Frederick Douglass asking, "What to the Slave Is the Fourth of July?" It includes Emily Dickinson, eccentric and "disloyal to civilization" (Rich, "Disloyal"). And it includes Mariano Vallejo's *Recuerdos*, which, as Genaro Padilla says in his introduction to that work, "by virtue of the author's social displacement . . . is pushed into an antithetical relation with other nineteenth-century American autobiographies which tend to celebrate the conjuncture between the progress of the American nation and that of the American individual" (Lauter et al. 2002).

So it follows that by the time my students read Thoreau, they understand that counterculturalism has been a basic component of the American personality since the first contact of Native Americans and Europeans. Thus they are much more comfortable now with a nineteenth-century iconoclast than they ever were before. We examine three elements of Thoreau's nonconformist philosophy: his valorizing of poverty over wealth, his rejection of American mercantile assumptions, and his uncompromising individualism.

Thoreau's primary notion of money is stated clearly in "Life without Principle": "The ways by which you may get money almost without exception lead downward" (Baym et al. 1901). He expands on this idea in "Resistance to Civil Government," saying that "the rich man . . . is always sold to the institution which makes him rich" (Lauter et al. 2022). A student, Robert, wrote: "It's true today. I read that nearly every congressman leaves Washington a millionaire. Lobbyists bribe them. We have the best government money can buy." But Thoreau's solution to the problem of wealth is to idealize poverty, to cultivate it "like a garden herb." He extols the advantages of being poor, reminding us that lack of money merely confines us "to the most significant and vital experiences" (2061; "Conclusion"). "Love your life, poor as it is," he urges us. "You may perhaps have some pleasant, thrilling, glorious hours, even in a poorhouse" (2050). He describes the houses of poor whites and Indians as "pleasant," "comfortable," even "picturesque" (Baym et al. 1733, 1743; "Economy"). Another student, DiAnna, disliked this attitude: "It's fine to tell people look on the bright side, but my life isn't picturesque. Me and 3 kids in 2 BR there's nothing picturesque about it. He didn't know how I live." In class we discuss Thoreau's critique of materialistic middle-class Americans obsessed with accumulating meaningless "gewgaws upon the mantlepiece" (1738). At the same time we notice how "Thoreau appears more interested in the idea of a box shelter than sympathetic to anyone in need of such a shelter" (McCarthy 325). In a classroom presentation, three students debated Thoreau's seemingly contradictory views. Each took a position: Robert, that Thoreau was an advocate of poverty; Jenny, that Thoreau was a voyeur of poverty; and Elizabeth, that Thoreau was an analyst of poverty. Never trying to reduce Thoreau to a perfectly logical unity, they laid out his views in a way that made his complexity understandable.

"This world is a place of business," complained Thoreau (Baym et al. 1900; "Life"). Indeed, he critiqued enterprise even more severely than he did other perceived outrages on the American moral, political, and ecological landscape such as slavery, territorial expansion, political institutions and processes, reformers, and the threatened destruction of the wilderness (Neufeldt, "Enterprise" 232). He lashed out against industrial opportunism, saying "a corporation has no conscience" (Lauter et al. 2016; "Resistance"). He ridiculed the notion of progress defined as technological advances: "We are in great haste to construct a magnetic telegraph from Maine to Texas; but Maine and Texas, it may be, have nothing important to communicate" (Baym et al. 1746; "Economy"). "We do not ride upon the railroad," he wrote. "It rides upon us"

(Lauter et al. 2035; "Where I Lived"). A rare instance of Thoreau admiring technology appears in the Journal, where he describes the autumn wind turning the telegraph wires into an Aeolian harp, "the manifest blessing of heaven on a work of man's." More typical is his scathing criticism of factories as causing ecological blight: "That water could never have flowed under a factory. How *then* could it have reflected the sky?" (*Selected Journals* 130, 117). My students and I discuss nineteenth-century industrialism and its effect on the daily lives of Americans, and we place Thoreau among those who stood against the mindless fascination with "internal improvements" (Lauter et al. 2035; "Where I Lived"). Peter, a student whose father worked for twenty years at the contaminated and now closed Fernald uranium processing plant near Cincinnati, wrote: "I think what Thoreau was saying is that internal improvements might get us color TV and microwave ovens, but also Fernald. Technology hurts us as well as helps us."

Much interest in Thoreau today stems from his reputation as a resister. But my students want to know how he managed to protest so firmly against American culture and institutions without paying a high personal price for his rebellion. The answer, we discover, lies in the relation between nonconformism and privilege. Thoreau was a Harvard graduate and thus part of America's intellectual elite (Bode 13); he was "borderline gentry to start with and downwardly mobile by his own perverse intent" (Buell, "Pilgrimage" 195). Thoreau, in a word, could afford to rebel. His friends bailed him out of jail; his mother and sisters brought him cookies at Walden; his connection with Emerson, Alcott, and other well-known literati lent him access to Boston publishers. These supports compensated somewhat for the comforts he gave up and brought him a degree of fame and success; yet at the same time he constructed a literary "self-mythography" (Hildebidle 39) according to which he stood outside the operative American value system. In short, Thoreau's privilege gave him the freedom to criticize American society. One of my students, Rashad, a Vietnam veteran, likened Thoreau to antiwar protesters on college campuses in the 1960s: "Those rich kids could protest all they wanted to because Daddy was paying the bill. Poor kids were getting killed meanwhile." And Bill, a middle-aged Appalachian man, related Thoreau to protesters at Antioch College who "took over a building for a rec center. They should have put all that energy into something that would benefit society, not just themselves." Indeed, Thoreau's philosophy advocated individualism over mass culture. "There will never be a really free and enlightened State," he wrote, "until the State comes to recognize the individual as a higher and independent power, from which all its own power and authority are derived, and treats him accordingly" (Lauter et al. 2029; "Resistance"). So extreme is his individualism that not only is he willing to break the law (1972) but he also acknowledges no truth in secondhand learning: "How can we *know* what we are *told* merely? Each man can interpret another's experience only by his own" (*Week* 365). My student Debbie's journal concluded with the following: "I looked up the word 'solipsism' and I think it applies to Thoreau. For him 'the self is the only existent thing.' He was such a good writer and he had so many ideas but finally they come down to solipsism."

In teaching Thoreau to two-year-college students, I have found three effective strategies. First of all, I have adopted the new Heath anthology; it provides thematic, political, and stylistic background material that helps us see Thoreau less as an anomaly than as part of an ongoing tradition in American literature. Second, I teach Thoreau primarily through theme (nature, slavery, counterculturalism) rather than exclusively through concentration on one work at a time. Finally, to let students see themes as they developed in Thoreau's writing, I range outside the anthology and include many selections from works not contained in the Heath (other parts of *Walden*, "Slavery in Massachusetts," some entries in the Journal, "Life without Principle," *A Week on the Concord and Merrimack Rivers*). I work, one might say, against Thoreau's own desire. He would have been pleased with his positioning in the Heath anthology, where he gets his own section, entitled "Henry David Thoreau: A Concord Individualist." But my teaching of Thoreau insists on connecting him to other people and movements in literary history, an approach that seems to help my sophomore students see him both alone and in relation.

"Baker Farm" and Historicism:
The Rainbow's Arch

Leonard N. Neufeldt

Thoreau's "Baker Farm," one of the least discussed chapters of *Walden*, begins with the narrator's clearly defined intention but soon describes the narrator chasing a rainbow, or, to be more precise, standing "in the very abutment of a rainbow's arch" (202). What follows is a brief meditation on Baker Farm folded into a meditation on one of the most talked-about topics in New England transcendentalist studies, the increasing calls for a return to historicism. "Baker Farm" and the scholarly commentary on it strike me as useful illustrative texts for our current debate over the need to recover historicism and to practice a "new" historicism. They may also serve to introduce undergraduates to these issues in the classroom.

In the quest for historicism, one might first note that Thoreau's chapter title was also the name of an actual farm a little more than a mile south of Walden Pond on the east shore of Fair Haven Bay, in Lincoln, Middlesex County. The farm got its name from its proprietor, James Baker (1796–1875), who, like numerous other mid-nineteenth-century family farmers of the region, was bogging marginal wetland meadows to turn them into profitable pasturage, sweet-hay fields (usually timothy or clover), or market-vegetable plots. Baker was keeping up with the times, so to speak. Indeed, several months after *Walden* appeared, he sold off twenty-five acres of potential cordwood southeast of his farm for $125 an acre—a handsome but not surprising price for woodlots near the railroad. The Baker Farm area was a favorite retreat of Thoreau and fellow walker Ellery Channing (who in 1849 published his "Baker Farm" poem, excerpts from which Thoreau used in his chapter by the same title). Apparently Thoreau had imagined this farm and house as a possible residence and writer's studio (*Walden* 81–82).

Six weeks after moving into his cabin at Walden Pond, Thoreau, like the *Walden* narrator, visited the derelict hovel and was surprised to find the Irish bogger John Field and his wretched family inhabiting the place. But neither Thoreau the journal keeper nor Thoreau the *Walden* narrator is surprised to discover an immigrant Irishman draining fields for others. In rural Massachusetts it was one kind of labor available to poor, unskilled, and functionally illiterate foreigners like Field, a recent arrival from a country in which the very poor made up one-third of the population. (According to the 1850 US Census figures, ninety-eight percent of the illiterate inhabitants of Middlesex County were foreign-born, most of them poor Irish.) In Ireland these pitiful land-rent, tenant, or migrant farmers had usually worked small plots of potatoes with spade and hoe, digging ditches through and around the wet land on which they cultivated their crop. For most, this work was their sole subsistence. Consequently, Field's work and the condition of his temporary dwelling would not have seemed unusual to Field: many of Ireland's poor lived in circumstances much worse than those described in "Baker Farm." Moreover, many of his fellow immigrants in inland towns were cleaning stables; digging foundations, canals, and ditches; carrying bricks, stone, mortar, cordwood, gravel, chestnut railroad ties, and iron rails like draft animals; and working long hours as domestics, almost invariably for inadequate wages.

Thoreau knew that the condition of Field's dwelling was not unusual for the region around Concord—many old houses and cabins on family farms and elsewhere had fallen into disrepair (Neufeldt, *Economist* 5–17). But none of Thoreau's writings, including his Journal, indicates that he was well informed about land-use practices, farming crises, crop failures, and the series of English parliamentary acts that, in the several years it took him to write his first three versions of *Walden*, killed more than one million in Ireland through famine and prompted a similar number to migrate to America, mainly through the ports of New York and Boston. In his scattered Journal notations on local Irish, Thoreau seems to distinguish between the relatively large number of wretched Irish who had settled in his area recently and the much smaller number of Irish artisans and farmers of means with whom he had grown up. Some of these earlier immigrants owned substantial properties in and around Concord by the time of the immigration of people like Field and his family.

"Enough," I can hear some of my colleagues say. "How can you possibly expect us to take your historical annotation seriously when history itself is the eye of a storm in English departments today?" My first answer is that in Thoreau's idea of economy there is a fundamental contrast between what the narrator and the Irish immigrant make of their houses, livelihoods, past, present, and future. Many Concordians viewed Thoreau pretty much as the narrator views Field: a ne'er-do-well who isn't eager to take good advice, wastes too much of his time in shiftless pursuits like fishing, and cannot figure out how to make a good living in an America of opportunity. The narrator notes this correspondence; he tells Field that he, too, "who came a-fishing here, and looked like a loafer, was getting [his] living like [Field]." But *getting a living* is a loaded expression in *Walden*, and the narrator immediately notes what in his opinion are crucial differences between himself and Field, underscoring his observations with a repetitive "I did not" and summing up the differences by remarking that Field "was discontented and wasted his life into the bargain" (205). My second answer is that I come to *Walden* as someone trained in historical as well as literary studies. As such, I have occasionally wondered why annotated texts of *Walden* offer virtually no historical glosses. My third answer is that although historical annotation of the kind just featured is neither old historicism nor new, it's not a bad way for a historicist to begin.

These answers are not meant to suggest that I dismiss the debate among literary theorists and critics over history. But I am persuaded that most claims made for and against historicism in current literary debates are locked into a priori determinations based on premises that cannot finally be proved and on analytical categories whose meaning or intent are in themselves neither obvious nor firm. In practice, historicism needs to be seen as an open question. In the first place, although history is usually assumed to refer to something objectively real, it refers to an entity only in uncritical commonsense thinking or in a pragmatically sanctioned operation in a particular situation. By itself, the term *history* is a floating signifier fastened only to pure possibility. A historical operation, however, anchors history to meaning, in that the operation is an act of meaning construction. In such an act, the meaning of history and a scholar's discernment of meaning are largely indistinguishable. Today historicists are no longer inclined to speak of objective history or the objective truth of history. Increasing numbers of them are in the business of trying to identify individual and collective meanings and to describe constructions of particular meanings over time or the expression of those meanings in behavior, even as they, the scholars, are themselves engaged in meaning construction. Most will agree that a past site, say, Concord of the 1850s, Baker Farm, or the world of Thoreau's horizons, cannot be definitively recovered. History is a story or some other kind of exegetical or explanatory construction around "facts" that we select from the past and that we accord a particular status. Making history and writing history are not categorically different from each other.

Second, history is a collective term for a variety of practices. We should regard it as normal that there are many different histories or historical practices, each dedicated to its assumptions about reality, to its concerns, methodologies, protocol of language, favorite analytical categories and questions—and to its results. The history of New England transcendentalism can be told many ways. If the historian's construction presents that history as a continuous, unified, and inevitable linear movement from past to present to imminent future, such a throwback to old historicism is not justified by the complex of people, cultures, social configurations, and events we refer to as the past. Such a plotting of history is a reminder of another aspect of the past, the kind of historiography that dominated historical scholarship in the nineteenth and early twentieth centuries.

To sum up the last few paragraphs: establishing the meaning of history must always be deferred, for at least two reasons—the status of history as imagined entity and its status as both the imagined and the actual horizon of the historian. Behind the term *history* are two questions: What kind of historicism? and How useful are the results? These are open questions that depend on the scholar's analytical categories and storytelling procedures as well as on the reader's relation to them. Although many historians of our generation concede everything just mentioned and admit, furthermore, that differences in assumptions, methods, and language characterize relations not only among their various subdisciplines but also among scholars within those subdisciplines, such a state of affairs, as far as I can tell, has not produced much metaphysical fright, epistemological bewilderment, or linguistic anxiety in history departments.

Although some literary new historicists have devoted much of their writing to questioning history and others to inventing wildly associative montages, the new historicism that commands attention is one in which "the historical subject" and traditional assumptions "of origin and telos" are problematized yet in which a "peculiar sense of the historical remains after the historical subject and the determinations of beginning and end have been dissimulated" (Schrag 46). To restate the problem of the historian's subject simply: historiography is principally the cultural product of a scholar engaging the past while influenced by her or his present and a desired future.

Scholarship on "Baker Farm" reveals the extent to which the critics' responses to Thoreau's text are implicated in attitudes (Thoreau's putative attitudes, his culture's, the critic's) toward past, present, and future. Thoreau's complicated attitude toward Field evokes an unusable past as typified by Field's Old World ways, but it also invokes a usable past—the rustic old family farms of Concord, unspoiled meadows and woods, good schooling, classical books, poetry. Yet Thoreau's uses of the past are inseparable from his present and desired future. Not that the past seeks to reproduce itself indefinitely or that it serves as the definitive origin and telic urge toward the present and the future. In "Baker Farm" and throughout *Walden*, the relation of past, present, and future to one another is nonlinear; they function simultaneously, and they are not necessarily commensurate. Imbued by the past, the narrator nonetheless can declare that "[a] man will not need to study history to find out what is best for his own culture" (205). That highly political statement appears in a literary work interested above all in culture-building, centered on self-culture, in the present and future.

Unlike most traditional Thoreau scholars, the majority of those I note in regard to "Baker Farm" reveal at least some interest in the relation of textual to political. Those interested in the political also respect historicism. To be sure, habitual old-historicist ways of linking past to present to future are evident in them. And, generally speaking, in the scholars' linking of the three what is most repressed is participation in the present, and what is least repressed are differences with the present (both Thoreau's and the critic's), differences prompted by moral, political, aesthetic, and personal desires for a future that edits the past in a spirit of suspicion.

In short, those scholarly commentators on "Baker Farm" inclined toward a new historicism resemble traditional Thoreau scholars in that the new scholars, too, tend to be children of desire, that is, utopian-minded. Yet it also bears noting that while two of them share the deconstructionist skepticism about the relation of word to world and of consciousness to both world and word about the world, all nonetheless assume that language gives a measure of consent to experience and to the world experienced. It is assumed that there is significant reciprocity between the symbolic action of *Walden* and the cultural development and social practices of Thoreau's time and place. As Stephen Greenblatt puts it, literary texts are not sealed off "from the minds and lives of their creators and their audiences" (5). The same reciprocity is assumed between our language and our world, between us and Thoreau's language, and between us and Thoreau's world.

The practical critical question is how to locate Thoreau in his world in the narratives, images, epigrams, allusions, citations, analogies, metaphors, and so on, of *Walden*. The vested interest here is to tease out of the text historically transmitted language and socially and personally constructed meanings. One could just as well focus on what Nancy Fraser calls the "symbolic or signifying dimensions of . . . political, social-institutional practices" (195). This approach is more common in history, sociology, and political science.

But what do these points have to do with "Baker Farm"? Let me begin an answer by noting the five literary scholars who have examined the chapter at some length. Three—Robert Sattelmeyer (" 'True Industry' " 193–97), Richard Bridgman (104–08), and Frederick Garber (*Thoreau's Fable* 181–88), especially Sattelmeyer—seem to share Gerald Graff's desire to recover "a historical perspective that was lost once academic literary studies became established and complacent" (2). Graff's chief fat-cat enemy is an institutionally commodified textualism fed by American ahistoricism and ministered to by critical schools focusing on a text's formal properties. That textualism is exemplified by two other discussants of "Baker Farm," Charles Anderson (132–43) and William Johnson (110–17). For *Walden*, Graff's renovation plan requires investigating in the literary text the sociopolitical manifestations of nineteenth-century American culture. But Graff also implicitly acknowledges both the limitations of any historical practice and the need to contextualize historically, socially, and institutionally one's own kind of historicizing so as not to view historicism as the rainbow's arch of utopian truth or perfect moral exhilaration.

Still regarded as a classic in Thoreau scholarship, and legitimately so, Sherman Paul's *Shores of America* devotes twenty-three pages to "social analysis" in *Walden* (301–23). "Baker Farm" does not appear in those pages, and sixteen pages later it is given less than a paragraph. A few years after that, Charles Anderson, in the interest of dismissing "social criticism," devotes twelve pages to demonstrating the poetic unity within "Baker Farm" and between the chapter and the work as a whole. In its poetic unity lies the "real significance" of this "magical" chapter (132, 135, 143).

Exploring what he calls the dark side of Thoreau, Bridgman, while not rejecting the relatedness and unity, discerns a quite different aspect. His psycho-history concentrates on the encounter with John Field and his family, an episode that occupies one-third of Thoreau's chapter. "Baker Farm" is disturbing, we are told, for its "bigotry and megalomania" (105); and Thoreau, identified completely with the narrator, is virtually relegated to the notorious Know-Nothing Party of his day. His bigotry, common for his time and place, is directed against immigrants, especially poor, uneducated Irish, and their unwillingness to relinquish Old World practices, some of which were not unique to the Irish and did not offend him when associated with a New Englander. Bridgman's charge that Thoreau's description of the Field family calls forth familiar stereotypes is probably correct; however, the particular stereotypes Bridgman has in mind in his ethnic- and class-based analysis may well be incorrect, and they remind us how powerfully attractive presentism is in cultural critique. As for Thoreau's critique, it links self-culture to proper American acculturation and focuses on character. His critique calls to mind the convincing case made recently by a social historian that the prevailing stereotype of the Irish immigrant among enlightened easterners in Thoreau's time

> drew more attention to aspects of interior character than the full range of behavior, condition, and appearance; it focused not on Irish religious affinities or political loyalties or economic condition but on interpersonal style, fundamental morality, and intelligence. . . . Behavior and condition were understood . . . to be correlates of character.   (Knobel 26)

And that character was usually seen as inferior. This view helps explain why Thoreau could also show sympathy and generosity toward the poor Irish he met, to the point of publicly demanding justice for them. It helps clarify, too, Thoreau's report in "Baker Farm" of a visitor's observation that "the shadows of some Irishmen [walking or standing] before him had no halo about them" (202). Coming to this statement with our current moral concerns about ethnic and class discrimination might obscure something badly in need of clarification: Thoreau's implicit notion of nationhood and the new nation, a notion strongly nurtured by his time and place. *Nation*, another one of those insubstantial words, was the subject of more than one construction; for Thoreau it was inseparable from a civil religion that he shared with his American culture yet that he also lambasted and opposed. The kind of moral superiority his visitor ascribes to New Englanders Thoreau ascribes to those who practice self-culture as he understands it. A halo can be explained empirically, which the narrator proceeds to do.

Explaining halos also greatly diminishes the seriousness of the narrator's temptation to "fancy [him]self one of the elect." Perhaps he has moments when he feels himself specially chosen by the gods, but he also characterizes himself (again tongue in cheek) as "a poor unarmed fisherman" routed by the gods with lightning. The gods seem to be largely on the side of the Concord establishment. This is the persona Sattelmeyer focuses on: Thoreau the Harvard graduate who likes to go bait-fishing while others work and who "look[s] like a loafer" (*Walden* 202, 203, 205). Concentrating on more of the chapter than Bridgman does, Sattelmeyer frames the visit to John Field's house by Thoreau's rambling across Baker Farm to fish at Fair Haven Bay only to be forced to seek shelter because of a sudden thundershower and by his return to Fair Haven Bay to continue fishing for pickerel in the shallows. Going fishing as well as writing about going fishing created a problem prompted by opposing cultural pressures, the common New England view of sportfishing as "a kind of social dereliction" and the traditional Old World view of it as genteel (Sattelmeyer, "'True Industry'" 193). Playing with and against these views, the narrator articulates a radical alternative to the American success myth and the Old World status myth. Seemingly free of both, Field becomes an ironic example of "thinking to live by some derivative old country mode in this primitive new country" (*Walden* 208), that is, to rely on Old World conventions to pursue his New World dream of success. What Sattelmeyer acknowledges but doesn't develop is how alien Field seems to Thoreau and how objectionable to him are particular Old World practices and prejudices (though hardly all of them). In this respect Thoreau is very much a part of his American culture, a culture always poised to resist former mentors and administrators within the psychological and ideological limits of a continuing relation to them—a subject examined recently by scholars like Robert Weisbuch, William Spengemann, and Lawrence Buell. As I have tried to show in my book, *The Economist*, this resistance to cultural containment characterizes Thoreau's relation to his country's doctrines of enterprise and success. Sattelmeyer also chooses to ignore Thoreau's priggishness, perhaps in response to Bridgman's preoccupation with it. Whereas Bridgman concentrates on the narrator's meeting with Field, Sattelmeyer is interested more in the fishing excursion that frames the Field episode. "Baker Farm" comprises both—and more than both in that it incorporates these two crucial elements in a larger narrative.

Garber's reading of "Baker Farm" internalizes the historical, identifying it with a play of discourses and images that reveal "Thoreau's fable of inscribing." The chapter ties in "several modes of discourse and a series of patterns of culture and possibilities in the world" and thus "begins to sketch out a history of *this* American place," which makes Thoreau's strategy "at least as political as it is sociocultural. Further, it is a comment on what *some*, the happy few to whom Thoreau ultimately speaks, are able to do." As Socrates does with Meno, the narrator "sets himself up as a parallel with Field, at once mentor and ironic mirror, though markedly better in the latter" (Garber, *Thoreau's Fable* 181, 183). Garber's discussion of that double role links him to both Bridgman and Sattelmeyer.

Yet the intrinsic nature of the cultural in Garber's reading gives *Walden* a stronger place in a history of Romantic irony and in a story of Thoreau's private quest for at-homeness than it does in Thoreau's New England and new America. For Thoreau, pastoralism is, as Garber notes, a way of locating himself in an intellectual, moral, imaginative environment where is both citizen and alien and often the two simultaneously. As such, the pastoralism of "Baker Farm" is future-oriented, corresponding roughly with the principle of accommodating the desires of the narrator and of those within his horizon to change, critique, reorientation, perhaps even private escape. Garber tries to join Thoreau in this possible site of an immanent critique of a way of life, whereas Bridgman largely displaces Thoreau's site and desires with his own, subjecting Thoreau to severe judgment. But Garber's mental, moral-aesthetic, and activist understanding of culture is also basic to Bridgman's and Sattelmeyer's expositions. Sattelmeyer further seems to imply that for Thoreau pastoralism is a language of complex desires tied to his lived experience and to the material production of those around him, a production in which he participates. Seen this way, pastoralism is a present-oriented attempt to image a coherent and structurally integrated life in a culture that desires holism. In this respect Sattelmeyer has affinities to a cultural historian and anthropologist. And these two implicit notions of the pastoral, the future-oriented and the present-oriented, Sattelmeyer seems to assume, operate simultaneously and in a contending rather than a linear, progressive fashion. Thus his analysis reveals stronger links than do the other two between "Baker Farm" and social practices.

What Sattelmeyer doesn't pursue in "Baker Farm" is the archaeological impulse, which is to say a past-oriented, preservationist approach to one's culture. This sometimes Arnoldian impulse both accepts and rejects one's cultural heritage (note, for instance, Thoreau's use of Benvenuto Cellini, Field, and Channing's poem). To be sure, the impulse is implied in Sattelmeyer's cursory notes on Thoreau's identification with the pursuits of hardy and honorable American pioneers, on the one hand, and, on the other, his uneasiness with elitist sport-fishing as mythologized in English social and literary traditions. I suggest that all three stances, the past-oriented, present-oriented, and future-oriented, are very much in evidence in "Baker Farm." And all three are usually involved in acts of historicizing, whether those acts are Thoreau's, the literary scholar's, or the historian's.

A discussion of "Baker Farm" that acknowledges all three impulses is Joan Burbick's rich but all too brief commentary. Thoreau's chapter, she suggests, poses

> significant questions about the relationship between the individual and cultural space, whose virtue is a protective, simplifying structure for human life, and whose terror is a stifling entrapment for the human spirit. . . . Thoreau has to redefine the vision of the "only true America."
> (66–67)

Yet "Thoreau's utopia of one stands against a cultural determination," and he "admits how inapplicable his vision of cultural space is to the family of John Field." He fights off his sense of ineffectualness with a call to pioneering and utopian adventure, thereby displacing the symbol of the settler with that of the saunterer (66–67).

What is most intriguing to me about Burbick's book, *Thoreau's Alternative History*, is that the three attitudes toward time she sees at work in Thoreau are at work in her analysis as well—simultaneously and in tension. Yet, following both the intermittent leads of an inconsistent Thoreau and the habits of old historicism, she also tries to separate the three in Thoreau and arrange them sequentially in a trajectory of progressive development. Her study reminds us how striking the difference can be between old historicism and a new historicist's understanding of attitudes toward the past, present, and future—the attitudes both in themselves and in relation to one another.

Considering all the practices that qualify nowadays as new historicist, the movement is as elusive as Thoreau's rainbow. Practically speaking, it can include all the historicist approaches noted in this essay together with the historical annotations. Indeed, such a multiple approach to *Walden* would undoubtedly be productive while largely keeping us out of the philosophical and historiographical predicaments inherent in Graff's advocacy of "real" historicism. It would also offer at least some protection from traps in the two principal contending views of Thoreau today regarding his culture: (1) Although apparently dedicated to cultural difference and opposed to the dominant cultural forces, Thoreau actually conformed to his culture's social, political, economic, and religious truths; (2) As Romantic-transcendental hero, Thoreau operated outside his culture. These two views are candidates for thoroughgoing deconstruction by a historicism that goes beyond the premises and habits of old historicism but also distinguishes itself both from hard and narrow and from airy and expansive cultural criticisms of our time. Such historicism would also resist the philosophical preciousness of those who are imprisoned by Nietzsche in ways that Nietzsche decried and the fantastic congeries and self-indulgent imagistic associationism practiced by scholars for whom the new historicism is little more than a refuge from historiography of any kind.

Walden: Text, Context, Pretext

Henry Golemba

Whether or not deconstruction began in America in 1971 with the appearance of Paul de Man's *Blindness and Insight*, it has expanded hugely since the early 1980s, when introductions to the subject like Jonathan Culler's *On Deconstruction* and Vincent Leitch's *Deconstructive Criticism* were published. Although people continue to call it "the most complex and forbidding of contemporary critical approaches to literature" (Murfin 304), modern scholars turn comfortably to the most sophisticated of deconstructionist ideas, and the theory's fundamental points have become so rooted in contemporary criticism that they sprout up casually in studies that do not mean to be deconstructive. Deconstructionists themselves are revealing the limits of their methodology or merging deconstruction with approaches that seemed irreconcilable with it a short time ago.

A text like *Walden* invites deconstructive reading. Its love of dismantling language and of reducing life to its lowest terms (91); its playfulness, or *jouissance*, as Jacques Derrida would say; its philosophical anarchy, as Walter Harding called it (*Thoreau Handbook* 132); its love of experimentation are all congenial with deconstructive moods. *Walden*'s cocky attitude, playing the "poor student" (*Walden* 4) who challenges everything others assert, accuses elders of offering not "the first syllable" (9) of valuable advice, and tells readers to pursue their own way just when they are becoming converted to Thoreau's way of thought (71), is an attitude consonant with deconstructive modes. Thoreau's rhetorical habit of giving with one hand while taking with the other and of unbuilding as he builds suits deconstruction perfectly.

Living in an Indian tepee has admirable advantage over owning (or being owned by) a house, *Walden* argues, and then the text has to do some mighty fancy footwork to explain why its hero is living in a cabin or small house. If we would just overcome materialism, we would not have to lock our doors or fear burglars, the narrator claims, yet someone walks off with his favorite book and he locks his manuscript securely in the drawer of his writing table. When we are told to take an abandoned toolbox whose dimensions are suspiciously like a coffin, drill a few holes in it, and convert it into an apartment, we feel that Thoreau is joking or at least exaggerating. Precisely when we feel confident about that interpretation, the narrator insists, "I am far from jesting" (29). "There is a solid bottom every where," the book concludes (330), yet the previous chapter has warned that we shall stagnate unless "all things be mysterious and unexplorable, that land and sea be infinitely wild, unsurveyed and unfathomed by us because unfathomable" (317–18). The contradiction between the solid and the unfathomable is essential to deconstructive practice and is the focus of this essay as it samples three broad deconstructive readings in terms of text, context, and pretext.

Where there are as many ways to begin as there are radii from a center, that is, infinite ways, one approach my classes have enjoyed is for small groups to read different parts of *Walden* with the understanding that each group will describe the voice it hears in the text as distinctly as possible. On the first discussion day, some students articulate a tender, gentle voice, while others—having read other selections—describe an aloof, almost smug, character. Some, having read parts of "Economy," hear an independent, severe critic, while others, having read "Former Inhabitants," discover a companionable man willing to listen sympathetically to another's story about how a fire destroyed his family history. Those who read this chapter are impressed by how desirous Thoreau is to hear all the stories the town's outcasts never had voice to tell, while others are bothered by his anti-Irish prejudice or his sexism in "Where I Lived." Some want the ground rules clarified; intrigued by the import of doubleness in "Solitude," they want to know if the adjective *poor* in "This doubleness may easily make us poor neighbors and friends sometimes" (135) applies to friends as well as neighbors. Those who choose "Higher Laws" describe how the writer as Chanticleer has become harsh and preacherly, while other students ask if we are supposed to take this man seriously, to believe that he is really as naive as he seems to be when, surprised to meet a man carrying a load of pottery to market, he says:

> I had read of the potter's clay and wheel in Scripture, but it had never occurred to me that the pots we use were not such as had come down unbroken from those days, or grown on trees like gourds somewhere, and I was pleased to hear that so fictile an art was ever practised in my neighborhood.   (261)

Why does this narrator sound like a noble leader at one point and the village fool at another, and why should the author choose to allow his narrator to appear that way? Since Thoreau spent ten years working through eight drafts of the manuscript, one would think such paradoxes represent more than a slip or a rhetorical typo.

Two main points always emerge from the first day of discussion. One is how diverse are the multiple voices that speak to us from the text, so many and so contradictory. To some students the "I" of this text's narrator is as varied as the characters in a novel. Of course, unifying threads run through the diversity—obviously the "I" or "Thoreau" believes in independence, loves nature, and laments materialism and conformity—yet much of the text seems concerned with variations on these central themes. Thoreau writes, "This is the only way, we say; but there are as many ways as there can be drawn radii from one centre" (11), and his book focuses as often on the infinite irradiations of radii as on the center.

The second point is how "fictile an art" Thoreau practices. Only naive readers can believe that *Walden* was written spontaneously or that its chapters fell like gourds from trees (gourds growing on trees?). Clearly this text is shaped, molded, and manipulated. The book's very first paragraph now shows to the class more fictile art than it did at the outset. Powerful shaping forces are at work, loosed by this man who instructs us to think of him as having "earned [his] living by the labor of [his] hands only" but who wants to be recognized for the labor of his mind and pen. This man "lived alone, in the woods," yet he loves "society as much as most" and was sometimes visited by twenty-five or thirty people at a crack (140). When we hear that he lived "a mile from my neighbor," we are now more attuned to how our hearing is being manipulated. In "A Yankee in Canada," Thoreau says that farms about a mile apart on the St. Lawrence River made for a crowded shore (21), but in *Walden*'s opening paragraph the same distance conjures a picture of solitude so complete that it borders on isolation. The suggestion is so strong that some readers will continue to picture Thoreau living like a hermit no matter what else the book portrays. The physical facts and geographical spacing are identical, yet the rhetorical format creates contrasting visions to suit two different books.

Some deconstructionists emphasize the play of point and counterpoint highlighted in the above discussion. Every significant part of the text has its antitext or con-text or countertext. To stress one idea is to invoke its opposite. To promote individualism is to admit the inevitability of conformity. To advocate self-reliance is to admit the necessity of community. To insist on independence is to echo America's greatest fear, that its union is about to disintegrate. Being rebellious is popularly accepted, and exaggeration is truth-telling. In his Journal, Thoreau expresses his pleasure in learning that the seeming opposites of *willed* and *wild* share an etymological root. In *Walden*, puns abound, including puns on *bound* as meaning a leap or limit, being tied up or destined. In the text at large, it is difficult to find a significant sentence that does not also have its antithesis or whose meaning does not evaporate when studied intensely. H. Daniel Peck eloquently says in this volume that "systematic study of [Thoreau's] Journal . . . will readily acknowledge its tendency to overwhelm comprehensive attempts at interpretation—to swallow up the very act of interpretation in its vast discursiveness." As with the Journal, the more one studies *Walden*, the more overwhelming it becomes.

Other deconstructionists are concerned more with placing an author's language play in its cultural context. In this volume, Michael West explains how Thoreau's wordplay mirrors Friedrich Schlegel's concept of the divine ironist. Others, like Richard Poirier, note Emerson's influence on Thoreau; for example, he cites Emerson's warning in "The Poet" that "every thought is a prison," including, presumably, this one (49, 82–83). Modern deconstructionists may sound like new historicists by demonstrating how *Walden*'s language of melting, thawing, fluctuating meanings—where every thought contradicts itself and important sentiments erase themselves as they are written—is also a language that is crucial to the Supreme Court's interpretations of the Constitution, to the teaching of the Bible in university courses, to politics, and to the other arts of

Thoreau's day. This last kind of deconstruction emphasizes the intertextuality of an era's discourse.

One need not confine oneself to the most illustrious and canonical authors and fields. A Thoreauvian language of self-erasure can be read also in the then nascent field of advertising, in the circus posters and museum displays of the day, and in P. T. Barnum's autobiography, which was published the same year as *Walden*. Or one can look to popular literature and find that Fanny Fern, one of the most widely read of all American authors, based her career on first citing and then contradicting an authority on etiquette. In other words: text and countertext. The basic theme of Martin Delany's *Blake; or, The Huts of America* (1859) is that no one can live without freedom, and yet freedom is impossible, especially for people of color. Living in an era marked by spectacular change on every front, Thoreau assures us that earth abides, that nature remains the same and follows its yearly cycles. Nevertheless, he could hear the sound of axes chopping down Walden Woods while he wrote these affirmations, and before he died, he advocated that Concord adopt the woods as a city park to preserve at least the semblance of its wildness.

Whether concentrating on the interplay of point and counterpoint within a specific text or preferring instead to locate the text in its cultural context, all deconstructors focus on deconstructing language to ground zero. It would make no sense to have a term like *deconstruction* if it ended up *re*constructing a resolution of the contradictions it had laid bare. Therefore, the perpetual process of unbuilding while building meaning must be respected. This essay began by referring to the solid and the unfathomable. Deconstructors champion neither. They do not pretend, as Hegel did in Thoreau's Romantic era, that antithesis will bring forth synthesis. Nor do they attempt to wrap all this confusion and contradiction in a humanistic package. They do not claim that literature is somehow good for us because it stretches the imagination or makes us better people or places the universe in cosmic harmony or what have you. Deconstructors operate more like biologists trying to describe dispassionately and apolitically what they see before them. They describe the counterbalancing centripetal and centrifugal forces from which a pot or a poem is shaped, but they do not take sides, claiming that centripetal is somehow superior to centrifugal force.

In fact, some critics go further and say that if deconstruction does indeed concentrate on the play of language, then it is a painful game. What does all this text and countertext business and their cultural context benefit? No resolution is offered. No rousing affirmation is sounded. No fruitful produce grows from this constant plowing over the fields of words. Deconstruction closely resembles the admissions in *Walden*'s "The Bean-Field," where Thoreau seems to step forth without the various poses of the "I" in order to make a series of confessions to "you, Reader" (164). He is not sure why he should make the earth (or this page) say beans (or one thing) instead of grass (or another). He certainly is not going to eat them (because they'll cause flatulence instead of inspiring the divine afflatus) but will trade them for rice (thus entangling the self-reliant, independent "I" with society and its market economy). The choice to cultivate the earth is not "natural" but the start of "a long war" (155); preferment is certainly less magnanimous than the sun, which takes no side but shines on crops and grass alike. Moreover, choosing to hoe beans will make Thoreau sweat, blister his feet, keep him from chasing loons and walking the woods, and generally make him the butt of ridicule from all passersby (fellow farmers whose criticism that he plants too late turns out to be right).

At any rate, he has made the earth say beans, for whatever reason, and that simple choice creates a host of problems. His thesis "I prefer beans" creates myriad antitheses. A simple act of love has created a universe of hate. Among his enemies he now numbers crows, frosts, skunks, woodchucks, brown thrashers, red mavis, worms, cool days, blackberries, salamanders, grass, "sweet wild fruits and pleasant flowers," "the ashes of unchronicled nations," and on and on. Worst of all, one day when the militia is practicing for war, Thoreau is slaying weeds and is so caught up by "a really noble and inspiring strain" of military music that he wishes for mightier foes than weeds. For a moment he feels he "could spit a Mexican with a good relish." Petty distinctions have led to mortal hatred and cannibalistic impulses, even to roasting another man on a spit and devouring him with a bit of relish (155–59, 161).

A deconstructor is attracted to chapters like "The Bean-Field" because they appear to go beyond simple proverbs or sentiments that, however inspiring, are obvious. Instead, a deconstructor likes to see writing where language is pushed to its limits, beyond any clear-cut resolution. Another reader might prefer to focus on noble thoughts like "[S]tep to the music which [you hear], however measured or far away" (326), but a deconstructor wonders whether that martial music may not emanate from a military band and as easily call us to murder our fellows as to explore ourselves. In short, a deconstructor prefers passages that expose an author's anxieties, passages that are truly rites of passage in that they mark the irreconcilable problems and impenetrable mysteries of life and of language.

Therefore deconstructors, whether they emphasize a close reading of text or its cultural context, are interested most of all in pretext: the conventions, expectations, demands, and rationalizations that are brought to bear on a text as readers engage in the act of reading. The deconstructive approach accentuates a persistent forming and reforming of meaning, a perpetual reshaping. It seeks to achieve a constant destabilizing of perspective and prejudice, a relentless exposure of ideology, of political and conventional prejudice. It means to set all things afloat, to keep language and our perceptions of language in an eternal state of flux. *Pretext*, after all, is derived from *praetexere*, Latin for "to weave in front." Deconstruction insistently reveals the weavings and unweavings readers create in the space between them and the words they are translating. In *Walden*, Thoreau produced a text wherein "[t]he volatile truth of our words should continually betray the inadequacy of the residual statement" (325).

The Genres of *A Week on the Concord and Merrimack Rivers*

Stephen Adams

The "drama" of Sunday in Thoreau's *A Week on the Concord and Merrimack Rivers* concludes "without regard to any unities which we mortals prize. Whether it might have proved tragedy, or comedy, or tragi-comedy, or pastoral, we cannot tell" (114). Many readers have shared a like uncertainty about *A Week* as a whole and have based criticisms of it on dubious assumptions about its genre. For example, James Russell Lowell was the first to berate what he called the work's digressions: "[T]hey are out of proportion and out of place, and mar our Merrimacking dreadfully. We were bid to a river-party, not to be preached at . . ." (Rev. 47). Because he assumes that *A Week* is essentially a book of travel and natural history, Lowell condemns as distractions the discursive essays that most modern critics consider essential to it. Students also find *A Week* troublesome, partly because they cannot fit it neatly into a familiar category or identify the conventions with which Thoreau is playing. Adding to their confusion is the lack of consensus among critics from Lowell on—even the experts cannot agree about how to classify this strange text.

The very confusion over the form or type of *A Week* makes a generic approach to teaching it rewarding. An exploration of the book's genres prompts students to generate insights into it and gain a better understanding of Thoreau and his period. Students develop a strong sense of intertextuality as they research Thoreau's models and his experiments with the conventions of literature that influenced his writings. The goal of this approach is not to classify for classification's sake, pinning the work neatly in a specimen case under a certain label, but to deepen and enrich the experience of reading the work. As Alastair

Fowler points out, "The processes of generic recognition are in fact fundamental to the reading process" (259). And according to Northrop Frye, "The purpose of criticism by genres is not so much to classify as to clarify traditions and affinities, thereby bringing out a large number of literary relationships that would not be noticed as long as there were no context established for them" (247–48). Most recently, Adena Rosmarin argues the case for generic criticism as pragmatic and exploratory, a way of identifying textual features we may not otherwise perceive. The genre approach offers various lenses or perspectives on *A Week*; each perspective emphasizes or highlights some aspects of the work that the others overlook.

A generic approach to *A Week* presupposes a certain sophistication and breadth of reading on the part of students—at the minimum, an introduction to literature course and some historical surveys. Most of us probably teach *A Week* in more advanced courses anyway, to students who have already read *Walden* and Thoreau's best essays. I assign *A Week* in courses for sophomores, juniors, and seniors who are predominantly humanities majors and familiar with the main forms and periods of literature.

The most effective way to examine the genres of *A Week* is to make the students active participants in the process. After an initial discussion or two about the concept of genre, neoclassical theories of types, and Romantic experimentation with mixing and modifying literary forms, I turn *A Week* over to class members. Students work in small groups, selecting one genre important to *A Week* and building a case for it, which they will present to their classmates. According to their level of sophistication, they use library resources ranging from basic discussions of genre (in handbooks such as those by Abrams; Holman and Harmon) to specialized texts on particular forms (Bakhtin and Payne on Menippean satire; Vinaver on romance), theoretical discussions of genre as a critical concept (Frye; Hernadi; Rosmarin; Todorov; Fishelov), and examples of generic criticism applied to *A Week*. I also encourage students to explore the texts that Thoreau mentions in *A Week* and uses as sources or models for his work. Students try to answer questions about the genre that their group has selected. For example, What are the characteristics and conventions of the genre? To what extent does *A Week* follow those conventions? How does Thoreau violate or bend them? To what effect and for what purpose? What expectations does he instill in readers by using elements of the genre, and to what extent does he fulfill those expectations? How does he combine the genre with others to expand, complicate, and enrich it? What elements of *A Week* are highlighted when it is read as an example of the genre? What insights into the book did the reader gain by exploring it in the light of the genre?

Below are some specific genres critics have identified as important in *A Week*.

Travel book   As Lowell suggests, *A Week* is most obviously an account of travel—of people, places, and things observed on a journey along the rivers named in the title. In the course of his excursion, Thoreau mentions many other travel works that influenced him—most notably Alexander Henry's *Adventures* ("a sort of classic among books of American travel" [218]) and Goethe's *Italian Travels*. He also discusses the art of "true and sincere travelling" and gives practical advice about what to take on a journey (304–06). As John Aldrich Christie documents, travel writing was the most popular genre of Thoreau's day; it provided a basic form for most of his other works too (*Thoreau*). (Even *Walden* can profitably be read as an account of a journey; after traveling a good deal in Concord, Thoreau sojourns in a place "as far off as many a region viewed nightly by astronomers . . . a withdrawn, but forever new and unprofaned, part of the universe" [*Walden* 88]). According to Sherman Paul, "the *Week* is a seventeenth-century book" like the works of Richard Hakluyt and Samuel Purchas, which are compilations of reports from various travelers during the age of exploration (*Shores* 204). Thoreau also incorporates Romantic innovations in travel writing—in his focus on the introspective traveler as much as on the travels, his poetic and expressive heightening of the narrative, and his melding of physical and mental travel. Thoreau's journey takes on spiritual-mythic-symbolic overtones; it is a voyage of inner as well as outer exploration. He not only records facts about the New England countryside that he visited but also attempts "some accurate information concerning that OTHER WORLD which the instinct of mankind has so long predicted" (*Week* 385). Robert Sattelmeyer ("Away from Concord") and Lawrence Buell (*Literary Transcendentalism*) explore *A Week* as a Romantic travel book that expands beyond the physical journey to become a transcendental excursion.

History The seventeenth-century books that Paul cites as models for *A Week* are essentially chronicles or histories of the New World. As Thoreau travels the two rivers, he gives much historical data about the localities he visits, re-creating the period when America was still new to the Europeans who claimed it. He quotes frequently from various historians, for their own sake and as a way of introducing topics that interest him. He includes many incidental observations on the concept of history and devotes an important internal essay in "Monday" to the subject (154–58). David Hoch explores *A Week's* exposition of history as a circle, and Joan Burbick traces Thoreau's abandonment of standard Romantic history to write a more accurate new "uncivil" history. Jamie Hutchinson, Linck Johnson (*Complex Weave*), and John Hildebidle also treat *A Week* as history writing.

Frontier narrative The history that matters most to Thoreau is colonial, the period when the territory that he visits constituted the American frontier. He keeps taking us back to that period by linking places to the Indians who originally inhabited them and to the whites who first explored and then expropriated them. He also plays the frontier hero himself, journeying into the wild beyond the boundaries of civilization, confronting "fresh and primitive and savage nature" (315). John and Henry Thoreau are "voyageurs" (22, 172) and heirs to the frontier heroes Henry celebrates (and questions) in *A Week*. Richard Slotkin and Leslie Fiedler treat the book as a western, tracing frontier narrative conventions in the many sections devoted to clashes between white settlers and Native Americans. They focus especially on the Hannah Dustan episode (320–24), an interesting example of the captivity narrative subgenre. As usual, Thoreau does not follow the conventions of a literary type straightforwardly; he plays with and modifies them, making something new of the old. He stretches the definition of frontier, exploring metaphorical "frontier territories of truth and justice" (112). He treats the frontier expansively as "wherever a man *fronts* a fact," and he challenges the reader to "build himself a log-house with the bark on where he is, *fronting* IT" (304).

Epic   Thoreau attributes to his frontier heroes (sometimes ironically) epic qualities. He often refers to and quotes from Homer, Vergil, Ossian, and Milton, inviting readers to place his book within the epic tradition. Brian Bond most fully explores the epic features of *A Week*: its invocation of the Muse, announcement of theme, catalog of heroes, epic similes, motif of heroic friendship, and so on. Thoreau's work incorporates both kinds of Homeric narrative, the account of a journey (*Odyssey*) and of warfare (*Iliad*). In common with epic writers, Thoreau attempts to define a people—to articulate its ideals, values, identity, hopes, and fears—through accounts of its heroes and the important events in its history. As in other Romantic adaptations of the epic (such as those by Wordsworth and Whitman), the hero becomes identified with the poet-narrator. The Romantic epic chronicles the growth of the poet's mind; wanderings and battles become symbolic, internal. But, as Raymond Adams insists, Thoreau does not take his own epic that seriously: "*A Week* is itself a mock-epic, mild and fluvial" (92). Thoreau uses epic conventions for commonplace subject matter. He regularly reminds us that his noble, heroic voyage is still also a summer vacation.

Myth   Just as the epic formulates a nation's myths, *A Week* can be analyzed as what Fiedler calls "a handbook of American mythology." Fiedler takes the subject of Thoreau's "new American mythology" to be "the Indian at the moment of first contact with the White invader" (104–05). But Thoreau also celebrates contemporary mythic figures, such as the old brown-coated fisherman (*Week* 24) and the "fabulous rivermen" who operate canal boats on the rivers (211). He devotes an important internal essay to myth or fable in "Sunday" (58–61) and refers to myth throughout the book, often in relation to genius and poetry. He defines the poet (perhaps self-reflexively) as "he who can write some pure mythology today without the aid of posterity" (60).

Romance   The many references to knights, adventures, castles, chivalry, treasure, and exotic places suggest another genre important for the content and structure of *A Week*: romance. Eric Sundquist treats the book as Thoreau's romance quest for "unravished and 'original' American frontiers . . . the lost state of Nature, the simple life of the Indian" (42, 45). Stephen Adams and Donald Ross explore the book as the kind of archetypal romance mythos central to Romanticism: a narrative with the poet for hero and with the theme of attaining an expanded consciousness. The Saddleback episode (180–90) is most clearly and explicitly couched in terms of romance, but Thoreau uses conventions of the genre and alludes to romance literature throughout *A Week*. His own quest for God and heaven provides the book's narrative spine, leading to the climactic ascent of Agiocochook and essay on natural life (378–88).

Pastoral   *A Week* is set in a romance landscape of castles and scaly monsters (8, 130, 195, 274), but it also explores "a leafy wilderness, a place for fauns and satyrs" (40) where New Englanders lead "poetic and Arcadian lives" (243). In *A Week*, as pastoral, a poet from the town celebrates the countryside and the virtues of a simple, rural life. The Thoreau brothers' vacation is a retreat from mainstream America, allowing them to criticize modern urban-industrial society from alternative perspectives. Bond lists the many pastoral conventions that Thoreau uses, including calendar structure (days of the week and change of seasons), catalog of flowers, encounters with rustic figures, and nostalgia for a rural golden age.

Elegy   Even more particularly, *A Week* can be viewed as a pastoral elegy. Thoreau conceived the work as a memorial tribute to his companion on the trip, his brother John, who died of tetanus in January 1842. (See Linck Johnson's *Complex Weave* for a detailed study of the book's evolution.) J. J. Boies calls it "a prose elegy analogous to Shelley's 'Adonais'" (355). Sundquist sees a more extensive scope to the work, calling it "a haunting elegy for the passing of the American Indian and an unspoiled state of Nature" (45). Daniel Peck too interprets the book as "essentially an elegiac and retrospective response to experience" (*Morning Work* 36): an elegy for John, certainly, but also an attempt to recover the lost realm of Indians and fishermen and to enter the timeless world of myth.

Autobiography   *A Week*'s roots in the historical fact of John Thoreau's death, its first-person narration, and its account of Thoreau's actual experience suggest that it might also be studied as autobiography for the light it sheds on Thoreau's life and character. Paul traces in the book Thoreau's "spiritual course from youth to maturity" (*Shores* 218). Richard Lebeaux uses the work as evidence for his Eriksonian psychobiography of Thoreau. He sees *A Week* as "an attempt to both expiate and deny guilt" over the death of his brother (*Young Man* 198) and finds indications in it of Henry's unresolved oedipal feelings and his deeply ambivalent relationship with John and with nature (*Seasons*, ch. 1). Yet there is little conventional biographical detail in the book. Frederick Garber sees *A Week* as a more subtle, experimental revelation of self: "It is not only, [Thoreau] argues, that we write *about* ourselves—most often we do not do so directly—but that we write ourselves *into* the text. In and through the act of writing, we seek to establish ourselves within the text, seeking, finally, to inhabit the text, to find a home place within it" (*Fable* 90).

Menippean Satire   If there is any one genre that provides an umbrella that encompasses the others featured in *A Week*, it might be satire. Adams and Ross consider the book a Menippean satire, which Frye defines as "a loose-jointed narrative form" that "relies on the free play of intellectual fancy" and tends to "expand into an encyclopedic farrago." Like other Menippean satirists, Thoreau covers a wide variety of topics, delights in "piling up an enormous mass of erudition about his theme," quotes frequently from various authorities, employs incidental verses (or what Lowell disparaged as his "worsification" [Lowell 51]), and features characters who are "stylized rather than naturalistic." The work "deals less with people as such than with mental attitudes" (Frye 309–11). *A Week* thus resembles other Romantic texts that combine the discursive and narrative in ways that make them difficult to classify. *Moby-Dick* is another American Menippean satire that tends to bewilder undergraduates.

In addition to the genres listed above, *A Week* contains examples of other literary types that students might explore: formal and informal essays on various topics, natural history writing (poetic, meditative science in the vein later tapped by Lewis Thomas), ecological theory, satire, reform propaganda, transcendental scripture writing, proverbs, self-improvement advice, prose poetry, and others.

Students might turn to nonliterary genres for additional insights into *A Week*. For example, several critics have compared the book to various kinds of contemporary painting, especially landscape painting (Thoreau's third epigraph promises "fair landscapes" [3]). John Conron and Kevin Radaker catalog similarities in theme and technique between luminist paintings and Thoreau's text: an emphasis on perception and contemplation; pervasive stillness, clarity, and light leading to epiphanies; a suggestion of infinite space and the sublimity of the quotidian; anonymity of the artist (an absence of brushstrokes in the paintings and the absence of specific biographical detail in Thoreau's book); and so on. Richard Schneider ("Landscape") extends the discussion of luminism and also examines important similarities between Thoreau and other nineteenth-century painters, including the Hudson River school, George Inness, and Winslow Homer.

The multiplicity of genres that students will discover in *A Week* should raise one persistent question that has bothered critics from Lowell on: the unity and coherence of the book as a work of art. Joseph Wood Krutch insists that "the whole is little more than a notebook" (96). Henry Canby is disturbed by "its digressiveness, its overstuffed quality as of a pudding into which the pantry has been dumped"; he calls it "an anthology carried upon a frame of a story . . . perilously like a library of the shorter works of Henry Thoreau" (272–73). Such statements invite students to debate the merits of the book and the grounds on which they make their own judgments.

Again, the goal of a generic approach is not to decide on one classification for the sake of tidy pigeonholing but to generate insights by viewing a work from various perspectives. Indeed, Thoreau seems to have designed his book to defy classification and to keep the reader actively involved in the process of interpreting it. According to Henry Golemba, "*A Week* seems attracted to but shies away from fulfilling a particular genre. . . . [Thoreau's] text would resist any efforts to find structural unities. Even a vague, oxymoronic category like 'tragi-comedy' is insufficiently loose to tether his text to a genre." The book exemplifies what Golemba calls Thoreau's "wild rhetoric," his attempt to avoid stagnation of meaning by writing texts that resist decoding (*Rhetoric* 153–54, 159). Thoreau formulated his rhetorical strategy in an early Journal entry: "Yes and No are lies—A true answer will not aim to establish anything, but rather to set all well afloat" (*Journal 1* 139).

By exploring the various genres of *A Week*, students set afloat possible readings that increase their appreciation of Thoreau's art and their knowledge of both literary history and the processes of interpretation. Students, I have found, often begin as committed partisans of the particular genre they have selected or been assigned. After all, they have invested considerable time and intellectual energy considering *A Week* under that rubric. In the debate that follows reports from the individual groups, however, most students indicate an increasing awareness of the complexities involved not only in interpreting Thoreau's first book but also in defining genres and approaching any significant text from various perspectives. As Thoreau suggests in *A Week* itself, the final destination is not as important as the continuing journey.

"Civil Disobedience" and the Problem of Thoreau's "Peaceable Revolution"

Michael Meyer

Many students who enroll in college-level American literature courses have at least heard of Henry David Thoreau, and very likely they have read an excerpt or two from the first two chapters of *Walden* and perhaps some or even all of "Civil Disobedience." If they recall their high school reading, what may have seemed to them a simple and sincere account of Thoreau is quickly rendered slippery, however, once they begin to learn, for example, that his given name was actually David Henry, that Thoreau is variously pronounced, and that "Civil Disobedience" appears—most probably—as "Resistance to Civil Government" in their textbooks. A little bit of learning can be disconcerting when even the name of a major author and a major work (perhaps the most widely read American essay ever written) are the source of confusion.

The order and pronunciation of Thoreau's names are easily explained by reference to his individualism and his French ancestry, but the question of the title "Civil Disobedience" is more complicated and is a sensible point at which to begin a serious consideration of the essay. If students read Thoreau in a recent standard anthology of American literature, they will find "Civil Disobedience" titled "Resistance to Civil Government" (see, e.g., Baym [Norton]; Elliott [Prentice Hall]; Lauter [Heath]; J. E. Miller [Harcourt]; and McQuade [Harper]). The essay was first printed in Elizabeth Peabody's 1849 periodical *Aesthetic Papers* under the title "Resistance to Civil Government," but four years after Thoreau's death, the essay appeared in *A Yankee in Canada, with Anti-slavery and Reform Papers* (1866) as "Civil Disobedience," the title by which it became world famous years later. In 1973, however, Wendell Glick argued, as editor of the new standard Princeton edition of *Reform Papers*, that the 1849 text and title were more accurate in reflecting Thoreau's intentions than the 1866 text and title (the only substantial differences between the versions are their titles, part of a sentence dropped from the 1866 text, and two brief passages added to the 1866 text). Opinion among Thoreau scholars is divided concerning which title the author intended, and though most American literature anthologies follow the Princeton edition's lead, ongoing research indicates that the more familiar title should be restored. Detailed discussions of this complex editorial matter can be found in Glick, Thomas Woodson, and Fritz Oehlschlaeger. I don't recommend spending a lot of time on such issues with undergraduates, but some familiarity with the arguments will go a long way toward explaining why the essay is known by two different titles.

The difference in tone between the two titles is significant and will prompt discussion. When asked to comment on the tone, students generally hear a more forceful kind of opposition in "Resistance to Civil Government" than they do in "Civil Disobedience." The *civil* in civil disobedience can be read two ways: Thoreau makes a case for disobeying unjust civil government and also for behaving civilly when engaged in disobedience against the state. The 1866 title indicates both who is to be disobeyed and the civility with which that disobedience is to be performed. *Resistance*, however, suggests a wider spectrum of protest, one not limited by any kind of decorum. If Thoreau was indeed revising "Civil Disobedience" just before his death in 1862, the beginning of the Civil War might well have influenced him to use *civil* disobedience, given the bloody *resistance* produced by the South's secession. Regardless of which title is chosen as authorial, the difference in tone raises an important question about the essay and Thoreau's political posture: Did Thoreau support passive resistance as the only means of ending slavery in America? With the raising of this question, the two titles can become an opportunity for students to explore Thoreau's attitudes toward reform in his later writings as well as in "Civil Disobedience."

Because "Civil Disobedience" has often been used as a showpiece of Thoreau's politics, reprinted more than "Slavery in Massachusetts" (1854) or "A Plea for Captain John Brown" (1859), Thoreau is commonly read as a committed pacifist and advocate of passive resistance to unjust laws.[1] Given the history and reputation of the essay, that reading is not surprising, because it is generally assumed that the essay is fully representative of Thoreau's attitudes toward reform and because the essay was invoked by Mohandas Gandhi to oppose British imperialism in India, by Martin Luther King, Jr., to oppose racial discrimination in the United States, and by antiwar activists to oppose the war in Vietnam. "Civil Disobedience" has come to be regarded as a quintessential embodiment of American individualism and is widely quoted by those who admire Thoreau's moral courage for claiming the law of conscience as a higher law than civil statutes. In addition, his determination not to cooperate with an unjust government—while accepting the full consequences of his disobedience as a means of calling attention to issues and effecting social change—has made him appear to be a social activist among contemporary reformers.

Though essentially an antiwar and antislavery piece, "Civil Disobedience" is also a withdrawal from what Thoreau regards as a corrupt government, in much the same way that *Walden* represents a withdrawal from the materialistic values of Concord. As strongly as he expresses contempt for the Mexican War and vents his hatred of slavery, he is also insistent on washing his hands of any complicity in these injustices: "The only obligation which I have a right to assume, is to do at any time what I think right" (65). It's worth reminding students that Thoreau's attitudes toward reform were informed by his transcendental efforts to live a spiritually meaningful life in nature rather than in society. Emerson's essay "The Transcendentalist" (as well as his essay "Politics") is invaluable for establishing a context in which to understand Thoreau's social thought. Emerson clearly has Thoreau in mind when he describes the transcendentalists' relation to society:

> [T]hey are not good citizens, not good members of society; unwillingly they bear their part of the public and private burdens; they do not willingly share in the public charities, in the public religious rites, in the enterprises of education, of missions foreign and domestic, in the abolition of the slave-trade, or in the temperance society. They do not even like to vote.   (1: 210–11)

Thoreau was deeply offended by injustice, but that did not mean he would abandon his real work of self-reform in favor of sustained social activism.

Gandhi, King, and many other political activists who have enlisted Thoreau in a particular cause would have found him an uneven and recalcitrant ally. Thoreau's Journal description of a reformer named Henry C. Wright visiting Thoreau's mother's house suggests just how much professional reformers offended him:

> I was awfully pestered with his benignity; feared I should get greased all over with it past restoration; tried to keep some starch in my clothes. . . . I wanted that he should straighten his back, smooth out those ogling wrinkles of benignity about his eyes, and, with a healthy reserve, pronounce something in a downright manner. It was difficult to keep clear of his slimy benignity, with which he sought to cover you before he swallowed you and took you fairly into his bowels.   (*Journal* 5 264)

Students familiar with his passage will understand that Thoreau found social reformers nearly as meddlesome as he did the government.

Thoreau's ambivalence about reformers was matched by his ambivalence about the means by which reform could be achieved. In "Civil Disobedience" he rejects voting and legislative actions as an adequate expression of moral conviction; for Thoreau voting "is a sort of gaming, like chequers or backgammon." He calls for deeper convictions: "A wise man will not leave the right to the mercy of chance, nor wish it to prevail through the power of the majority" (69–70). In the early 1840s Thoreau placed his faith entirely in the individual as the driving force of reform. In "Paradise (To Be) Regained" (1843), he calls for the "prevalence of *a* man" (emphasis added) who "must first succeed alone, that we may enjoy our success together" (42). For Thoreau, love could create the individual moral reform that would in turn transform the world. Like Emerson, who argued in "Politics" that "the power of love, as the basis of the State, has never been tried" (*Works* 3: 128), Thoreau, along with many of his contemporaries who believed in individualistic reform outside the usual political arenas of parties and organizations (as Nye has explained [32–70]), envisioned the possibility of a better world through a faith in self-reform rather than in social reform.

This faith is considerably tempered in "Civil Disobedience," because the author has to acknowledge that the machinery of the state is driven by forces love is inadequate to match. He argues that tax resistance can clog the government's capacity "to commit violence and shed innocent blood." What is interesting about this position is not that it determines whether tax resistance is an effective strategy (it had utterly no influence in Thoreau's time) but that it reveals Thoreau's having to shift his ground to sustain his faith in moral law. Even more important is the sentence that follows his proposal for tax resistance: "This is, in fact, the definition of a peaceable revolution, if any such is possible" (76). The final phrase takes on a powerful significance in the light of the country's inability to resolve the slavery issue during the 1850s, when nonviolent resistance—whether practiced individually or collectively—could not effectively further the cause of abolitionism.

By 1854, Thoreau's disgust concerning the cowardliness represented by the Fugitive Slave Law and subsequent court decisions turns vituperative in "Slavery in Massachusetts," where he attacks the press and the church as well as the government in a speech delivered to the Massachusetts Anti-slavery Society on 4 July. His frustration and impatience with the ineffectiveness of any proposed "peaceable revolution" is powerfully presented in his parody of those who would be content to wait for the government to reform itself:

> Do what you will, O Government! with my wife and children, my mother and brother, my father and sister, I will obey your commands to the letter. It will indeed grieve me if you hurt them, if you deliver them to overseers to be hunted by hounds or to be whipped to death; but nevertheless, I will peaceably pursue my chosen calling on this fair earth, until perchance, one day, when I have put on mourning for them dead, I shall have persuaded you to relent. Such is the attitude, such are the words of Massachusetts.
>
> Rather than do thus, I need not say what match I would touch, what system endeavor to blow up. . . .   (102)

Though his "thoughts are murder to the State, and involuntarily go plotting against her" (108), Thoreau did not discover the embodiment of those thoughts until John Brown attacked Harpers Ferry in 1859 in what would be a futile effort to create insurrections among slaves in the South. That Brown failed and that nearly everyone, including abolitionists, initially repudiated him as a fanatical madman did not matter to Thoreau. For in Brown he found a "transcendentalist above all" (115) who offered more than passive resistance to the violent oppression of slavery: "I think that for once the Sharps' rifles and the revolvers were employed in a righteous cause. The tools were in the hands of one who could use them." Thoreau did not take issue with Brown's use of violence; instead he endorsed it and refused to worry about reconciling his earlier faith in individual passive nonviolence and his present unqualified support of Brown: "The question is not about the weapon, but the spirit in which you use it" (133).

Students who read "A Plea for Captain John Brown" alongside "Civil Disobedience" are often surprised to see how violently the idea of a peaceable revolution competed with other means of reform. Thoreau, however, ultimately retreated from this issue because he was, as a transcendentalist, essentially apolitical. His skirmishes with slavery would not deter him from his primary concern with self-reform and idealistic principles; he always chose eternity over the times. The real issue, finally, was his own freedom. Though he could not put slavery or the Civil War out of his mind, he wished that he could. A letter to an abolitionist friend just before the Civil War expresses his apolitical temperament: "I do not so much regret the present condition of things in this country . . . as I do that I ever heard it." The advocate of peaceable revolution in "Civil Disobedience" and the staunch supporter of Brown's violent means in "A Plea" hopes that his reader "ignores Fort Sumpter [sic], and Old Abe, and all that, for that is just the most fatal, and indeed the only fatal weapon you can direct against evil ever; for as long as you know it you are a *particeps criminis*" (*Correspondence* 611).

To his credit, Thoreau could not ignore the most important political issues of his time, and his inconsistencies about the means by which reform should be effected reflect a complex competing set of values that students can examine in their latency in "Civil Disobedience" and in their intense expression in "Slavery in Massachusetts" and "A Plea." A familiarity with the range of Thoreau's attitudes toward reform encourages students to go beyond reductively labeling him a pacifist, a revolutionary, or an apolitical individualist and allows them to begin the serious business of understanding his struggles to be, as he puts it on the first page of *Walden*, "a sojourner in civilized life."

NOTE

[1]All page references to these three essays are from Thoreau, *Reform Papers*.

"Civil Disobedience"
(or Is It "Resistance to Civil Government"?)
in a Composition Course

Laraine Fergenson

When one considers teaching "Civil Disobedience" to a composition class, one confronts at once two difficult and important subjects: Thoreau as a writer and the general goals of college writing courses. Journals that emphasize the teaching of writing are filled with articles that analyze the conflicting expectations of the composition course. According to David Chapman, some instructors see it as a service course offered by an English department to teach students the standard academic prose that will be their means of demonstrating in future courses what they have learned and the "serviceable" prose they will use in their careers (40). Others see the composition course as a means of introducing students to great literature, thus promoting cultural literacy. Still others see it as inculcating humanistic values along with a spirit of critical inquiry and independent thought (Brown; Comley) and thus helping to fulfill a larger function served by the university—that of "teaching for democracy" ("Education for Democracy"). Radical pedagogy goes further and sees the role of the composition course as encouraging students to question—in the hope of altering—the status quo (Berlin; Paine; Freedman; Shor; and Sporn). The composition course is also seen as having an epistemological function, using writing to explore a subject and systematize one's understanding of it. Proponents of this view see writing not merely as a way of demonstrating what one has learned but also as a method of learning (Berlin 484; Chapman 44). Obviously these different goals must sometimes jostle one another, but a composition course can and often does combine them. One reason for the popularity of Thoreau's "Civil Disobedience" despite its difficulties as a prose model is that it helps the class meet these varied expectations.

Studying Thoreau's exquisitely crafted sentences and learning about his painstaking methods of composition can help students develop a love of good prose style and the motivation to improve their own writing. Exposure to a classic writer like Thoreau certainly promotes cultural literacy. In fact, one reason that I teach Thoreau even to my basic writing classes is to acquaint the students with a major figure in American literature and with some major ideas in American cultural history. Obviously "Civil Disobedience" teaches democratic and humanistic values, and its comments on government earn it a place in the syllabus of many radical teachers. And yet, admirably suited as "Civil Disobedience" is to fulfill all these expectations, it presents certain difficulties in the writing class.

First, the essay appears to violate a cherished precept of composition textbooks by not having a single, clear thesis, one statement on which the entire piece is focused. Furthermore, "Civil Disobedience" cannot be characterized under the rubric of any single basic mode of writing such as description, narration, argumentation, or analysis. When it *is* classified under one of them, the classi-fication is often argumentation (Brent and Lutz xiv). In a rhetorical index Charles Muscatine and Marlene Griffith place the essay in the categories "The Personal Note" and "Contesting Argument," with a further reference to it in the section "Exposition of Ideas" (v–vii). Of course, many essays combine modes and have an implied thesis rather than a simple thesis statement, but students may be confused by Thoreau's essay because it attempts so much. It is helpful, therefore, to explain in a lecture or to elicit through class discussion the different threads Thoreau weaves together and the different rhetorical modes he employs.

The essay discusses the relation between the individual and society, and it explores the nature of government (abstract mode). It makes both a reasoned and an impassioned plea for individuals to follow conscience when the civil law conflicts with the "higher law" and to resist the state in protest against the par-ticular evils of slavery and the Mexican War (argumentative and persuasive modes). It relates Thoreau's arrest, his impressions during his night in jail, and his release the next day (narrative and descriptive modes).

Students may note that "Civil Disobedience" seems to contain paradoxical or self-contradictory statements, especially in the discussion of the relation between the individual and society. Jacques Barzun finds in the essay "a series of strong im-pressions, lucidly expressed but uncoordinated—indeed totally inconsistent" (250). Although Barzun seriously overstates the case, asserting that the essay's "meanderings are enough to disqualify it as political thought" (253), there is an undeniable tension in "Civil Disobedience" between Thoreau's conceptions of in-dividual action and mass action (Fergenson 115). His famous "definition of a peaceable revolution" is prefaced with the sentence "If the alternative is to keep all just men in prison, or give up war and slavery, the State will not hesitate which to choose" (*Reform Papers* 76). But Thoreau states earlier that "[t]here is but lit-tle virtue in the action of masses of men" (70)—and he places this remark in a con-text that strikes at the basis of American democracy, for it occurs in the paragraph that starts, "All voting is a sort of gaming, like chequers or backgammon, with a slight moral tinge to it . . ." (69). Thoreau does not really explain how, if the de-mocratic process is such a chancy means of bringing about the right, humanity can ultimately reach the ideal that concludes the essay: the "really free and enlight-ened State" that "comes to recognize the individual as a higher and independent power, from which all its own power and authority are derived . . ." (89).

There are several ways to deal with the conflict between the straightforward prose model that is likely to be described in the composition textbook and this wonderful but problematic essay with its "looseness of structure" (Schneider, *Thoreau* 150) or what Barzun calls "meanderings." The approach one takes will be determined by the level of the class.

For advanced classes in rhetoric and for some fairly sophisticated freshman composition classes, a thorough discussion of the contradictions in "Civil Disobedience" is instructive. The undeniable position of "Civil Disobedience" as a masterpiece of American literature and one of the most influential essays in world literature makes us reconsider the prose-model approach and reevaluate accepted advice on writing. For example, a class might contrast Thoreau's method in "Civil Disobedience" with the discussion of an essay's thesis in leading books on rhetoric, the following description being representative: "A thesis is a sentence that establishes your writing commitment by stating the main idea you are going to develop. The thesis sentence usually appears in the first paragraph of your essay" (McCrimmon, Trimmer, and Sommers 27). The class might discuss the dominant impression as a refinement of the concept of thesis. For despite the diversity of Thoreau's goals in the essay, the reader does come away with a clear dominant impression: that Thoreau is asserting the moral ascendancy of the individual conscience over laws that violate human rights. Further, an instructor might ask a class to discuss the contradictions in "Civil Disobedience" in the light of the frequently proffered advice that a good essay consistently supports the writer's point of view. Students may decide that while a *good* essay hews to the rule of consistency, a *great* one may violate it. But students should be reminded that so does many a bad essay.

An instructor may avoid the problems mentioned above by assigning only a portion of the essay. Some object to this practice, and I do not advocate it for most freshman composition classes—and certainly not for advanced writing classes. For developmental students, however, who are seriously pressed for time in which to master the material they will need before they can pass the university-mandated writing test and who might have great difficulty in reading all of "Civil Disobedience," presenting an excerpt is practical and justifiable. It is better to expose students to a portion of Thoreau's great essay than to make them wait for another opportunity—which may never materialize. In my experience, basic writing students enjoy and benefit from reading an excerpt of "Civil Disobedience." In fact, what Barzun calls Thoreau's impressionistic method actually favors such an approach. The two paragraphs that contain the famous definition of "peaceable revolution" (74–77) are the structural and moral center of the work. They set forth the specific issues on which Thoreau disagreed with the government and the specific form that his protest took. They contain enough information to stand alone, but of course the instructor can provide some background. Moreover, these two paragraphs are short enough for an instructor to review thoroughly in class, giving, if need be, a line-by-line explication de texte. After their initial encounter with Thoreau, some students will be motivated to read the rest of "Civil Disobedience," and they should certainly be encouraged to do so, with the offer of extra discussion time during office hours.

Two problems that a writing instructor may encounter in teaching "Civil Disobedience" appear at first to be totally different, but they are really opposite sides of the same coin. Some students uncritically accept Thoreau's ideas without reflecting on any of their inherent difficulties, while others just as uncritically reject the ideas as leading to anarchy—without considering their tremendous importance.

More critical students rightly ask the question "*Whose* conscience should be above the law?" They also question Thoreau's ultralibertarian view of government as an obstacle to free trade (64), pointing out that some of his statements could come straight out of the mouths of conservative politicians who oppose any government regulation—politicians who, among my urban and generally liberal students, are distinctly unpopular.

I am pleased when students point out such difficulties in Thoreau's views of government, for too many students simply let them pass without the scrutiny they demand. For those who uncritically accept Thoreau's ideas, one might raise questions such as the following essay topic:

> Thoreau says that the only way a person in his situation meets the government is by being told to pay taxes. Is this the only way that most people today deal with their government? (You might consider the following: the courts, departments of public assistance, school systems, town meetings, and health-care programs.)   (Fergenson and Nickerson 385)

One might also question Thoreau's statement that "[l]aw never made men a whit more just" (*Reform Papers* 65), pointing out that it was written more than a century before the antidiscrimination laws passed in the 1950s and 1960s—laws inspired by one of Thoreau's most important followers, Martin Luther King, Jr.

In fact, one practical approach to "Civil Disobedience" is to teach works by Martin Luther King along with it. King's statement of his debt to Thoreau, published as "A Legacy of Creative Protest," and his "Letter from Birmingham Jail" can help students appreciate Thoreau's ideas. Since "A Legacy" is brief, it can be read in class or distributed when the instructor assigns Thoreau. It begins:

> During my early college days I read Thoreau's essay on civil disobedience for the first time. Fascinated by the idea of refusing to cooperate with an evil system, I was so deeply moved that I re-read the work several times. I became convinced then that non-cooperation with evil is as much a moral obligation as is cooperation with good. No other person has been more eloquent and passionate in getting this idea across than Henry David Thoreau. As a result of his writings and personal witness we are the heirs of a legacy of creative protest. It goes without saying that the teachings of Thoreau are alive today. . . .

Students are usually impressed by the passion of King's response to Thoreau. His having found the essay so moving that he reread it several times motivates students who, frustrated by its long paragraphs and complex structure, may have difficulty reading it even once. Moreover, King's assertion of its importance as a moral guide and a source of "creative protest" overcomes the resistance of some students who find in Thoreau a formula for anarchy.

King's "Letter from Birmingham Jail" deals even more effectively with the problem of the uncritical rejection or acceptance of Thoreau's ideas, for here King faces an important issue that Thoreau dodges: the possibility that people following their consciences might violate a just law, for example, court-ordered integration. King acknowledges that there is a "legitimate concern" over the breaking of law and that "it may seem rather paradoxical" to break some laws while urging people to uphold others. But he distinguishes carefully between just law, which "uplifts human personality," and unjust law, which degrades it. "In no sense do I advocate evading or defying the law, as would the rabid segregationist," he writes. "That would lead to anarchy." To strengthen his point, King presents many instances from ancient to modern times when civil disobedience was necessary. He asserts: "It was 'illegal' to aid and comfort a Jew in Hitler's Germany. Even so, I am sure that, had I lived in Germany at the time, I would have aided and comforted my Jewish brothers" ("Letter" 82–84). King's words, so healing in today's divisive climate, help students confront the unresolved issues in Thoreau's essay and strongly affirm what Thomas Brown calls the ethical center of the composition course.

Although instructors inevitably spend much time discussing the crucial ideas of "Civil Disobedience," in a composition course questions of style too must arise. Thoreau is known to us not because he spent one night in jail to protest war and slavery but because he wrote about his experience and set forth his ideas in elegant prose. He is a consummate literary craftsman, and students of writing can learn from a careful examination of his sentences, his paragraphs, and his revisions. Many authors of composition textbooks cite passages from "Civil Disobedience." In *Writing Well*, Donald Hall excerpts the three paragraphs beginning with "The mass of men serve the State thus, not as men mainly, but as machines . . ." (*Reform Papers* 66–67) and asks students to study Thoreau's transitions (177–179). In *Words and Ideas*, Hans Guth states that "[a] complex, elaborate sentence is often appropriate for detailed explanation or argument" (331) and cites two sentences from "Civil Disobedience." His choices are excellent, including the sentence "There will never be a really free and enlightened State, until the State comes to recognize the individual as a higher and independent power, from which all its own power and authority are derived, and treats him accordingly" (89). One might choose many other sentences for their balance, rhythm, and aphoristic force. An instructor can ask a class to examine the paragraph that begins, "I have never declined paying the highway tax, because I am as desirous of being a good neighbor as I am of being a bad subject . . ." (84) as an example of parallel structure.

A writer who produced such carefully crafted sentences had to be very conscious of the importance of style and method. The many passages that Thoreau wrote on the art of writing make fascinating and instructive reading. Two collections of such passages, one by Richard Dillman (*Thoreau's Comments*) and one by Eva Burkett and Joyce Steward, are helpful guides to Thoreau's views on prose style. Dillman has grouped Thoreau's ideas on such topics as grammar, word choice, and revision. These quotations can provide points of departure for discussions of Thoreau the writer.

Thoreau's comments on revision are particularly interesting for anyone concerned with the writing process. According to the introduction in the Princeton edition of *Reform Papers*, manuscript evidence "suggests that Thoreau may have put ['Civil Disobedience'] through a number of drafts en route to publication" (228). Unfortunately, except for a few fragments, the preliminary drafts of the essay are lost, making it impossible to provide the kind of detailed study of the evolution of this text that J. Lyndon Shanley has done for *Walden*. Nevertheless, some interesting textual questions can be raised.

We have two versions of Thoreau's essay, the original one published in 1849, which was titled "Resistance to Civil Government," and the slightly altered version from *A Yankee in Canada, with Anti-slavery and Reform Papers*, posthumously published in 1866. It is the latter version that bears the title "Civil Disobedience." In the absence of proof that Thoreau himself made the changes, the editors of the Princeton edition have published the 1849 text, giving the changes in their notes. We find an interesting revision on page 78. The 1849 text reads, "When I converse with the freest of my neighbors, I perceive that . . . they cannot spare the protection of the existing government, and they dread the consequences of disobedience to it to their property and families." The revision, which reads, ". . . they dread the consequences to their property and families of disobedience to it" (327), is clearly an improvement. Although we cannot know with certainty that it was Thoreau's improvement, Walter Harding feels that it was, for *The Variorum Civil Disobedience*, which he edited, reprints the 1866 version "on the assumption that it was based on a corrected copy made by Thoreau" (27).

One example of a revision that we know was Thoreau's shows us the writer trimming the fat from his prose. For the 1849 edition Thoreau deleted the words "since, which is not a little" from a sentence that originally read, "The character inherent in the American people has done all that has been accomplished since, which is not a little; and it would have done somewhat more, if the government had not sometimes got in its way" (*Reform Papers* 64, 323). George Orwell once advised, "If it is possible to cut a word out, always cut it out" (139). Here Thoreau cut out *six* words to make the sentence leaner and clearer.

Another revision that Thoreau might have made was the change in the essay's title. The debate over what the essay should be called can be explained to students. An instructor, pointing out that titles are important since they convey the first impression of an essay, can ask students to discuss why Thoreau might have made this change and what different effects the two titles produce.

The controversy over the title epitomizes the difficulties of this essay; we do not even know with certainty what to call it, and in fact, the difference between the two titles reflects not only one of the ambiguities of the text but also the different interpretations of Thoreau's political ideas, for "Civil Disobedience" is less strident than "Resistance to Civil Government." But despite the problems "Civil Disobedience" presents, it is one of the most important texts that writing students can study, and its rewards more than compensate both the instructor and the students for its difficulties. It is one of the most influential essays ever written. That fact alone makes an acquaintance with it highly desirable for composition students on all levels. Its importance as an expression of humanistic values and its proven power to promote social change demonstrate the far-reaching effects of great writing.

"Life without Principle" and
Cape Cod as Foils to *Walden*

Richard J. Schneider

Walden is, as Michael Gilmore has suggested, "a book at odds with its own beliefs" (178), a book full of contradictions. As such it is especially troublesome for students who are in the earliest stages of cognitive development and have not yet made the leap to what John Keats called negative capability, the ability to handle uncertainty and to be "content with half knowledge" (261). What begins as a problem, however, can become a key to Thoreau's value for undergraduate students, because like so many college students Thoreau grapples throughout his works with the tension between the certainty of dualism and the uncertainty of multiplicity. This struggle can be seen within *Walden* itself, but its implications for Thoreau and for students become clearer when *Walden* is compared with other of Thoreau's less frequently taught works.

I use the terms *dualism* and *multiplicity* with specific reference to theories of cognitive development in undergraduates, theories developed by such psychologists as William Perry and Robert F. Rodgers. (The following summary of these ideas is based on Rodgers, "Teaching" 99–104.) Perry originally described the cognitive development of students as being in nine stages, but he and others have since condensed those nine stages to five. In the first three, students assume that all knowledge and all questions can be handled in dualistic terms of right or wrong, truth or falsehood. Their assumption is that absolute right or truth exists, at least in principle, and that the purpose of a teacher is to make them aware of that right or truth. In such dualistic thinking uncertainty is dealt with as nonexistent (stage 1), as an error imparted by an incompetent teacher (stage 2), or as acceptable only when experts have not yet had a chance to determine the truth (stage 3).

In stages 4 and 5, the accommodation of multiplicity and the synthesis of varied points of view occur. In stage 4, students recognize that uncertainty is the most common condition of real life, except perhaps in a few special cases like religion. In such a world students believe that all opinions must be equally valid, since there are no absolute bases for judgment in most areas of life. Therefore commitment to any one decision is impossible. In stage 5 all knowledge is viewed as uncertain, even in such strongholds of absolutism as religion. However, students now accept the need to make value judgments based on nonabsolute criteria, can synthesize such criteria from various sources, and can make a commitment, knowing that the criteria for their decision are relative and realizing that their commitment will need to be reassessed periodically in new contexts. Studies based on these five stages have revealed the depressing fact that probably no more than fifteen percent of graduating college seniors, even at elite institutions, are likely to have reached level 5 (Rodgers, Remarks).

Thoreau himself demonstrates a strong desire to resolve important issues dualistically. The most obvious example in *Walden* is the certainty of his pronouncement, "The greater part of what my neighbors call good I believe in my soul to be bad, and if I repent of any thing, it is very likely to be my good behavior" (*Walden* 10). This good-versus-bad dualistic attitude is what puts off many students about the opening chapter of *Walden*, "Economy," particularly students who are also dualistic thinkers and who have a worldview opposed to Thoreau's (see Dillman's essay in this volume). Thoreau goes on to express the dualist's confidence that absolute truth is attainable: "When one man has reduced a fact of the imagination to be a fact to his understanding, I foresee that all men will at length establish their lives on that basis" (11). Dualistic readers sympathetic to Thoreau's optimism admire Thoreau for apparently having done just that with the fact of Walden Pond.

Thoreau's search for the hard bottom of truth, much discussed in criticism in recent years (see Michaels and Boone), is now generally understood to be one of the main themes of *Walden*. However, that discussion has also made it clear that Thoreau's search for the hard bottom of truth does not arrive at a conclusion as firm as either Thoreau or his dualistic readers might wish. Although he physically sounds the bottom of Walden Pond without much difficulty, he breathes a sigh of relief that "[w]hile men believe in the infinite some ponds will be thought to be bottomless" (287). A careful reading of *Walden* suggests that Thoreau values this principle of uncertainty as much as he does his optimism about finding absolute truth. One could argue that in *Walden* he has merely swapped the certainties of materialism for the certainties of transcendentalism. Yet there is also the recognition that truth is various, that each person must discover his or her own truth: "I would have each one be very careful to find out and pursue *his own* way, and not his father's or his mother's or his neighbor's instead" (71). There are as many ways of living, he reminds us, "as there can be drawn radii from one centre" (11).

It is only by taking a look at Thoreau's whole writing career that a reader can fully understand how Thoreau coped with uncertainty. This method is problematic, since few teachers and none of their students have time to read all of Thoreau. It is possible, however, to provide students with key passages from Thoreau's other works to suggest how he struggled with the conflict between certainty and uncertainty, thereby inviting students to confront their own dualistic outlooks and to consider some ways for coping with uncertainty. The pedagogical strategy is to call their attention to key contradictions in *Walden* and then to use sample passages from Thoreau's other works to demonstrate how Thoreau struggled elsewhere with each contradiction.

One contradiction in *Walden* that should be easy for most students to recognize is his attitude toward business. In "Economy," he describes with pitying eye the inhabitants of Concord who "in shops, and offices, and fields . . . have appeared to [him] to be doing penance in a thousand remarkable ways" (4). He also points out the foolishness of the farmer who sells his cattle for profit: "The farmer is endeavoring to solve the problem of a livelihood by a formula more complicated than the problem itself. To get his shoestrings he speculates in herds of cattle" (33).

Yet despite Thoreau's frequent condemnations of commerce, students must also be reminded of his favorable comments on the benefits of commerce. In "Sounds," he watches the many products being carried by the railroad as it whizzes by Walden Pond, and he observes, apparently without irony, that "[w]hat recommends commerce to [him] is its enterprise and bravery." "Commerce," he continues, "is unexpectedly confident and serene, alert, adventurous, and unwearied. It is very natural in its methods withal" (118, 119). So does Thoreau think businesspeople are greedy or heroic? That should be the question running through the minds of dualistic students, and it should lead to significant class discussion.

The next step is to give students excerpts from Thoreau's most-often delivered lecture, "Life without Principle," in which he announces that he "will leave out all the flattery," especially regarding business, and "retain all the criticism" (*Reform Papers* 156). Thoreau here seems to be even more firmly dualistic and absolute than in *Walden*. He condemns "this world" as "a place of business. . . . It is nothing but work, work, work." Greed is so pervasive that "[he] cannot easily buy a blank-book to write thoughts in; they are commonly ruled for dollars and cents." He is no longer willing to credit commerce with the virtues of enterprise and bravery. Now it is an absolutely damned occupation. "The ways by which you may get money almost without exception lead downward," he preaches. His unequivocal judgment now is that "there is nothing, not even crime, more opposed to poetry, to philosophy, ay, to life itself, than this incessant business" (156, 158). Here, of course, the dualists in class will immediately take sides for or against Thoreau's condemnation of business.

This is the time to remind them of the changes Thoreau saw in Concord in the seven years between his departure from Walden Pond in 1847 and his first delivery (under a different title) of "Life without Principle." After the arrival of the railroad, Concord had rapidly moved toward being a suburb of Boston. Farmers were increasingly selling crops and herds for profit rather than using them for sustenance and barter, thus losing their self-reliance. They were also selling off their woodlots to meet the growing urban demand for fuel. In 1849 many young men headed west for the California gold rush, as clear an example of sheer greed as Thoreau would ever see. In short, he had plenty of reason for pessimism, and plenty of evidence for an absolute judgment against capitalism.

Lest the antibusiness dualists in class start feeling too smug, however, the teacher will need to remind them that throughout the last decade of his life Thoreau continued to participate in the world of business by lecturing and by writing for publication, both activities bringing in a modest income. He also continued to survey his neighbors' woodlots, thus contributing to the drastic reduction in the Concord woods. And he could not escape entirely involvement in the family pencil factory, which he had to take over after his father's death. Hypocrisy? Perhaps. But it might be revealing to engage students in a discussion of Thoreau's objection to the gold rush and the gold rush's connection to the trend today in state government to rely on lotteries to balance state budgets. The discussion is likely to reveal ambivalent attitudes among students: there will be some who object to gambling in theory but are quite likely to buy a lottery ticket now and then. The point is that it was no easier for Thoreau to maintain an absolute view of right and wrong than it is for us. He too sometimes had to make transcendental truth subject to context and circumstance.

Throughout his life Thoreau clung to a profoundly dualistic outlook about some topics, such as economics and slavery (see his John Brown essays). In his views of nature, however, multiplicity asserted itself. His description of his "checker game" with the loon is perhaps his best expression in *Walden* ("Brute Neighbors") of this openness to multiplicity. The loon, though humanized as a checkers opponent, is also a mysterious, even sinister, figure. It probes to the bottom of the pond, where Thoreau cannot go except with a line and sinker. The loon prepares the reader for what may be the most important passage in *Walden*, Thoreau's description, in "Spring," of a basic human paradox:

> At the same time that we are earnest to explore and learn all things, we require that all things be mysterious and unexplorable, that land and sea be infinitely wild, unsurveyed and unfathomed by us because unfathomable.
>
> (317–18)

This equal emphasis on learning all things and on the mysterious and unexplorable acknowledges the call of multiplicity and uncertainty, a call that became stronger the more Thoreau studied nature.

To understand fully Thoreau's attempt to deal with this paradox, one would have to study his Journal thoroughly. But to demonstrate to students the power of multiplicity and uncertainty even for a transcendentalist, sample passages from either *The Maine Woods* or *Cape Cod* can serve. Thoreau's descriptions of nearing the peak of Mount Katahdin and of descending over the "burnt lands" in the "Ktaadn" chapter of *The Maine Woods* demonstrate powerfully how his transcendental assumptions about the goodness of nature could be tested by a truly sublime landscape. However, I prefer passages from *Cape Cod*, because they seem to contain experiences more permanently unsettling to Thoreau's transcendental assumptions.

The shipwreck passage from the first chapter of *Cape Cod* should stir consideration of Thoreau's multiple views of nature. As he and his companion wait in Boston for a boat to the Cape, they read in the newspaper of a shipwreck near Cohasset. They catch a stagecoach to Cohasset and arrive in time to see the full effects of nature's fury on the victims of the wreck, which Thoreau describes with powerful journalistic economy:

> I saw many marble feet and matted hands as the clothes were raised, and one livid, swollen and mangled body of a drowned girl . . . to which some

rags still adhered, with a string, half concealed by the flesh, about its swollen neck; the coiled-up wreck of a human hulk, gashed by the rocks or fishes, so that the bone and muscle were exposed, but quite blood-less—merely red and white—with wide-open and staring eyes, yet lus-treless, dead-lights. . . .   (5–6)

Thoreau presents this description objectively, trying hard to resist its horror by retreating to a transcendental rationalization that is not quite convincing. "Why care for these bodies?" he asks. Although they are dead, the consolation is that "they emigrated to a newer world than ever Columbus dreamed of, yet one of whose existence we believe that there is far more universal and con-vincing evidence—though it has not yet been discovered by science . . ." (10). The teacher should ask students whether they are convinced by this transcen-dental-Christian apology for death. Some will notice that Thoreau is clinging desperately to the idealist's certainty of an afterlife, yet at least a few will sense that he is not completely convinced himself.

Much of *Cape Cod* is filled with descriptions of phenomena on the Cape that defy certainty. In calling students' attention to these phenomena, I remind them that Thoreau was a surveyor by trade, that he was known for the excep-tional accuracy of his surveys, and that an inability to measure a thing would be very disconcerting to such a person, would in fact make it unknowable. A few examples should illustrate the point (for additional examples, see my essay on *Cape Cod* or its revised version in my book *Henry David Thoreau*).

Thoreau and his companion see something large and black cast up on the beach behind them, too far to be clear. As he walked toward it, he says, "it took successively the form of a huge fish, a drowned man, a sail or a net, and finally of a mass of tow-cloth." He describes such phenomena as being both "exceed-ingly grotesque" but also "much larger and more wonderful than they actually are" (84). The word *wonderful* expresses his delight at the novelty of the chang-ing view, but *grotesque* suggests some disgust at the object's uncertainty of pro-portion and his inability to measure it accurately.

Some pages later, Thoreau describes one of many optical illusions or mirages that he sees on the Cape: an elevated plateau that seems to slope downward "very regularly" but on closer inspection turns out to be "interrupted by broad valleys or gullies," some of them "circular, a hundred feet deep without any outlet" and hiding houses or even whole villages. These elusive valleys make Thoreau uneasy when he imagines that "[they] might tumble into a village be-fore [they] were aware of it, as into an ant-lion's hole, and be drawn into the sand irrecoverably." On such plateaus, Thoreau finds it "impossible to estimate distances in any weather" (104, 105).

A third example, perhaps the most unsettling for Thoreau, is the incident in "The Highland Light," in which the lighthouse keeper tells him that the sun sometimes appears to rise over the ocean fifteen minutes before it actually does. Thoreau tries two physical explanations for this phenomenon, but neither is convincing. If even the sun, nature's symbol of God, is deceptive, then the existence of absolute truth is called into question. One can trust only one's own insights, not the light of nature: "[I]t behooves us old stagers to keep our lamps trimmed and burning . . . and not trust to the sun's looming" (136, 137).

Thoreau comes to Cape Cod thinking that it is only a larger Walden Pond, but the more he observes the ocean, the more he realizes that unlike Walden Pond the ocean is, from a human perspective, truly bottomless:

> As we looked off, and saw the water growing darker and darker and deeper and deeper the farther we looked, till it was awful to consider, and it appeared to have no relation to the friendly land, either as shore or bottom,—of what use is a bottom if it is out of sight, if it is two or three miles from the surface, and you are to be drowned so long before you get to it, though it were made of the same stuff with your native soil?— . . . I felt that I was a land animal.   (96)

The ocean here is disturbingly unknowable and sends Thoreau back to land in retreat from the possibility that there is another kind of nature than the one at Walden Pond. At the beginning of *Cape Cod*, Thoreau claims to have been "little salted" by his experiences on Cape Cod, but the above passage suggests that he was quite deeply affected by the multiple and elusive realities of the Cape and the ocean.

It is now time to return the students to the passage in *Walden* from which we began our excursions into "Life without Principle" and *Cape Cod*. Immediately after his assertion in "Spring" that it is good for nature sometimes to be "mysterious and unexplorable," he argues that "[w]e can never have enough of Nature. We must be refreshed by the sight of inexhaustible vigor, vast and Titanic features, the sea-coast with its wrecks" (318). The question for the students here is whether or not Thoreau is in fact refreshed by the ocean's titanic features in *Cape Cod*.

Thoreau optimistically proclaims:

> I love to see that Nature is so rife with life that myriads can be afforded to be sacrificed and suffered to prey on one another. . . . With the liability to accident, we must see how little account is to be made of it. The impression made on a wise man is that of universal innocence. . . . Compassion is a very untenable ground.   (318)

This transcendental affirmation seems convincing enough when applied, as it is here, to a dead horse in the woods. It seems considerably less convincing when Thoreau tries it on the human dead from the wreck of the *Saint John*.

It is good now to engage students in a discussion of their doubts concerning absolutes of religion that they have been taught are not to be questioned. Through such discussion they may become more sympathetic to Thoreau's concern that "[w]e will not be shipwrecked on a vain reality" (326)—that is, on apparent realities that prove finally to need questioning.

In *Walden*, Thoreau expresses his struggle to move from dualistic thinking to stage 5 multiplistic thinking. Exposing students to some of the later developments in this struggle in "Life without Principle" and *Cape Cod* should help them to see its progress and to move in that direction too. Time and again in *Walden* and elsewhere, Thoreau emphasizes the limitations of our knowledge. In *Walden* he says "Most have not delved six feet beneath the surface, nor leaped as many above it. We know not where we are" (332). Furthermore, "We may not arrive at our port within a calculable period"—perhaps not until we are dead like the corpses of the *Saint John*. "[B]ut," he adds, "we would preserve the true course" (71), a course the truth of which will be constantly shifting, like the sands of Cape Cod. Thoreau addresses *Walden* especially to students. He himself was a lifelong student. Through his example students have the opportunity to learn that to be a student, to be a human being, is finally to be constantly at odds with one's own beliefs.

Thoreau's "Walking"
and the Ecological Imperative

David M. Robinson

The student who encounters Thoreau's "Walking" will find it a familiar work, in that it speaks with surprising directness to our ecological concerns today. As our economic, political, and ethical choices become increasingly bounded by our ecological predicament, Thoreau's desire to "speak a word for Nature, for absolute freedom and wildness" ("Walking" 205) has a correspondingly stronger contemporary ring. The course of history has made Thoreau's unique voice a prophetic one. For the teacher, "Walking" can be an important enabling text, a text for framing a classroom discussion on ecological questions and setting those questions in a historical perspective.

Much of the initial appeal of "Walking" is its ability to capture in briefer scope *Walden*'s sharp-edged skepticism about the deadening routines of conventional life. "I confess that I am astonished," Thoreau remarks, "at the power of endurance, to say nothing of the moral insensibility, of my neighbors who confine themselves to shops and offices the whole day for weeks and months, aye, and years almost together" (208). What undergraduate can resist this, especially in an afternoon class late in the week? The appeal of the essay goes deeper, of course, but we should not forget that Thoreau was engaged in an act of persuasion and that his celebration of the modern sacrament of walking is aimed at inculcating fundamental changes in the way men and women lead their daily lives. "Walking," that is to say, is an essay in ethics, for in it Thoreau calls for both a revision of the patterns of ordinary life and a revivification of the quality of moral aspiration that underlies them. A striking and important moment in the text—certainly a promising point of entry for any teacher—is Thoreau's description of his daily schedule, one he seems to have settled on after returning from his experiment at Walden Pond (Richardson 252–54; Sattelmeyer, "Remaking" 56–57). "I think that I cannot preserve my health and spirits," he declares, "unless I spend four hours a day at least—and it is commonly more than that—sauntering through the woods and over the hills and fields, absolutely free from all worldly engagements" (207). This freedom from engagements is what Thoreau principally meant when he said in *Walden* that he loved a "broad margin" to his life (111). In "Walking," he admits at times having "stolen forth for a walk at the eleventh hour, or four o'clock in the afternoon, too late to redeem the day," and feeling as a result "as if [he] had committed some sin to be atoned for" (208). The afternoon, then, that part of the day that Thoreau had set aside for his rambles, was an essential period of self-recovery, one that complemented the essential but here unmentioned "morning work" of reading and writing, the scholar's more typical pursuits (see Peck, *Morning Work* x–xi). The teacher's first task in presenting "Walking" should be to emphasize the place of sauntering in Thoreau's daily life, to make the essay seem more than a hymn to undisciplined wildness and absolute freedom. Sherman Paul sensibly reminds us that Thoreau did not "relinquish civilization" in "Walking" but instead "saw the possibility of a higher cultivation" in the wild (*Shores* 416). The wild provided him with a discipline of awareness, and as Stephen Adams and Donald Ross, Jr., have explained, "Thoreau celebrates in 'Walking' not so much physically wild nature as a psychologically 'wild' way of looking at the woods and fields near his Concord home" (143). But in a first encounter with the essay, the student is likely to be overwhelmed by Thoreau's spirited rhetoric, in which sauntering is depicted as a gesture of independence from the conventional and the routine. "I wish to make an extreme statement," Thoreau warns us, "if so I may make an emphatic one, for there are enough champions of civilization: the minister and the school committee and every one of you will take care of that" (205).

This tactic of exaggeration ("engaging obstreperousness," as James McIntosh put it [286]) is best expressed in Thoreau's challenge to conceive of the demands of walking as absolute; walking is a mode of experience that, to be valid, must supersede all others. Like a religious convert, the "saunterer" must abandon everything to partake in the sacrament of the walk. "We should go forth on the shortest walk, perchance, in the spirit of undying adventure, never to return,—prepared to send back our embalmed hearts only as relics to our desolate kingdoms" (206). Thoreau's challenge is blunt: unless one is prepared never to return home, one cannot really experience a walk. The walker must embody a "chivalric and heroic spirit" and remain determined to ignore the restrictions of conventional life (206). The fanciful extravagance of the passage sets the tone for the essay, which contains some of Thoreau's most engaging prose.

Students are likely to find further appeal in the symbolic geography Thoreau includes in "Walking," which focuses on the west as the direction of the saunterer's desire. "I believe that there is a subtle magnetism in Nature," he tells us, "which, if we unconsciously yield to it, will direct us aright. It is not indifferent to us which way we walk" (216). Thoreau's description of his intuitive directedness is a version of the symbolic moral reasoning that Emerson expounded in *Nature*, and students who come to "Walking" after reading Emerson will find this description of walking a good exemplification of Emerson's claims that moral direction can emanate from nature and that ethical and spiritual principles parallel physical laws. Thoreau is saying that a walker will, by a kind of natural inclination, always discover the "right" direction to walk when he or she embarks on a ramble. In fact, Thoreau claims that in his walks he is usually led in roughly the same direction, by an internal compass. Whenever he leaves his house for a ramble, "strange and whimsical as it may seem, . . . I finally and inevitably settle southwest," or, as he notes even more precisely, "between west and south-southwest" (217). Thoreau praises the southwest as that "right" direction toward which nature always steers him, the repository both of wild, unclaimed nature and of human hope.

This claim is perhaps the essay's most fanciful and extravagant, and it is useful now to bring classroom discussion down to earth by pointing out that Thoreau is universalizing his geographical situation,making his love of the Old Marlborough Road, which leads southwest from Concord, into a kind of ethical imperative. The observation should generate student response along these lines: Doesn't the direction that you are drawn to walk depend on where you start from? on where you live? The simple facts of Concord's geography can thus provide the teacher with an excellent opportunity to ground the essay in the historical specifics of its composition, to comment on Thoreau's strategic use of exaggeration, and to demonstrate the extent to which his primary audience was always Concord, as Robert Milder and Stephen Railton have recently shown. To approach "Walking" as a local essay is also to emphasize its historicity and to underline to one's students the value of understanding Thoreau's historical situation as a prerequisite for assessing the ecological lessons that we can now draw from "Walking."

Thoreau's strategy is to present his own local rambles as an instance of the westward migration of European culture and thus to use them in the construction of a mythical narrative that, as scholars have noted, underlies the essay (Garber, *Imagination* 40; Richardson 230–33; Adams and Ross 149–52). "Eastward I go only by force; but westward I go free," Thoreau writes, meaning that he willingly accepts the guidance of nature and that in going west he gains a sense of freedom. "Every sunset which I witness inspires me with the desire to go to a West as distant and fair as that into which the sun goes down" (219). Thoreau's "West" is in fact a name for a vague yearning or desire, a mood of restless alienation from the settled and conventional. The image of a beckoning western sunset is a version of the better-known, much pondered declaration of *Walden*: "I long ago lost a hound, a bay horse, and a turtle-dove, and am still on their trail" (17). When the student of Thoreau begins to see how he links these desires with the cultural symbol of the west in ways that are both compelling and problematic, the essay opens as an expression of our culture's own contradictory desires. Thoreau's gesture of walking from Concord westward ("Stepping Westward" was an early alternative title to the piece [Paul, *Shores* 414; Adams and Ross 146]) is a symbolic walking away from civilization toward the unsettled and the wild. "I must walk toward Oregon," he declares, "and not toward Europe" ("Walking" 218). But Oregon, be assured, is a real place as well as a symbolic one, and the historical reality of the American West became an increasingly important part of a reader's comprehension of the essay. In the 1850s Thoreau's declared preference of Oregon to Europe had enormous cultural appeal, and the enactment of that preference over the next half-century profoundly altered the continent. "Walking" can help students recognize that the lyric wildness Thoreau celebrates as essentially western is inextricably bound up with the historical tragedy of the American West and with the continuing ecological tension, particularly acute in the West, between the desire to preserve the wild and the desire to make use of it. The irony of

"Walking" is that its affirmation of the wild, which makes the essay relevant to us now in an ecological sense, is difficult to extricate from the ethic of possession that we associate with the western migration and the doctrine of manifest destiny.

The problem caused by Thoreau's conflation of west and wild is an instance of the larger difficulty inherent in the use of the wild as an ethically normative concept—a dilemma that contemporary sociological writers have also confronted. Gary Snyder's *The Practice of the Wild* and Wendell Berry's *Home Economics* offer examples of the continuing importance of wildness as an ethical category and examples also of the problems that attend both the definition and valuation of the wild. Thoreau was not unaware of these problems in working out the essay, and his response to them was influenced by his encounter with Coleridge's concept of polarity (Sattelmeyer and Hocks). William Rossi has explained how polarity helped Thoreau understand and reconcile the duality between the imperative toward self-culture and the demand for "the Wild as indomitably, radically Other" ("Limits" 94). Thoreau expounds the wild as a source of inexhaustible vigor and force, which he contrasts with the enervation of civilization. This contrast is the fundamental polarity of the essay. The wild is valuable not only because it embodies positive values but also because it serves as a negating counterforce to civilization. The wild is from the first defined by civilization and thereby bounded by the very system of values it attempts to oppose.

Walter Benn Michaels has called our attention to a version of this problem in *Walden*, where nature, having been given value because of its otherness, cannot maintain that value and still reflect back to us any sense of self-recognition (137–38). To assign value to a thing because of its otherness threatens to prevent our aspiration toward it as ethically normative. "The West of which I speak is but another name for the Wild," Thoreau tells us, "and what I have been preparing to say is, that in Wildness is the preservation of the World" ("Walking" 224). With this justly familiar quotation the essay shifts direction, transposing the idea of the wild from the category of the absolutely other to a concept that has ethically redemptive potential. It is at this point, in other words, that Thoreau turns back toward the world that he initially scorned. If we accept Rossi's explanation of the polar structure of the essay, Thoreau's turn back is in fact necessitated by the energy of his departure. "The farther the walker moves out, in his ideal walk, *into* nature," Rossi explains, "the more (and more deeply) his thinking engages culture" ("Limits" 97). Thoreau's larger strategy is thus to use the wild to purify and preserve in a new and redeemed form the world of civilization. He could equate west and wild because they both were denials of civilization. But his goal remained that of the ethical philosopher: to bring change in lives inevitably bounded by civilization.

The teacher of "Walking" must therefore strive to show how the appeal of Thoreau's praise of the wild is part of a deeper ethical purpose to inform ordinary life with a sense of openness and renewed vitality. "Life consists with wildness. The most alive is the wildest" (226). But this declaration takes on practical authority only when Thoreau ties it into the reclamation of human concerns and intentions.

> Not yet subdued to man, [the wild's] presence refreshes him. One who pressed forward incessantly and never rested from his labors, who grew fast and made infinite demands on life, would always find himself in a new country or wilderness, and surrounded by the raw material of life. He would be climbing over the prostrate stems of primitive forest-trees.
> (226)

The image is remarkably timely, given the ongoing debates about forest preservation, wildlife habitat, and the limits of human economic activity. We live in a day in which not only humanity's economic appetites but also its recreational inclinations tend toward the steady reduction of what can be considered the wild. The chief ethical dilemma of our culture is to find a way to limit human desires and appetites. We cannot blame Thoreau for not foreseeing the technological advances that would actually threaten those "primitive forest-trees" providing the stage for his encounter with the spiritually invigorating wilderness. To receive his essay now, the student must first be brought to the historical perception that Thoreau could not have imagined the changes that have made our wilderness, his moral touchstone, so fragile. But Thoreau did understand that the gesture of expansion and exploration he elaborated is itself bounded by the very concept of the wild. The wild in "Walking" ultimately reinforces a sense of human limit and humility, and that reinforcement is part of an overall strategy of rekindling hope.

The great temptation in teaching "Walking" is to expend a huge measure of time and energy on its rhetorically brilliant beginning, to the exclusion of the "quiet reversal" (McIntosh 287) that marks its end. Thoreau's displacement of the rhetoric of exaggeration with humility is best revealed in his frank admission that he himself is not the wild, free personality his essay has praised. "For my part, I feel that with regard to Nature I live a sort of border life, on the confines of a world into which I make occasional and transient forays only . . ." (242). This confession is especially striking because of its relation to the essay's earlier declaration that any true walk must be undertaken with the expectation that the walker may be required never to return. Thoreau admits the "occasional and transient" quality of his walks and tells us that he has never entered into nature with the complete surrender he proclaimed as necessity at the essay's opening. The irony of this turn is deepened by Thoreau's additional confession of inability to follow any discernible direction offered by nature: "Unto a life which I call natural I would gladly follow even a will-o'-the-wisp through bogs and sloughs unimaginable," he says, "but no moon nor firefly has shown me the causeway to it" (242). Students may be inclined to ask what became of the "subtle magnetism" that Thoreau had declared would "direct us aright."

His description of his "border life" in nature undercuts the central declaration of faith that informed so much of the essay's discussion of the west and the wild.

The contradiction is inherent, I believe, in making wildness a normative term for the ethical life. The wild and the good cannot cohere completely if the wild is defined as utterly nonhuman. Thoreau also struggled with this problem in the chapter "Higher Laws" in *Walden*. Insofar as wildness does become an ethical category for him, it functions as an ameliorating quality of human endeavor, thus obviating its identity as something other—the very identity that provided its normative capacity to begin with. Thoreau suggests this difficulty in a sentence that is wildly contradictory: "Nature is a personality so vast and universal that we have never seen one of her features" ("Walking" 242). This is a remarkably confident proclamation of ignorance, important for its explicit confession of a limit to human comprehension and thus to human power.

The confident saunter into the wild at the beginning of "Walking" therefore becomes a humble recognition of the separate existence of nature, a moment of insight articulated at other key points in Thoreau's work, such as the "burnt lands" passage in "Ktaadn" or the end of the chapter "Spring" in *Walden*. "Thus has wildness been gentled," McIntosh comments (287), and this gentler quality is in part marked by Thoreau's return to the realm of daily life with its responsibilities and concerns. Significantly, he now uses the western setting sun as the emblem not of his yearning but of his return to the domestic and the social. He describes an evening in which the sunset bathed the hillsides in a "golden flood" and "seemed like a gentle herdsman driving us home at evening" (247). "Walking" begins by teaching the value of the wild as a potential human quality, but it concludes by demonstrating that nature can set a limit to both human desire and human capability. Thoreau's discovery of the limits of his wildness, a lesson of humility, is as crucial to him as his discovery of his capacity for wildness—and it may be, for readers now, an even more important lesson.

NOTE

I would like to acknowledge support from the Center for the Humanities, Oregon State University, in preparing this essay.

Teaching Thoreau's Journal

H. Daniel Peck

How is it possible to teach Thoreau's Journal? Here we have a two-million-word document, written over the course of twenty-four years (1837–61), whose size alone makes it the unlikeliest of texts for classroom consideration. Furthermore, the Journal significantly changes in form and character during its long development, so that any portion of it will necessarily fail to represent the whole.

Even if one could find a fully representative selection, wouldn't the teaching of such a selection create another kind of distortion? Because a journal is characterized by provisionality—it is always of the moment, *in* the moment—any selection from it, no matter how judiciously chosen, places boundaries around words that are meant to have no boundary. As Sharon Cameron has pointedly asked, regarding the difficulty of quoting from the Journal, "Where . . . , in any given case, are we to begin and end a quotation when the work's most pervasive critique derides the stability of such demarcations?" (20).

Unlike works that Thoreau published, or intended for publication, during his lifetime, the Journal is written in a radically open form. For all its idiosyncratic features, *Walden* generally conforms to nineteenth-century expectations for narrative; it concludes with "Conclusion." The Journal, however, is a work that by its very nature has no end. One day's entry ceaselessly gives way to another, and even when Thoreau speaks with certitude about some topic, we know that the form of his Journal always allows him, indeed, beckons him, to take that topic in an entirely different direction: tomorrow, or next week, or in five years.

Problems in selecting representative passages from the Journal are, of course, unimportant if we are considering the Journal simply as a workshop for the development of Thoreau's ideas and as a place where he drafted his other works. If this is our approach, then in teaching the Journal we aren't teaching a work at all but simply examining it as a way toward understanding those texts that we have designated as literary: *Walden*, *A Week on the Concord and Merrimack Rivers*, "Walking," and so on.

Increasingly, however, scholars are being drawn to the view that the Journal is an integral work. Perry Miller took that position in 1958, calling the Journal "a deliberately constructed work of art" (*Consciousness* 4) and pointing to a passage from the early 1850s in which Thoreau speculates on the possibility that "thoughts written down thus in a journal might be printed in the same form with greater advantage—than if the related ones were brought together into separate essays" (*Journal 4* 296). Scholars since have supported Miller's assertion by showing that in 1850 Thoreau ceased tearing out pages from his Journal for use in drafting other works and began instead to copy passages so that his Journal would remain intact. (See Thoreau, *Journal 3* ["Historical

Introduction"] 480–81.) Furthermore, there is considerable evidence in the Journal itself—beyond the passage cited by Miller—to indicate that Thoreau understood his Journal as a work and that, especially after 1850, he was devoted to pursuing its imaginative possibilities.

That Thoreau sometimes wrote several days' entries at a single sitting and often recounted his nature walks in the present tense contributes to our growing awareness of the Journal's fictionality. Certainly, by the early 1850s Thoreau's journal keeping had developed into a highly self-conscious and artful method: he generally walked in the afternoons, taking notes along the way, and wrote out his observations in his Journal on subsequent mornings.

As facts like these became better known to scholars during the 1980s and 1990s, a consensus formed about the Journal's literary integrity, even as the exact nature of that integrity remained elusive. Further, we have begun to find in the Journal a complex but discernible set of philosophical intentions. Not only do contemporary critics argue for the Journal's standing independently as a work; some would claim it is Thoreau's most important work (Cameron; Howarth, *Book*; Peck, *Morning Work*).

Such appraisals need not displace teachers' traditional use of the Journal as a tool for helping students better understand Thoreau's other works. This use typically involves examining passages in *Walden* that were drafted first in the Journal and tracking their stylistic development. But given what we now know about Thoreau's intentions for his Journal, such a use, by itself, appears limited. It assumes a relation between the Journal and Thoreau's other works that is a relation only of influence or derivation, whereas our present understanding of that relation suggests a dialogue.

The Journal and *Walden*, for example, are works written in different modes, yet they unmistakably participate in a set of common projects in moral economy and philosophy, literature, and natural science. A fuller vision of these works emerges as we hear each speaking to the other, each including and excluding things from its discourse according to its own procedure (see my essay "Crosscurrents"). One well-known example of the difference is the way Thoreau explains why he left Walden Pond. The *Walden* explanation is simply "I had several more lives to live" (323), with all the rich sense of expectancy that this phrase implies. The Journal's reason is more complex:

> But Why I changed—? Why I left the woods? I do not think that I can tell. I have often wished myself back— I do not know any better how I ever came to go there—. Perhaps it is none of my business—even if it is your's. Perhaps I wanted a change— There was a little stagnation it may be—about 2 o'clock in the afternoon the world's axle—creaked as if it needed greasing—as if the oxen labored—& could hardly get their load over the ridge of the day— Perhaps if I lived there much longer I might live there forever— One would think twice before he accepted heaven on such terms—   (*Journal 4* 275)

On the face of it, this passage tells us more about *Walden*'s development than it does about the Journal's—that is, how Thoreau remade a realistic and sober assessment of his years at the pond into the rhetorical flourish that closes *Walden*. But this is to regard the Journal's account as conveying Thoreau's bottom-line, "real" thoughts on the matter rather than as portraying yet another version of experience. And isn't the Journal version as much a fiction as the one that appears in *Walden*, and shouldn't it also be subjected to critical scrutiny? By this logic, we might find it profitable to study *Walden* as a way of better understanding the Journal, a reversal of the usual procedure.

The pedagogical issue, then, is not whether to teach the Journal when taking up Thoreau in the classroom. How, given what we now understand about the Journal's centrality to Thoreau's literary life and its intimate, dialogic relation with his other major works, can we *not* teach the Journal?

But reaching this conclusion, we are left with the same vexing questions with which we began. Students asked to read and absorb the entire Journal would be long in the tooth by the time they graduated from college, and, in any case, even reading the entire Journal with great care and insight does not ensure anything other than rich confusion.

The daunting problems of reading the Journal apply, though in a different way, to teachers as well. Teachers can claim a certain control over most texts they teach; this may mean only that they have read a work through more often than have their students and therefore have a more secure starting point for thinking about it. But how many teachers, even specialists in nineteenth-century American literature, have read all of Thoreau's Journal? How many can claim control over it? Even those scholars who have made a systematic study of the Journal (I confess to being one of them) will readily acknowledge its tendency to overwhelm comprehensive attempts at interpretation—to swallow up the very act of interpretation in its vast discursiveness.

I hope it is clear from these remarks that I have no simple solution to the formidable problems of teaching Thoreau's Journal, even as I believe that teachers must teach it. Like the Journal's own procedures, the teaching of the Journal will always be an experiment, and perhaps the best we can hope for is that the experiment will prove interesting. In the end, teachers must settle for one pedagogical compromise or another, and my effort here is simply to offer some possible approaches.

One approach involves the use of anthologies that select passages from various points in the Journal's twenty-four-year development. Over the years, a number of such collections have appeared, beginning in 1927 with Odell Shepard's *The Heart of Thoreau's Journals*. At this writing several anthologies, including Shepard's, are in print in paperback editions. Their advantages are low cost, wide availability, and the inclusion of a rich and varied selection of passages. Because their editors have made the selections with an eye to Thoreau's most eloquent moments, his "gems," these books show students how beautifully crafted the Journal is. As Alfred Kazin once said, "It is not natural for a man to write this well every day" (188), and the remarkably consistent beauty of the Journal's prose is certainly one of its most striking features.

Most of the anthologies of Thoreau's Journal are organized chronologically, but one currently in print—*Henry David Thoreau: A Writer's Journal*, edited by Laurence Stapleton—provides a thematic structure within a larger chronological framework. It is divided into six chapterlike sections with titles ("Simply Seeing" and "Standing at a Distance" are two of them) that suggest the principles by which passages were selected from all the thousands that might have been taken from any given period. The thematic force of the titles indicates the relation between this volume and the long tradition of publishing selections from the Journal. For example, in the late nineteenth century Thoreau's friend Harrison Blake produced a four-volume selection of Journal passages that was organized by the seasons, and a 1910 anthology was made of passages about birds from the 1906 edition of the Journal.[1]

The obvious problem with such collections is that students are led into the Journal through someone else's conceptions of its dominant topics, themes, and issues—a particularly dangerous procedure given how complex and multifaceted the Journal is. Perhaps the purely chronological form of anthology, with no headings except the years from which passages are selected, gives a clearer view of the Journal's overall development. One such volume currently in print—*The Selected Journals of Henry D. Thoreau*, edited by Carl Bode—provides selections from every year of the Journal; the editorial commentary that prefaces each section tells what went on in Thoreau's life during that year, thus providing a shorthand biography. But, in the end, chronologically based anthologies will be just as selective as those with an overtly topical or thematic organization. When an editor has excerpted two or three hundred pages from the Journal's seven thousand (in the 1906 edition), that editor has necessarily made severe and restrictive decisions about what is representative or interesting and what is not.

But for classroom use the most serious problem with both thematically and chronologically organized anthologies is that they lose the sense of the Journal's dailiness—the rhythm of observation and reflection that became a discipline for Thoreau in the Journal's mature period. The Journal's eloquent prose, when taken outside the context of its dailiness—the interruptions, hesitations, stranded thoughts, rhetorical fumbling, and *in*eloquent prose—loses the ground from which eloquence comes into being. To read the Journal for its gems is to miss the nature of Thoreau's enterprise.

The Journal, in its fullness, exhibits an extraordinarily wide-ranging imagination that reaches out ceaselessly and often randomly to relate the diverse things of this world. This process—what I have elsewhere called the relational imagination (*Morning Work*, chapter 3)—is ultimately at the service of an evolving vision of the cosmos. Omitting the Journal's random elements and the play of those elements restricts our perception of Thoreau's vision as much as omitting the cetology chapters from *Moby-Dick* limits our view of Melville's vision. Another analogy would be trying to read Whitman's *Song of Myself* without the catalogs.

In discussing the advantages and disadvantages of using anthologies, I mean to make this larger point: As important as it is for students to learn the characteristic topics in Thoreau's Journal, it is more important still for them to learn the process of his journal keeping. And the only way to teach that process is to give students an extended, uninterrupted portion of the text (which may involve some inconvenience, as I indicate below). It almost doesn't matter what portion we choose—with one important qualification. The Journal before 1850 is fragmentary, with many missing and lost pages; further, it was not until the early 1850s that Thoreau came to understand his journal as a work. For these reasons I would choose for classroom examination a period from the 1850s or early 1860s.

The period between 1850 and 1854, the year *Walden* was published, is particularly rich in intellectual discovery for Thoreau. During these years he absorbs European Romanticism, sets the direction for his natural history projects, and refines his political and moral attitudes toward slavery. The insights earned result in major new developments in the composition of *Walden*, but they have their first expression in the Journal, appearing there in distinctive, often dramatic, form. For this reason, a text chosen from the early 1850s will always provide exciting reading for students, though they should be alerted that the intellectual intensity of this period makes it somewhat unrepresentative of the Journal as a whole.

It is a commonplace of Thoreau criticism to say that the Journal in the late 1850s and early 1860s, when it is dominated by empirical observation associated with the writer's natural history projects, lacks interest for modern readers. But, in fact, the later Journal has its own fascinating aspects. In it, we see Thoreau confirming his understanding of natural law and moving toward a more consolidated vision of the cosmos. "It takes us many years," he writes on 5 May 1860, "to find out that Nature repeats herself annually. But how perfectly regular and calculable all her phenomena must appear to a mind that has observed her for a thousand years!" (*Journal* [1906] 13: 279).[2] As this sentence indicates, the later Journal has its own form of eloquence and presents opportunities for teachers who emphasize Thoreau's relation to nature.

What, then, is a viable time frame of the Journal for classroom consideration? The answer to this question depends, of course, on one's pedagogical purposes and on the amount of time to be devoted to the Journal. If one's schedule is tight, a month or a season of any year after 1850 could serve at least to acquaint students with Thoreau's procedures and some of his issues. My own preference is a full year, which can mean following Thoreau either through a calendar year or through an annual cycle beginning at any point. Such a strategy is faithful to the Journal's development, because Thoreau thought in calendrical terms. The Journal was, among its many uses to him, a vast calendar of annual phenomena, a calendar whose purpose was to study the nature of time and change. The symbolic significance of seasonal variation is at least as important an issue in the Journal as it is in *Walden*.

Once the teacher has decided on a period of the Journal to read with students, a text must be found for them. The emerging Princeton edition certainly is the best choice, not only because of its accuracy and relative completeness (it restores many passages set aside by the 1906 editors) but also because it is more faithful to Thoreau's punctuation. For example, the dash with which Thoreau so often closes a thought—preserved in the Princeton edition—conveys the active, transitive force of his journal style. Arguably, the dash is as important to Thoreau's journal prose as it is to Emily Dickinson's poetry.

The Princeton edition now runs to five volumes, taking the Journal to March of 1853. The obvious disadvantage of this hardcover edition is its cost, but with a relatively small class copies made available in the library may suffice. An alternative is the paperback volume *A Year in Thoreau's Journal: 1851*, which reproduces a full, uninterrupted year of the Princeton text. In any study of the Journal, regardless of which text the students are reading, copies of all existing Princeton Journal volumes should be made available in the library, for their invaluable historical introductions and textual commentaries.

If the teacher wants to focus on a period beyond the point where the Princeton edition leaves off, the 1906 edition can serve reasonably well. One fact to keep in mind is that the farther one goes into the Journal chronologically, the more complete and generally reliable the 1906 edition tends to be. Most college and university libraries own it, either in the original Houghton Mifflin edition or in one of the two reprints.

For most pedagogical purposes, the shortcomings of the 1906 edition are not significant. When using it, I advise my students that its running heads and month divisions were put there by editors, and I alert them to some of the edition's other idiosyncrasies. By showing the students a facsimile of a page or two of the Journal manuscript (available in the Princeton edition volumes), I can give them a vivid sense of Thoreau's actual format. Comparison of the Journal's printed format in the 1906 version with that in the Princeton version can itself become an interesting topic for discussion, since editorial formats inevitably reflect prevailing critical assumptions about the nature of literary textuality (see Neufeldt, "Praetextus").

Using the 1906 edition has one large pedagogical advantage: it affords the possibility of asking every student in a seminar-sized class to read from a different period in the Journal. Each student in the class can check out from the library one of the following thirteen volumes: Princeton volumes 3, 4, and 5, which cover the period from 1850 to 1853, and the 1906 edition volumes 5 through 14, which take the Journal from 1853 to its close in 1861. Oral reports from the students can then create a composite view of the Journal's development, with all the shifting emphases that that development exhibits.

Once there is a text and students reading it, what should the teacher say to them? The most important thing, I believe, is not to overinstruct. We teachers and scholars ourselves are just coming into knowledge of the Journal and therefore have not the kind of intimacy or fluency with it that we have with works like *The Scarlet Letter*. It's altogether possible that our students' responses to the Journal will be state-of-the-art insights, and we ought to encourage firsthand engagement most of all.

At the outset of teaching the Journal, it is useful to sketch the broad outlines of its development, pointing especially to the shift in the early 1850s toward a self-consciously literary form. Then questions *about* form can follow: If Thoreau saw his Journal as a literary work, then in what senses is it literary? What does it share with other confessional forms, such as letters, diaries, memoirs, and autobiographies? How does Thoreau's Journal resemble those forms, and how does it differ from them? For example, does the fictionality of Thoreau's Journal (alluded to earlier) resemble the fictional qualities of autobiography? One thing to be gained from such discussions is an enlargement of the students' sense of what is literary.

Comparing the Journal with *Walden*, in the ways I indicated above, can be effective in focusing discussion of the Journal's mode and formal characteristics, as long as the students' attention is not excessively drawn to the more familiar work. Especially rich comparisons, I have found, result from a discussion of the ways that both the Journal and *Walden* elide dimensions of experience, each work creating its own distinctive version, or fiction, of a life. Such a discussion pries students away from their initial assumption that the Journal is merely a source for the text of *Walden*. They should come to understand that both works, despite their different modes, are texts whose relation to each other is more dialogic than hierarchical.

Because so much of the Journal is given to landscape description, nature writing provides another excellent context for comparative study. Works in this genre with informal, diary-like structures, like John Muir's *My First Summer in the Sierra* (1911), are especially useful to compare with the Journal. As I suggest elsewhere ("Better Mythology"), the legacy of Thoreau's Journal to the work of later nature writers is procedural and formal as well as thematic, and the most rewarding classroom discussions emphasize both aspects.

The journals of other writers, such as Emerson (*Emerson in His Journals*), can provide further contrasts, through which students will quickly discover the unusual and distinctive features of Thoreau's journal keeping. It is always fruitful to have them keep their own journals while they are reading Thoreau's; this gives them firsthand experience of the formal and psychic demands of journal writing. But this kind of exercise needs to be carefully structured, so that the focus is on Thoreau's (rather than on the students') prose.

Related to all the issues raised by comparison is the issue of audience. To whom does the writer of the Journal speak? To posthumous readers? To another version of the writer's self? To a Thoreau whose future reading of his present writing might help him grasp the direction and meaning of change?[3] Once we have engaged the Journal around the issue of audience, we have discovered yet another relation between the Journal and other forms of literature.

In the end, however, it is a mistake to lead students to believe that all questions pertaining to the Journal reduce to matters of style and mode of presentation. The Journal was many things for Thoreau, but most of all it was a living endeavor, a way of being in the world. Thoreau himself would have considered it trivial to engage the Journal solely in formal terms, because for him it was a vast project aimed at developing and expressing a comprehensive vision of nature and human life. To miss his sheer, outrageous ambition is to miss one of the Journal's essential aspects.

NOTES

[1]For a description of how Blake made his selections from Thoreau's manuscript, see Howarth, *Literary Manuscripts* xxi–xxiii. The collection of the Journal's passages about birds is Thoreau, *Notes*.

[2]Teachers unfamiliar with the 1906 edition of Thoreau's complete works should note its double numbering of the fourteen Journal volumes it contains. One numbering gives their position in the full twenty-volume set; the other is independent. In this volume all references to the 1906 edition of the Journal use the independent numbering. The reference of this note, therefore, is to the thirteenth volume of Thoreau's *Journal*, which is the nineteenth volume of Thoreau's *Writings*.

[3]Cameron provocatively explores the possibility of Thoreau imagining a posthumous audience (81–83, 98–104). For the idea of the Journal as a medium for understanding change, see my *Morning Work* 44–46, 90–102.

Thoreau in the Wilderness

David G. Fuller

During spring interim, a colleague and I conducted an experiment by offering a course, Thoreau and the Wilderness Experience, that gave us the opportunity to teach Thoreau in an uncommon but appropriate way. We believed that students, by reading selections of his works and going on a wilderness trip, would develop a deeper appreciation for Thoreau and a better understanding of his literature. The plan was to read selected works of Thoreau, canoe in the wilderness as Thoreau did in Maine, keep a journal, and write an essay for publication in a course book. As it turned out, the class, the wilderness experience, and the writing far exceeded our expectations.

Our assumption in planning the course was that an intellectual grasp of Thoreau would be made more meaningful when reading was combined with experience. Thoreau acknowledges in *Walden* "[t]o read well, that is, to read true books in a true spirit, is a noble exercise . . ." (101–02), but he warns that "while we are confined to books . . . we are in danger of forgetting the language which all things and events speak without metaphor, which alone is copious and standard" (111). The copious language that speaks without metaphor is the language of nature and life experience, a language embodied in Thoreau's notion of wildness. His question, "Will you be a reader, a student merely, or a seer?" (111), made us see our students not only as scholars and readers of books but also as alert observers of and participants in the wilderness. Our aim was to lead the participants, as Thoreau writes in *Walden*, to "become essentially students and observers" (99) capable of understanding his literature and the copious language of the wilderness.

The course included three-hour class meetings and a ten-day canoe trip in the Boundary Waters Canoe Area (BWCA) in northern Minnesota, a primitive region designated restricted wilderness. Although the BWCA is approximately 1,600 miles and 150 years away from Thoreau's Maine wilderness, it is strikingly similar to what Thoreau encountered in his three trips described in *The Maine Woods* and therefore an ideal setting for an experience of Thoreau's wildness.

The students possessed little if any experience with either the wilderness or Thoreau. We required them to read *The Maine Woods*, selections from *Walden*, and John McPhee's *The Survival of the Bark Canoe*, which includes a description of McPhee's trip retracing one of Thoreau's itineraries in Maine. The class discussions were lively, with students sharing a variety of responses to passages in *The Maine Woods* and noting Thoreau's observations and experiences in the wilderness. Anticipating their own sighting of moose, they were particularly interested in his specific and sensitive descriptions of moose and other wildlife. We discussed Thoreau's remarks about distinctions between the civilized and primitive; his comments about Native Americans, particularly Joe Polis; and his exclamation "*Contact! Contact! Who* are we? *where* are we?" (*Maine Woods* 71). The *Walden* chapters "Solitude," "The Ponds," "Higher Laws," and "Spring" offered us many opportunities to make connections among Thoreau's views on the significance of water, one's relation to the wilderness, and the meaning of spring. Finally, McPhee's book provided an important modern perspective on Thoreau's journey and allowed us to envision the connection between the trips in Maine and our forthcoming trip to the wilderness in Minnesota.

The second Sunday in May our group departed for northern Minnesota, and the following day we were on the water and paddling and portaging nearly fifteen miles. Observing the students' exhaustion and silence at the first campsite, I was reminded of Thoreau's remark at the end of the essay "Ktaadn" that the wilderness of Maine was "even more grim and wild than you had anticipated, a damp and intricate wilderness, in the spring everywhere wet and miry" (80). It was obvious that the students did not realize what it meant to leave the comforts of home and rely on rustic conveniences. Nonetheless, over the next ten days we experienced Thoreau's wilderness, as he described it, a "country full of evergreen trees, of mossy silver birches and watery maples, the ground . . . strewn with damp and moss-grown rocks—a country diversified with innumerable lakes and rapid streams . . ." (80).

The days of paddling and carrying equipment across difficult portages ended in quiet, restful evenings, with all participants writing in their journals. Students experienced the solitude and could identify with Thoreau's remark, "I never found the companion that was so companionable as solitude" (*Walden* 135). They recorded and contemplated each day's events in their journals, a practice to which Thoreau (they knew) devoted countless hours, and later, around the campfire, they talked about their reading and the incidents of the day—the loons, bears, eagles, wolf and moose tracks, rapids, and portages. Topics of the talk both during the day and in the evening were notably similar to the subject matter of *The Maine Woods*: where to find firewood, when to begin the meals, how to deal with the insects or the weather, how to locate campsites. Recognizing the connections between the actual experience and the details in the literature, the students appreciated more fully Thoreau's literature and special sense of nature and the wilderness.

At the end of the ten days, they were much more comfortable in the wilderness than they had been at the beginning of the trip. They were also more receptive and aware of the sense of wilderness in Thoreau's writing. In fact, the reading and the trip seemed to inspire a new appreciation of Thoreau. A former Boy Scout leader, admitting that before the trip he believed that what Thoreau wrote could have been "written in one-third of the space," said that he now thought much more of Thoreau for his love and respect for the wilderness. Others expressed similar feelings, but the influence of the trip and the reading became obvious in the essays the students wrote on our return.

The essays gave simple and sincere accounts of the participants' experiences; they contained both sensitive readings of Thoreau and alert observations of the wilderness. It was apparent that the writers used their journals, as Thoreau had done, as a basis for the essays. In many ways the essays resembled Thoreau's own accounts in *The Maine Woods*: close descriptions of the flora and fauna, observations of the people on the trip, and insightful remarks about the writer's connections to the wilderness.

One student, who had never experienced the wilderness and who was a bit fearful of leaving the comforts of home, drew parallels between Thoreau's campsites and those of our trip. She referred to a line from her journal, "It is amazing how each day we inhabit a strange campsite, which by nightfall seems naturally like home," and remembered Thoreau's observation that a place chosen as a camp becomes like home. Her essay focused on ambivalence of place, on a new sense of wilderness. She acknowledged that living in the wilderness had helped her put "a lot of things in perspective" about what was important in her life and what she could live without. She concluded that Thoreau had captured for her the "essence of this feeling."

The essays showed that the students now recognized more clearly the distinction between the civilized and the primitive. One wrote: "For the first time in my life I was angry to hear a motorized vehicle, as it seemed to disturb the beauty of the wilderness. Being the mechanical-minded person that I am, I never thought that I would see the day that I would resent such an otherwise minor consideration. I could now relate to Thoreau as he spoke of an untouched natural environment." Another student noted, "On our last day back into civilization we heard the grating sound of whining motorboats." She recalled a passage from *The Maine Woods* in which Thoreau responds to the disconcerting sound of a gunshot and says that the "crashing noise" affected him "like an insult to nature" (192).

Another writer showed a special interest in the subtle balance between the perceived dangers and safety of the wilderness. She wrote that when one is faced with dangers in the wilds of northern Minnesota, one should heed Thoreau's warning not to stop to be scared since there are "more terrible things to come" (*Journal* [1906] 2: 45). She remembered her fear when she heard the "hollow drumming" of the ruffed grouse; she felt her heart "beating in unison with the drummer's tune." With that recollection she pointed to Thoreau's remark that the partridge's beat "falls still with a remarkably forcible, almost painful, impulse on the ear" (*Journal* [1906] 5: 144). Attempting to understand this fear, she noted Thoreau's observation that experience is in both "the fingers and head" and that the "heart is inexperienced" (*Journal* [1906] 1: 358). She seemed to come to terms with her fear, writing, "But once the canoe has penetrated into the heart of Quetico-Superior's darkness and the hands and head have become experienced in her glory, you find yourself moving into the darkness of your own inexperienced heart."

She recognized the profound tranquillity of the wilderness. Although being lost in the woods had seemed at first a terrible prospect, she now accepted Thoreau's statement that "[n]ot till we are lost, in other words, not till we have lost the world, do we begin to find ourselves, and realize where we are and the infinite extent of our relations" (*Walden* 171). By leaving the familiar comforts and security of civilization and going to the woods, she concluded, she was able to better understand herself and her relationship with others. "These moments of solitude for self-exploration are as much longed for by the Quetico-Superior paddler as by Thoreau, and you soon learn to relish them above all others."

A thirty-year-old mother of two wrote that she wanted to get away "to front only the essential facts of life" and learn how to canoe. She explained that out of necessity she had stayed at home for almost five years, and it was now time to see if she "could still function as an individual" outside the family and live by the rule "Simplicity, simplicity, simplicity!" (91). She observed, "It was this wildness and its voices that I wanted to experience." She noted that the course and trip had allowed her, as Thoreau put it, "to live deep" (91), and she concluded that she had indeed "lived deep for over a week; a deliberate life of beauty, new impressions, fellowship, solitude, and simplicity." She said she "wanted to carry the wilderness with [her] for a while."

The essays, often quoting from Thoreau's works, included observations and details similar to those in *The Maine Woods*. For example, many of the essays contained references to loons. Two writers remembered the loon calls in the BWCA and agreed with Thoreau's observation that loons sometimes sound "singularly human" to the ear (*Maine Woods* 224).

Without a doubt, the most rewarding feature of the essays was the provocative connections made between our canoe trip and Thoreau's experience and philosophy. The essays demonstrated to my colleague and me that the participants in our course had become students and observers of both Thoreau and the wilderness. One student put it this way: "How little did I realize the full impact that Mr. Thoreau would finally have on my life." The effect on the students and instructors alike came from a unique opportunity to connect his books and his sense of the wild. In our course, students did indeed experience the reading of Thoreau in his true spirit—and the reading of that other, equally noble and copious, language of the wilderness.

"Monarch of All I Survey":
Thoreau among Engineering Students
Wesley T. Mott

With respect to landscapes,—

"I am monarch of all I *survey,*
My right there is none to dispute."
—Thoreau

"[I]nstead of engineering for all America," Ralph Waldo Emerson lamented in his eulogy for Henry David Thoreau, "he was the captain of a huckleberry-party" (Emerson, "Thoreau" 480). For many readers this quip has fixed the image of Thoreau as an irresponsible, fuzzy-brained transcendentalist. Engineering majors, however, can find Thoreau accessible in ways that might surprise English professors who assume that the prickly idealist will alienate students preparing for a rigorous profession. Thoreau's renowned skill at determining metes and bounds provided him with income, sharpened his naturalist's talent for precise observation and measurement, and presented an opportunity (sometimes an excuse) to get outdoors. With his insistence on exactness and his uncanny grasp of the actual, he drew on surveying—on engineering—for more than tropes for *Walden.*

In teaching Thoreau to engineering majors, I brandish three marvelous propaganda tools: the lithograph of Walden Pond, based on Thoreau's own survey, from the first edition of *Walden;* H. F. Walling's 1852 map of Concord, which uses Thoreau's pond surveys and credits "H. D. Thoreau, Civil Engineer"; and the Duke University civil engineering professor Henry Petroski's beautifully illustrated article "H. D. Thoreau, Engineer." (See also Petroski's "An American Pencil-Making Family," *The Pencil: A History of Design and Circumstance.*) Henry Thoreau *was* a surveyor—and thus by the preprofessional standards of his day also a civil engineer. Because he refined the ingredients of and manufactured his family's award-winning pencils, I am not beneath claiming him as a chemical and mechanical engineer as well.

Beyond the classroom, Thoreau and *Walden* have proved particularly well suited to a distinctive project degree requirement at Worcester Polytechnic Institute. All students at WPI (most of whom are science or engineering majors) must complete an interactive qualifying project (IQP), which is usually undertaken in the junior year and is the equivalent of three courses. Students, usually in teams of two to four, examine the interaction of science or technology with an issue having social or humanistic implications. Topics may be suggested by faculty members, students, or an outside party acting as a "client." The team submits a preliminary proposal to its adviser that demonstrates familiarity with the topic, sets objectives, and gives a timeline. Because the IQP presumes that writing is collaborative and a means of learning, this proposal—and its continual revision—often becomes the basis of meetings held at least weekly with the adviser. The balance of the week is spent working on-site with the host organization, doing research, and holding team meetings as determined by the students.

The IQP, it must be stressed, is not an internship, nor is it busywork or a feeble gesture in making the humanities "relevant" to the professions. Students are expected to do original research culminating in a substantial report (from fifty to more than two hundred pages); a copy is sent to the sponsoring organization, and a copy is permanently deposited in the WPI library.

The IQP is designed, according to the college's literature, as a key to promoting "humanistically educated engineers." William Grogan, who pioneered WPI's project-based curriculum, is fond of quoting graduates who tell him that a project in their technical field got them their jobs but that the IQP changed their lives. Indeed, Thoreau, who wrote *Walden* "to wake [his] neighbors up" (84), has exerted his transforming power on three recent IQPs.

In 1989, when Tom Blanding and his Thoreau Country Conservation Alliance (TCCA) were urgently calling attention to the imminent threat of two commercial developments within historic Walden Woods, Malcolm FitzPatrick, a civil engineering professor, and I proposed the IQP topic Which Way Walden? Four students—Daniel Berk, James Callahan, Stephen Lotterhand, and Bernardino Nanni—registered for this topic, embarking on a project with three goals: "(1) to study the history of the Walden Pond reservation, including past debates about its use and maintenance; (2) to assess the current debate between developers and preservationists by examining local ordinances, state law, and sound civil-engineering practice; and (3) to prepare a written report incorporating this background and a plan for management of the area." Only Berk had read *Walden* before starting the IQP, which seemed a straightforward exercise in rational problem solving.

But this IQP team, like most, discovered that in the real world, knowledge, let alone wisdom, is found less in formulating neat plans of work than in challenging one's preconceptions, coping with obstacles, dealing with different kinds of people. Perhaps most important, the team members discovered that neither scholarship nor their own professional activities were value-free. Early objectives of finding the solution to the dilemma of Walden Woods soon evaporated as the students observed the gifted and committed people already struggling with the issue. Working with Vidar Jorgensen, a TCCA board member, they made more limited but more concrete contributions, such as identifying landowners within Walden Woods, an important step in creating an inventory of the 2,680-acre tract. And they found that their mapping skills were really needed. Their final ninety-seven-page IQP report was not the cautious analysis of "rights in conflict" we had all initially expected; it was a committed defense of the cultural and ecological uniqueness of Walden Woods, accompanied by original maps systematically laying out such land-use factors as zoning, hydrogeology, and traffic. The tone of the report is far from the charged urgency of Thoreau's opening of "A Plea for Captain John Brown" ("I do not wish to force my thoughts upon you, but I feel forced myself" [*Reform Papers* 111]). But the four students to varying degrees were changed by their project. They found that research results need not be coldly neutral. And they found, to their great satisfaction, that engineering and the humanities are not necessarily adversarial. Their own talents and education could be used in the service of a cause higher than mere commercial development.

The second Thoreau IQP—Thoreau Country Mapping Project: The Concord Region (1989–90)—was initially conceived as an attempt to update (and, where possible, to correct) Herbert Gleason's classic 1906 map of "Thoreau Country." The Gleason map, still historically significant, is not drawn to scale and contains topographical inaccuracies. Tracey Barnes, Scott Odierno, and Melissa Perry were sponsored by Tom Blanding, who suggested that such a map could both heighten awareness of the immediate battle to save Walden Woods and set an example for future efforts to identify and preserve sites farther afield that had important associations with Thoreau. The students, advised by Malcolm FitzPatrick and me, worked closely with Walter Brain, a TCCA director and expert on Thoreau sites, and Edmund Schofield, president of the Thoreau Society; they consulted with Anne McGrath and Dick O'Connor, of the Thoreau Lyceum; with Concord town officials; and with members of regional environmental groups.

As had the first IQP team, the second team confronted the obstacles of time, limited resources, and technical complexity. Not trained cartographers, they quickly accepted that they would not be able to physically produce an updated map. What they did accomplish was to translate the Gleason map to the scale of a United States Geological Survey topographical map of the Concord region and analyze natural features and human landmarks separately by laying sheets of tracing paper over the master map on a light table. Their report contained guidelines for a cartographer to consider. The stunning Walden Woods map eventually produced by the TCCA and the Walden Woods Project drew on professional resources beyond the capabilities of the IQP team, but the students had the satisfaction of being among the first to struggle with the accuracy of Gleason's map. Moreover, they envisioned the wider implications of preserving "Thoreau country." They created a computer database of the placenames in *Walden*, *A Week on the Concord and Merrimack Rivers*, and the first two volumes of the Princeton edition of the Journal as a tool for both scholars and conservationists. Each entry includes the name of the site, location by town and state, an identifier (e.g., river, town, hill), source in Thoreau's writings, and dates associated with the site.

The third Thoreau IQP exemplifies ways in which undergraduate non-English majors can conduct research that complements the professional interests of their advisers—on a level of sophistication normally associated with graduate students. In 1990, I was actively involved, along with my colleague Kent Ljungquist, in planning events for The Thoreau Society Jubilee, a two-week fiftieth-anniversary celebration that featured panels, lectures, musical performances, tours, and exhibits. Craig Perno, a computer science major who had expressed interest in Thoreau, agreed to an IQP that would help us meet one of our commitments: to arrange an exhibit titled *Thoreau as Surveyor and Engineer* at the college's Gordon Library, since WPI was hosting several of the jubilee's programs and sessions. Perno did not simply outline Thoreau's career as surveyor and the use of surveying tropes in his writings; he grounded his research in nineteenth-century surveying literature to determine the practices and equipment Thoreau would have used. Working with the college librarian Albert Anderson (who loaned to the exhibit his first-edition *Walden*) and the WPI archivist Lora Brueck, Perno selected photos, maps, and period surveying instruments and wrote the cards for the exhibit installed by Brueck. Besides writing the required IQP report, he participated in the 9 July 1991 Thoreau jubilee session "Thoreau as Surveyor and Engineer" along with the leading authorities on the subject, Marcia Moss, curator of the Concord Free Public Library, and Henry Petroski, of Duke University. Perno's poised, enthusiastic talk was warmly received by an audience of Thoreau aficionados—a remarkable feat for a junior computer science major and evidence of the confidence a student can derive from a well-done IQP.

However fundamental classroom knowledge may be, the IQP is a synthesis offering special benefits. To the external clients it means a real service: relatively sophisticated consulting and a written report at no cost other than giving students the opportunity to do original research. The three Thoreau projects tangibly helped organizations whose mission is to foster appreciation of Thoreau's writings and philosophy and to preserve a literal part of his legacy.

To faculty members the IQP affords a continually fresh teaching experience and gives new perspectives on familiar subjects. Though IQPs often build on earlier projects with new crops of students, an adviser has "several more lives to live." Thoreau, after an IQP, cannot seem narrowly literary or the domain only of English departments. Indeed, the IQP is interdisciplinary as well as genuinely collaborative (a current pedagogical buzzword) not only for students but also for faculty members, who typically coadvise with members of other departments. The need to reach beyond the standard course format, moreover, nudges the professor to confront that older cliché—the real world beyond the ivory tower, the world in which the writers we teach actually lived and moved and had their being. In my own case, advising the Walden Woods IQP led directly to active involvement with the Walden Woods Project organized by recording artist Don Henley to raise money to purchase the threatened tracts of land identified by the TCCA.

In richly rewarding ways, IQPs infuse both classroom and scholarship with new materials, insights, and approaches. Faculty members and students at WPI share the belief that teaching, research, and service—the triad we all pay lip service to—can indeed be a seamless whole. Whatever the topic, an IQP fosters a sense of personal investment in the subject.

Faculty members at colleges and universities without project-based curricula and without the advantage of proximity to Concord can still adopt IQP-type programs. It might be difficult to allocate three courses' worth of credit to a Thoreau project, but many colleges at least offer independent study opportunities. Exhibits are not only possible but sought and appreciated at most institutions. And interdisciplinary faculty-student teams would be welcome in many communities engaged in land-use controversies and other conservation issues like those facing Walden Woods.

In this regard, the IQP responds to Thoreau's own critique of a college education that defrauds the student. He does not mean "exactly" that students should balance intellectual training with manual labor:

> I mean that they should not *play* life, or *study* it merely, while the community supports them at this expensive game, but earnestly *live* it from beginning to end. How could youths better learn to live than by at once trying the experiment of living? . . . I would not pursue the common course, which is merely to send [youths] into the neighborhood of some professor, where any thing is professed and practised but the art of life.
>
> (*Walden* 51)

Those at WPI who worked on Thoreau know that they have done far more than merely study him; they have contributed their professional talents to issues that mattered to him. They have come to appreciate the effect of their prospective engineering careers on that hitherto abstract world of society and culture we profess. The creative tension between the literary and the technical that the Thoreau IQPs demand is the hallmark of Thoreau himself. What else does he celebrate in *Walden* but a dialectic of the intellectual and the physical, the spiritual and the natural, the private and the social, the ideal and the literal?

Emerson's infamous assessment of Thoreau is invoked by two diametrically opposed camps: those who accept the sentence at face value and those who turn it back on Emerson as a sign of his obtuseness. For both, paradoxically, the remark serves as the definitive pronouncement on Thoreau's supposed lack of ambition, his failure to engage in the affairs of the world. Emerson's statement, I think, is more subtle than as usually read, expressing not bald condemnation but bittersweet whimsy, a personal sense of loss. Whatever Emerson meant, he could not have foreseen the ways in which Thoreau continues to speak directly even to engineers.

Sauntering after Sixty:
Thoreau in the Elderhostel Program

Gordon V. Boudreau

> When we can no longer ramble in the fields of Nature,
> we ramble in the fields of thought & literature. The old
> become readers—Our heads retain their strength when
> our legs have become weak.
>
> —Thoreau

> What sort of fruit comes of living as if you were a going
> to die? Live rather as if you were coming to life. How
> can the end of living be death? The end of living is life.
> Living is an active transitive state to life— Life in the
> green state.
>
> —Thoreau

No one in the pantheon of American authors has written more pointedly of the value of a continuing, liberal, and liberating education than Henry David Thoreau, though he was very apt to express his concern in negatives: "How vain to try to teach youth, or anybody, truths! They can only learn them after their own fashion, and when they get ready" (*Journal* [1906] 13: 67). A glance at the history of the Elderhostel program drives home the fact that many in our population over sixty years of age are indeed ready. The program, which in this country began in 1976, has already accommodated more than three-quarters of a million people in sessions usually of a week's duration. Sessions now are offered at 1,800 colleges, universities, conference and environmental education centers, retreat houses, and the like. In 1992, nearly 250,000 hostelers participated in programs offered in all fifty states, the ten Canadian provinces, and over forty-five countries around the world.[1] With the swelling of the gray generation, the movement will likely continue to grow. Moreover, these students—who seek no credit, take no exams, submit no papers—return again and again. In a session held at the Stella Maris retreat house on the shores of Skaneateles Lake in upstate New York, one veteran hosteler was attending his ninety-fifth session, another his forty-third, and a married couple their twenty-eighth together.

These participants vary a great deal, to be sure. In recent sessions at Stella Maris and Le Moyne College, attendees included a toolmaker; a former chief justice of the supreme court of an eastern state; an ophthalmologist; a Chinese linguist who had spent some thirty years in the Far East serving the State Department; a building contractor; a woman who, convinced that the door to becoming a college professor of English was closed to her, had instead become a lawyer; a Roman Catholic nun who was actively opposing a toxic landfill in upstate rural New York; and a former chair of the chemistry department of a major university.

What these Elderhostelers almost surely have in common, whatever their diversity, is a habit of reading and so the knowledge of the affective potency of words. In idle moments, one can almost always find an Elderhosteler at work on a crossword puzzle. Since Thoreau was himself a "chain reader," in the view of Robert Richardson (*Life* 245), and owned half a dozen dictionaries, a common ground of subject and audience seemed assured in my focusing on Thoreau's love of words. What I did not expect in my first presentation was a dash of resistance—of animosity, even—toward our nation's most persistent gadfly: Thoreau, "a tough butt for the choppers" (*Journal* [1906] 8: 140), may still rub as many the wrong way as he does the right way. "What good did he ever contribute?" one gentleman stridently queried, seeing in Thoreau an exemplar of the unproductive, even as Emerson had. Some students may have had painful encounters with such challengers of the establishment as Thoreau inspired or gave sustenance to, especially in the late 1960s and early 1970s, perhaps in their own families, businesses, professions.

Women in these groups—typically there are more women than men—seem more sympathetic to Thoreau, especially for his love of nature. Still, one particularly contentious woman was incensed at Thoreau; she called him a phony who never strayed beyond the range or aroma of Emerson's kitchen. "Was he gay?" she asked. "Was his mother domineering?" "Was he a . . ."—here she hung fire over the most damning charge—"a hippie?" The spirit of Lowell and Holmes still has its proponents concerning Thoreau's reputation, even in Concord.

One of the problems in teaching an Elderhostel session is uncertainty about the students' familiarity with Thoreau's works. While some may have read the whole of *Walden* and perhaps "Civil Disobedience," few if any will have read *A Week on the Concord and Merrimack Rivers* or such nature essays as "Autumnal Tints" and "Walking." And if they once studied *Walden* at college, it was during the depression or in the years during or bracketing World War II. Where, in short, was I to begin, and with what assumptions? In addition, there were the constraints of time. Programs vary at different sites, to be sure. In some a professor might have a whole week. As one of five Le Moyne College scholars in a week-long program, I was allotted but a single day.

I began the first of my three seventy-five-minute sessions by noting that Thoreau was invoked to propagandize the causes of three simmering movements that simultaneously came to a boil in the spring of 1971: the antiwar movement, the civil rights movement, and the ecological movement. To place Thoreau in the context of his own time, I next briefly traced the religious, philosophical, and literary antecedents of transcendentalism and the displacement of the former age's conception of a mechanical universe, represented metaphorically as a clock, by its conception of the universe as organic, represented as a tree or seed.

Soon there were questions about the meaning of *transcendental* and about Kantian notions of a priori knowledge. A passage from Sampson Reed's oration "On Genius," given at Emerson's Harvard commencement in 1821, effectively conveyed not only the transcendentalists' perception of the process of learning but the organic metaphor as well. In his address, Reed challenged John Locke's notion that we enter the world with a mind that is a tabula rasa, asserting instead that "the mind of the infant contains within itself the first rudiments of all that will be hereafter, and needs nothing but expansion, as the leaves and branches and fruit of a tree are said to exist in the seed from which it springs" (67). The etymology of *education* (*e-ducere* 'to draw out from'), the excitement of the transcendentalists over the "kindergarten" (garden of children) experiment, and the teaching theories and practices of such zealots as Bronson Alcott, Elizabeth Palmer Peabody, and Margaret Fuller—all these illustrated the transcendentalists' attraction to the a priori theory and the organic metaphor.

An appeal to shared experiences also seemed to work. Why should particularly affecting statements seem to us not merely true but in a sense foreknown—for instance, passages preserved in the margins of our high school or college notebooks, passages such as Shakespeare's "Lilies that fester smell far worse than weeds" (sonnet 94) or the advice in *Hamlet*, "to thine own self be true" (1.3.78)? Does the shock of recognition testify to a prior knowledge? Do Shakespeare's words of themselves make truths, or do they dis-cover, ex-press from the tips of our inarticulate tongues what is wombed in our unconscious? I once read of an East Indian telling an anthropologist that stories told to their children did not teach but only reminded them of what they already knew. Or, as Frederick Douglass put it, reading "one of Sheridan's mighty speeches . . . gave tongue to interesting thoughts of my own soul, which had frequently flashed through my mind, and died away for want of utterance" (*Narrative* 55).

Another effective appeal I made was to the students' artistic experience, since most had suffered some birth pangs of creativity, whether in language, music, or painting. How do we know when our word choice is absolutely right, the word one with the thing, the curve true, the chord resonant? Or, conversely, how do we know—know just as surely—that it isn't right? In such matters, the two chief definitions of poet may be pertinent: the poet as maker, and quite proud of the results of his labor, as Poe in his "Philosophy of Composition" recounts—or fables—how he wrote "The Raven"; and the poet as seer, as Michelangelo was, discovering what was implicit in the stone, the ideal figure that he could only reveal by his workmanship and, humbled by the vision, that he could only imperfectly render by his art. Is artful language invented? assigned? Or is it instead a skin? Are words the scoriae of nature, as Emerson suggests (*Nature* 23), and the right word a realization, a revelation, an uncovering? Are words agreed-upon tokens, counters for meaning? Or are they meaning itself? As I taught, glowing countenances suggested that experiences in living had given many of the students a sense of matters that I was only educing. At two sessions, participants related the transcendentalist theory of language with Noam Chomsky's theory of a natural grammar.

Having thus presented the a priori idea, held out a metaphorical object (the seed) to grow in the mind, and appealed to their personal experiences of wrestling with the angel Art, I next briefly described the Concord of Thoreau's day and the early career of Emerson: his resignation from the ministry, his trip to Europe (a "reorientation," as Joel Porte brilliantly describes it in his chapter "Eastering" [*Representative Man* 53–69]), and the publication of *Nature* in 1836. Only then did I deal with the influence of Emerson on his neighbor Thoreau, which began in 1837 and prompted Thoreau to record his observations in what would become a two-million-word journal.

The students were curious about mundane matters. Quite simply, what did Thoreau look like? Reminded of Robert Frost's preference in potatoes for the kind that still had some dirt on them, real potatoes, I referred to the "Wanted" poster Walter Harding had distributed at a 1978 Thoreau program on psychology and the literary artist. It described a five-foot-seven, 127-pound societal nemesis who had chopped off one toe as a child, who had false teeth and piercing blue eyes, who had once—by accident or negligence—set a woods afire, and who after graduating from Harvard—which, he affirmed, taught "all of the branches but none of the roots" (Harding, *Days* 51)—had tried to reduce the necessity of working to six weeks out of the year. I then related the adventures that led to the two books published in his lifetime: his two-week journey on the Concord and Merrimack Rivers in the boat he and his brother John made, the shocking death of John by tetanus, and Henry's removal to Walden Pond where, in a cabin of his own construction, he wrote his first book and began his second, his masterpiece, *Walden.*

I next turned to the chapter "Language" in Emerson's *Nature*, reading aloud his famous dicta: "1. Words are signs of natural facts. 2. Particular natural facts are symbols of particular spiritual facts. 3. Nature is the symbol of spirit" (*Works* 1: 17). Then I lingered over Emerson's illustrations—"spirit" (wind), "transgression" (crossing a line), "supercilious" (raising of the eyebrow)—which interestingly uncover the fossil history of words (18). Such examples suggest, contrary to Locke's belief that language is an arbitrary creation of humanity, that nature itself determines language.

But while Emerson discussed the etymology of the word *spirit*, it was Thoreau who discovered the spirit or anima in the book of nature unfolding at his cabin door. "It is the characteristic of all religion and wisdom to . . . detect the *anima* or soul in every thing" (*Journal 1* 483), Thoreau wrote, and he indicated his means of detection by insisting that "the highest that we can attain to is not Knowledge, but Sympathy with Intelligence" ("Walking" 240). As a result, his most intimate experiences of animate nature grew from analogies, from putting himself in a posture of sympathetic identification, of under-standing: cornering a woodchuck and then using baby talk to communicate with it (*Journal 4* 453–55); standing on tiptoe on a knoll, flapping his arms and mimicking the honking of geese (*Journal* [1906] 7: 258); standing beside a swamp for hours, immersing himself in the bullfrog's study to study the bullfrog (Harding, *Days* 403–04). "All perception of truth is the detection of an analogy," Thoreau asserted. "[We] reason from our hands to our head" (*Journal 4* 46).

Not content to detect nature's anima, he wished to express it as well, insisting that "a history of animated nature must itself be animated" (*Journal* [1906] 13: 154). And his animated descriptions of a kitten, a fox, a rooster (*Journal* [1906] 14: 314–15; 8: 175–77; 11: 190–91), and a squirrel (*Walden* 273–75) each seem to appropriate the spirit of the animal he is at pains to describe, even to the rhythm and cadence of its movements. A few well-chosen examples go far to demonstrate this quality.

Moreover, sympathy with nature drew Thoreau insistently to the roots of living things, which for him included words. In "Walking," he wrote that the poet who would "give expression to Nature" is he who "transplanted" his words to the page "with earth adhering to their roots" (120). In their vital roots, both nature's and humanity's languages were expressions of the anima. In *A Week*, Thoreau observed that "a man's real faith is never contained in his creed." Digging into the soil of the word *religion*, he unearthed its root, *ligature*. Thus *religion* meant for him to "tie back" or reconnect. But he found that for most, what should be the "umbilical cord connecting them with divinity" was instead a cord that bound, cutting off circulation (*Week* 78, 64, 78). As for him, he practiced his religion in his sauntering, which connected him with the spirit of nature. In this sense he was a religious fundamentalist, a born-again saunterer ("*Ambulator nascitur, non fit*," as he wrote in "Walking" [207]), his worship generating a prose of joyous, vital mimicry of life at its source, life "near the bone" (*Walden* 329).

To exemplify his penchant for analogy, I foraged among index cards, mostly notes taken from his Journal when I was writing a book on Thoreau (*The Roots of* Walden). Some of his analogies reveal his quirkiness; others his penetration and expressive genius; still others his sense that all of nature has meaning, is a sentence, a language to be read with sympathy. "There are two sides to every sentence; the one is contiguous to me, but the other faces the gods, and no man ever fronted it" (*Journal 1* 220).

One of the most interesting—if not always appealing—aspects of Thoreau's personality is his contrariness; his penchant for seeking the paradoxical; his Protestant-ism; his reversals, the reversal even of his own name, which he changed from David Henry to Henry David; his sense of (for some the absence of) humor. From my accumulated notes I gave examples of stimulating (or irritating) contradictions and paradoxes. In matters of religion, Thoreau took a sometimes perverse delight in mocking the clergy or institutional religion. "I see dumb-bells in the minister's study, and some of their dumbness gets into his sermons"; and "Lectured in basement (vestry) of the orthodox church, and I trust helped to undermine it" (*Journal* [1906] 14: 111 and 9: 188). But he also suggested, in "Life without Principle," a worship of great depth and intimacy: "I have walked into such an arena [a lyceum] and done my best to make a clean breast of what religion I have experienced, and the audience never suspected what I was about" (*Reform Papers* 168).

About the elderly, too, Thoreau wrote sometimes with sympathy and generous understanding, as in the epigraphs to this essay (*Journal 3* 178–79; 30, respectively) but sometimes with scorn and obduracy: "Practically, the old have no very important advice to give the young, their own experience has been so partial, and their lives have been such miserable failures" (*Walden* 9). His remarks about women, not tempered for late-twentieth-century sensibilities, drew such scornful hoots during the class that I uneasily calculated the distance and trajectory to the nearest exit. For example: "In the east women religiously conceal that they have faces—in the west that they have legs. In both cases it is evident that they have but little brains" (*Journal 4* 311).

Among Thoreau's expressions concerning language, the following, read and left to smolder, seemed to fetch the fire:

> For our aspirations there is no expression as yet, but if we obey steadily, by another year, we shall have learned the language of last year's aspirations.   (*Journal 1* 244)

> I look around for thoughts when I am overflowing myself. While I live on, thought is still in embryo—it stirs not within me. Anon it begins to assume shape and comeliness, and I deliver it, and clothe it in its garment of language. But alas! how often when thoughts choke me do I resort to a spat on the back—or swallow a crust—or do anything but expectorate them.   (*Journal 1* 15)

> A written word is the choicest of relics. It is something at once more intimate with us and more universal than any other work of art. It is the work of art nearest to life itself. It may . . . not only be read but actually breathed from all human lips; . . . carved out of the breath of life itself.
>   (*Walden* 102)

In describing my brief experience teaching these vibrant, appreciative, sometimes opinionated, even crusty and outspoken learners, I admit to the impulse of urging my fellow Thoreauvians to join in that stimulating and professionally invigorating enterprise. Many pathways beckon, and the field widens to view: in a 1993 catalog that lists some five thousand Elderhostel offerings in the United States, only twelve indicate Thoreau content, and of those only three focus exclusively on Thoreau (*Elderhostel*).[2] Not one of those twelve Elderhostels is offered west of the Mississippi, only four are outside New England, and none is farther south than New York.[3]

As for the academic communities' estimate of the value of teaching in the program, one favorable indicator is a description, in the 1991 *MLA Elections: Candidate Information Booklet*, of a candidate for the position of special-interest delegate in Continuing Education. Having taught for some fifteen years "in retirement communities and public libraries, at Elderhostels and alumni convocations," Donald Gray (Indiana Univ., Bloomington) offers his assessment that the "pleasure and power" of teaching in the program are "undervalued by administrators and insufficiently appreciated by faculty," a perception he hopes to correct (9).

Among participants, the value of the program is undisputed. For though the students are of an age to be put out to pasture, as the saying goes, as a group they affirm Thoreau's belief that

> [i]t is foolish for a man to accumulate material wealth chiefly, houses and land. Our stock in life, our real estate, is that amount of thought which we have had, which we have thought out. The ground we have thus created is forever pasturage for our thoughts.   (*Journal* [1906] 9: 350)

While many of the Elderhostelers may have known this for years, some, I suspect, are just discovering that there can be frolicsome times in the high pastures of thought and that Thoreau's final sentences in *Walden* ring true: "There is more day to dawn. The sun is but a morning star."

NOTES

[1]Elderhostel catalogs are sent to every public library in the United States. Individuals may request catalogs by writing to Elderhostel, 75 Federal Street, Boston, MA 02110-1941. The eligibility age level for attendance was recently reduced from sixty to fifty-five. For a firsthand account of the Elderhostel movement, see Mills.

[2]One of the three takes place in Maine, though run through the Vermont Elderhostel agency. The program offered has the following description: "Thoreau Country Canoe Trip (Outfitted): West Branch of the Penobscot River in Maine (10 Elderhostelers plus guide). Intermediate paddlers, 50 mile, 10 day canoe trip. Focus on *The Maine Woods*. Nine-night program—Sunday to Tuesday. Hulbert Outdoor Center, Fairlee. Charge: $525."

[3]By state, the number of Elderhostel course offerings with Thoreau content are Massachusetts, four; New York and Vermont, two each; Illinois, Maine, New Hampshire, and Wisconsin, one each. Of the five thousand course offerings nationwide, those with Thoreau content constitute only 0.24 percent. By far the most frequently featured author in Elderhostel course offerings is, not unexpectedly, Shakespeare. The most popular American authors are Dickinson, Frost, Poe, and Twain.

CONTRIBUTORS AND SURVEY PARTICIPANTS

The following scholars and teachers of Thoreau's work contributed essays for this volume or participated in the survey that preceded and provided material for the preparation of this book:

Stephen Adams, *University of Minnesota, Duluth*
Jonathan Bishop, *Cornell University*
Stanley S. Blair, *Monmouth University*
Gordon V. Boudreau, *Le Moyne College*
Lawrence Buell, *Harvard University*
Hennig Cohen, *University of Pennsylvania*
Gary Collison, *Penn State University, York*
Bradley P. Dean, *East Carolina University*
Richard Dillman, *Saint Cloud State University*
Monika M. Elbert, *Montclair State University*
Laraine Fergenson, *Bronx Community College, City University of New York*
Robert Franciosi, *Grand Valley State University*
David G. Fuller, *Northern State University*
Frederick Garber, *State University of New York, Binghamton*
Michael T. Gilmore, *Brandeis University*
Henry Golemba, *Wayne State University*
Gary R. Hall, *University of California, Los Angeles*
George Hendrick, *University of Illinois, Urbana*
John Hildebidle, *Massachusetts Institute of Technology*
Ronald Wesley Hoag, *East Carolina University*
William Howarth, *Princeton University*
Alan Howell, *California Polytechnic State University*
M. Thomas Inge, *Randolph-Macon College*
Linck C. Johnson, *Colgate University*
Katsumi Kamioka, *Kochi University, Kochi City*
Koh Kasegawa, *Aoyama Gakuin University, Tokyo*
Richard Lebeaux, *Keene State College*
David Ledel, *North Lake College, TX*
Elaine Marshall, *Barton College*
Frank J. McGill, *University of Colorado, Boulder*
T. S. McMillin, *Oberlin College*
Deborah T. Meem, *University College, University of Cincinnati*
Michael Meyer, *University of Connecticut, Storrs*
Wesley T. Mott, *Worcester Polytechnic Institute*
Leonard N. Neufeldt, *Purdue University, West Lafayette*
Elisa New, *University of Pennsylvania*
H. Daniel Peck, *Vassar College*
Robert D. Richardson, Jr., *Wesleyan University*
Herbert J. Risley, *Valparaiso University*

David M. Robinson, *Oregon State University*
William Rossi, *University of Oregon*
Scott Slovic, *University of Nevada, Reno*
Lorrie Smith, *Saint Michael's College*
Michael West, *University of Pittsburgh, Pittsburgh*
Lonnie L. Willis, *Boise State University*
Annette M. Woodlief, *Virginia Commonwealth University*

WORKS CITED

In the following bibliography, reprints are indicated for the reader's convenience. If multiple reprints of an essay or book exist, only the most recent one is listed.

Abrams, M. H. *A Glossary of Literary Terms.* 4th ed. New York: Holt, Rinehart, 1981.

Adams, Florence Bannard. *Fanny Fern; or, A Pair of Flaming Shoes.* West Trenton: Hermitage, 1966.

Adams, Raymond. "Thoreau's Mock-Heroics and the American Natural History Writer." *Studies in Philology* 52 (1955): 86–97.

Adams, Stephen, and Donald Ross, Jr. *Revising Mythologies: The Composition of Thoreau's Major Works.* Charlottesville, UP of Virginia, 1988.

Adamson, Joseph. "The Trials of Thoreau." *ESQ: A Journal of the American Renaissance* 36 (1990): 137–72.

Albrecht, Robert C. "Thoreau and His Audience: 'A Plea for Captain John Brown.'" *American Literature* 32 (1961): 393–402.

Altherr, Thomas L. "'Chaplain to the Hunters': Henry David Thoreau's Ambivalence toward Hunting." *American Literature* 56 (1984): 345–61.

Anderson, Charles R. *The Magic Circle of* Walden. New York: Holt, Rinehart, 1968.

Anderson, Douglas. *A House Undivided: Domesticity and Community in American Literature.* Cambridge: Cambridge UP, 1990.

Andrews, William L. *To Tell a Free Story: The First Century of Afro-American Autobiography, 1760–1865.* Urbana: U of Illinois P, 1986.

Anhorn, Judy Schaaf. "Thoreau in the Beanfield: The Curious Language of *Walden.*" *ESQ: A Journal of the American Renaissance* 24 (1978): 179–96.

Baker, Houston A., Jr. *Long Black Song: Essays in Black American Literature and Culture.* Charlottesville: UP of Virginia, 1972.

Bakhtin, Mikhail M. *Problems of Dostoevsky's Poetics.* Trans. R. W. Rotsel. Ann Arbor: Ardis, 1973.

Barbour, Brian M. *American Transcendentalism: An Anthology of Criticism.* Notre Dame: U of Notre Dame P, 1973.

Barzun, Jacques. "Thoreau the Thorough Impressionist." *American Scholar* 56 (1987): 250–58.

Baym, Nina. "Thoreau's View of Science." *Journal of the History of Ideas* 26 (1965): 221–34.

———. *Women's Fiction: A Guide to Novels by and about Women in America, 1820–1870.* Ithaca: Cornell UP, 1978.

Baym, Nina, et al., eds. *The Norton Anthology of American Literature.* 4th ed. Vol. 1. New York: Norton, 1994.

Begiebing, Robert J., and Owen Grumbling, eds. *The Literature of Nature: The British and American Traditions.* Medford: Plexus, 1990.

Bercovitch, Sacvan. *American Jeremiad*. Madison: U of Wisconsin P, 1978.

Bergon, Frank, ed. *The Wilderness Reader*. New York: NAL, 1980.

Bergstrom, Robert F. "Less Erroneous Pictures of Whales: Open Structures in Teaching *Moby-Dick*." *Approaches to Teaching Melville's* Moby-Dick. Ed. Martin Bickman. New York: MLA, 1985. 96–103.

Berlin, James. "Rhetoric and Ideology in the Writing Class." *College English* 50 (1988): 477–94.

Berry, Wendell. *Home Economics*. San Francisco: North Point, 1987.

Berthoff, Anne E. *Forming, Thinking, Writing: The Composing Imagination*. Rochelle Park: Hayden, 1978.

Bickman, Martin. Walden: *Volatile Truths*. New York: Macmillan, 1992.

Bier, Jesse. *The Rise and Fall of American Humor*. New York: Holt, Rinehart, 1968.

Bishop, Jonathan. "The Experience of the Sacred in Thoreau's *Week*." *English Literary History* 33 (1966): 68–91.

Blanding, Thomas. "Walton and *Walden*." *Thoreau Society Bulletin* 107 (1969): 3.

Bloom, Harold, ed. *Modern Critical Views of Henry David Thoreau*. New York: Chelsea, 1987.

———. *Modern Critical Views of* Walden. New York: Chelsea, 1987.

Bly, Robert. "The Greatness of Thoreau." *American Poetry Review* 15.5 (1986): 5.

Bode, Carl. Introduction. Thoreau, *Portable Thoreau* 1–27.

Boies, J. J. "Circular Imagery in Thoreau's *Week*." *College English* 26 (1965): 350–55.

Bond, Brian C. "Thoreau's *A Week on the Concord and Merrimack Rivers*: A Generic Study." Diss. Bowling Green State U, 1972.

Boone, Joseph Allen. "Delving and Diving for Truth: Breaking Through to Bottom in Thoreau's *Walden*." *ESQ: A Journal of the American Renaissance* 27 (1981): 135–46. Rpt. in Myerson, *Critical Essays* 164–77.

Borck, Jim Springer, and Herbert B. Rothschild, Jr. "Meditative Discoveries in Thoreau's 'The Pond in Winter.'" *Texas Studies in Literature and Language* 20 (1978): 93–106.

Borst, Raymond R. *The Thoreau Log: A Documentary Life of Henry David Thoreau, 1817–1862*. New York: Hall, 1992.

Boudreau, Gordon. *The Roots of* Walden *and the Tree of Life*. Nashville: Vanderbilt UP, 1990.

Brent, Harry, and William Lutz, eds. *Rhetorical Considerations*. 3rd ed. Cambridge: Winthrop, 1980.

Bridgman, Richard. *Dark Thoreau*. Lincoln: U of Nebraska P, 1981.

Broderick, John C. "Imagery in *Walden*." *University of Texas Studies in English* 33 (1954): 80–89.

———. "The Movement of Thoreau's Prose." *American Literature* 33 (1961): 133–42.

———. "Thoreau's Proposals for Legislation." *American Quarterly* 7 (1955): 285–90.

Brodhead, Richard. *Hawthorne, Melville, and the Novel*. Chicago: U of Chicago P, 1976.

Brown, Thomas H. "Maintaining an 'Ethical Center' in the Composition Course." *CEA Forum* 19.3–4 (1989): 1–2.

Buell, Lawrence. "American Literary Emergence as a Postcolonial Phenomenon." *American Literary History* 4 (1992): 411–42.

———. *Literary Transcendentalism: Style and Vision in the American Renaissance.* Ithaca: Cornell UP, 1973.

———. "Melville and the Question of Decolonialization." *American Literature* 64 (1992): 217–37.

———. *New England Literary Culture: From Revolution through Romance.* Cambridge: Cambridge UP, 1986.

———. "The Thoreauvian Pilgrimage: The Structure of an American Cult." *American Literature* 61 (1989): 175–99.

———. "Transcendentalism." *The Columbia Literary History of the United States.* Ed. Emory Elliot. New York: Columbia UP, 1988. 364–78.

Buranelli, Vincent. "The Case against Thoreau." *Ethics* 67 (1957): 257–68.

Burbick, Joan. *Thoreau's Alternative History: Changing Perspectives on Nature, Culture, and Language.* Philadelphia: U of Pennsylvania P, 1987.

Burke, Kenneth. *A Rhetoric of Motives.* Berkeley: U of California P, 1969.

Burkett, Eva M., and Joyce S. Steward. *Thoreau on Writing.* Conway: U of Central Arkansas P, 1989.

Cameron, Sharon. *Writing Nature: Henry Thoreau's Journal.* New York: Oxford UP, 1985.

Canby, Henry Seidel. *Thoreau.* Boston: Houghton, 1939.

Cavell, Stanley. *The Senses of Walden.* New York: Viking, 1972. Expanded ed. San Francisco: North Point, 1981.

Chai, Leon. *The Romantic Foundations of the American Renaissance.* Ithaca: Cornell UP, 1987.

Channing, William Ellery. *Thoreau: Poet-Naturalist.* Ed. F. B. Sanborn. Boston: Goodspeed, 1902.

Chapman, David W. "Conflict and Consensus: How Composition Scholars View Their Discipline." *Profession 87.* New York: MLA, 1987. 43–45.

Christensen, Francis, and Bonniejean Christensen. *A New Rhetoric.* New York: Harper, 1976.

———. *Notes toward a New Rhetoric.* Rev. ed. of *A New Rhetoric.* New York: Harper, 1978.

Christie, John Aldrich. *Thoreau as World Traveler.* New York: Columbia UP, 1965.

———. "Thoreau on Civil Disobedience." *ESQ: A Journal of the American Renaissance* 54 (1969): 5–12.

Christy, Arthur. *The Orient in American Transcendentalism.* New York: Columbia UP, 1932.

Clapper, Ronald. "The Development of *Walden*: A Genetic Text." Diss. U of California, Los Angeles, 1967.

Colyer, Richard. "Thoreau's Color Symbols." *PMLA* 86 (1971): 999–1008.

Comley, Nancy. "Review: Critical Thinking/Critical Teaching." *College English* 51 (1989): 623–27.

Conron, John. "'Bright American Rivers': The Luminist Landscapes of Thoreau's *A Week on the Concord and Merrimack Rivers*." *American Quarterly* 32 (1980): 144–66.

Cornis-Pop, Marcel. *Hermeneutic Desire and Critical Rewriting*. New York: St. Martin's, 1992.

Culler, Jonathan. *On Deconstruction: Theory and Criticism after Structuralism*. Ithaca: Cornell UP, 1982.

de Man, Paul. *Blindness and Insight*. New York: Oxford UP, 1971.

Dedmond, Francis B. "Economic Protest in Thoreau's Journals." *Studia Neophilologica* 26 (1954): 65–76.

Delany, Martin R. *Blake; or, The Huts of America*. Boston: Beacon, 1970.

Derrida, Jacques. *The Ear of the Other: Otobiography, Transference, Translation: Texts and Discussion with Jacques Derrida*. Trans. Peggy Kamuf and Avital Ronell. Ed. Christie V. McDonald. New York: Schocken, 1985.

———. *Writing and Difference*. Trans. Alan Bass. Chicago: U of Chicago P, 1978.

Dettmar, Kevin J. H. "Ransacking the Root Cellar: The Appeal to/of Etymology in *Walden*." *Strategies: A Journal of Theory, Culture, and Politics* 1 (1988): 182–201.

Dillard, Annie. *Teaching a Stone to Talk: Expeditions and Encounters*. New York: Harper, 1983.

Dillman, Richard. "The Psychological Rhetoric of *Walden*." *ESQ: A Journal of the American Renaissance* 25 (1979): 79–91. Rpt. in Myerson, *Critical Essays* 147–63.

———. "Reader Response to Thoreau's *Walden*." *Reader: Essays in Reader-Oriented Theory, Criticism, and Pedagogy* 19 (1988): 21–36.

———. *Thoreau's Comments on the Art of Writing*. Lanham: UP of America, 1987.

———. "Thoreau's Human Economy." *ESQ: Journal of the American Renaissance* 25 (1979): 20–25.

———. "Thoreau's Philosophy of Audience." *Bucknell Review* 31.2 (1988): 74–85.

———. "Thoreau's Philosophy of Rhetorical Invention." *Bucknell Review* 31.2 (1988): 60–73.

———. "Thoreau's Philosophy of Style." *Bucknell Review* 31.2 (1988): 86–96.

Douglas, Ann. *The Feminization of American Culture*. New York: Knopf, 1977.

Douglass, Frederick. *My Bondage and My Freedom*. Rpt. of 1855 ed. Introd. Philip S. Foner. New York: Dover, 1959.

———. *Narrative of the Life of Frederick Douglass, an American Slave*. Ed. Houston A. Baker, Jr. New York: Penguin, 1982.

Drinnon, Richard. "Thoreau's Politics of the Upright Man." J. Hicks 154–68. Rpt. in Thoreau, Walden *and "Civil Disobedience"* (Norton) 366–77.

Duban, James. "Conscience and Consciousness: The Liberal Christian Context of Thoreau's Political Ethics." *American Literature* 60 (1987): 208–22.

Eckstorm, Fanny. "Thoreau's *Maine Woods*." *Atlantic Monthly* July-Aug. 1908: 16–18+. Rpt. in Harding, *Thoreau: A Century* 103–17.

Edel, Leon. *Henry D. Thoreau*. Univ. of Minnesota Pamphlets on American Writers 90. Minneapolis: U of Minnesota P, 1970.

"Education for Democracy: A Statement of Principles." *American Educator* 11.2 (1987): 10–18.

Egan, Kenneth V., Jr. "Thoreau's Pastoral Vision in 'Walking.'" *American Transcendental Quarterly* 57 (1985): 21–30.

Eiseley, Loren. *The Night Country*. New York: Scribner's, 1971.

Elderhostel: United States and Canada Catalog: Summer 1993 Programs: Jul, Aug, Sep. 10. Boston: Elderhostel, 1993.

Elliott, Emory, et al., eds. *American Literature: A Prentice Hall Anthology*. Vol. 1. Englewood Cliffs: Prentice, 1991.

Emerson, Edward. *Henry Thoreau as Remembered by a Young Friend*. Boston: Houghton, 1917.

Emerson, Ralph Waldo. *The Collected Works of Ralph Waldo Emerson*. 4 vols. to date. Joseph Slater, gen. ed. Cambridge: Belknap-Harvard UP, 1971– .

———. *Emerson in His Journals*. Ed. Joel Porte. London: Cambridge UP, 1982.

———. "Thoreau." *Lectures and Biographical Sketches*. Cambridge: Harvard UP, 1904. 449–85. Vol. 10 of *The Complete Works of Ralph Waldo Emerson*. Rpt. in Thoreau, *Walden and "Civil Disobedience"* (Norton) 320–33.

Erikson, Erik. "The Life Cycle: Epigenesis of Identity." *Identity: Youth and Crisis*. New York: Norton, 1968. 91–141.

Erlich, Michael. "Thoreau's 'Civil Disobedience': Strategy for Reform." *Connecticut Review* 7.1 (1973): 100–10.

Eulau, Heinz. "Wayside Challenger: Some Remarks on the Politics of Henry David Thoreau." *Antioch Review* 9 (1949): 509–22.

Fairbanks, Jonathan. "Thoreau: Speaker for Wildness." *South Atlantic Quarterly* 70 (1971): 487–506.

Feidelson, Charles. *Symbolism and American Literature*. Chicago: U of Chicago P, 1953.

Fergenson, Laraine. "Thoreau, Daniel Berrigan, and the Problem of Transcendental Politics." *Soundings* 65 (1982): 103–22.

Fergenson, Laraine, and Marie-Louise Nickerson. *All in One: Basic Writing Text, Workbook, and Reader*. 3rd ed. Englewood Cliffs: Prentice, 1992.

Fern, Fanny. *Ruth Hall and Other Writings*. Ed. Joyce W. Warren. New Brunswick: Rutgers UP, 1986.

Fiedler, Leslie A. *The Return of the Vanishing American*. London: Cape, 1968.

Finch, Robert, and John Elder, eds. *The Norton Book of Nature Writing*. New York: Norton, 1990.

Fink, Steven. *Prophet in the Marketplace: Thoreau's Development as a Professional Writer*. Princeton: Princeton UP, 1992.

———. "Variations on the Self: Thoreau's Personae in *A Week on the Concord and Merrimack Rivers*." *ESQ: A Journal of the American Renaissance* 28 (1982): 24–35.

Fischer, Michael R. "*Walden* and the Politics of Contemporary Literary Theory." Sayre, *New Essays* 95–113.

Fishelov, David. *Metaphors of Genre: The Roles of Analogies in Genre Theory*. University Park: Penn State P, 1993.

Fisher, Marvin. "Seeing New Englandly: Anthropology, Ecology, and Theology in Thoreau's *Week*." *Centennial Review* 34 (1990): 381–94.

Fleck, Richard. *Henry Thoreau and John Muir among the Indians*. Hamden: Archon, 1985.

Foerster, Norman. "Thoreau as Artist." Harding, *Thoreau: A Century* 123–35.

Ford, Milton E. *Life Journey: Literature and the Search for Meaning in the Stages of Life*. Grand Rapids: Triumph, 1987.

Foster, Edward Halsey. *The Civilized Wilderness: Backgrounds to American Romantic Literature*. New York: Macmillan, 1975.

Fowler, Alastair. *Kinds of Literature: An Introduction to the Theory of Genre and Modes*. Cambridge: Harvard UP, 1982.

Franklin, H. Bruce. *Prison Literature in America: The Victim as Criminal and Artist*. Westport: Hill, 1978.

Fraser, Nancy. "On the Political and the Symbolic: Against the Metaphysics of Textuality." *Boundary 2* 14 (1986): 195–209.

Freedman, Carl. "Marxist Theory, Radical Pedagogy, and the Reification of Thought." *College English* 49 (1987): 70–82.

Frost, Linda. " 'The Red Face of Man,' the Penobscot Indian, and the Conflict of Interest in Thoreau's *Maine Woods*." *ESQ: A Journal of the American Renaissance* 39 (1993): 21–47.

Frothingham, Octavius Brooks. *Transcendentalism in New England: A History*. 1876. Philadelphia: U of Pennsylvania P, 1959.

Frye, Northrop. *Anatomy of Criticism: Four Essays*. Princeton: Princeton UP, 1957.

Furst, Lillian R. *Fictions of Romantic Irony*. Cambridge: Harvard UP, 1984.

Galligan, Edward L. "The Comedian at Walden Pond." *South Atlantic Quarterly* 69 (1970): 20–37.

Garber, Frederick. *Thoreau's Fable of Inscribing*. Princeton: Princeton UP, 1991.

———. *Thoreau's Redemptive Imagination*. New York: New York UP, 1977.

———. "Unity and Diversity in 'Walking.' " *ESQ: A Journal of the American Renaissance* 56 (1969): 35–40.

Gilmore, Michael T. *American Romanticism and the Marketplace*. Chicago: U of Chicago P, 1985.

Gleason, Herbert. *Thoreau Country*. San Francisco: Sierra Club, 1975.

Glick, Wendell. " 'Civil Disobedience': Thoreau's Attack upon Relativism." *Western Humanities Review* 7 (1952): 35–42.

———. *The Recognition of Henry David Thoreau*. Ann Arbor: U of Michigan P, 1969.

———. "Scholarly Editing and Dealing with Uncertainties: Thoreau's 'Resistance to Civil Government.' " *Analytical and Enumerative Bibliography* 2 (1978): 103–15.

———. "Thoreau and Radical Abolitionism." Diss. Northwestern U, 1950.

Goldman, Irene C. "Feminism, Deconstruction, and the Universal: A Case Study of *Walden*." *Conversations: Contemporary Critical Theory and the Teaching of Literature*. Ed. Charles Moran and Elizabeth Penfield. Urbana: National Council of Teachers of English, 1990. 120–31.

Golemba, Henry. *Thoreau's Wild Rhetoric*. New York: New York UP, 1990.

———. "Unreading Thoreau." *American Literature* 60 (1988): 385–401.

Graff, Gerald. *Professing Literature*. Chicago: U of Chicago P, 1987.

Greenblatt, Stephen. *Renaissance Self-Fashioning from More to Shakespeare*. Chicago: U of Chicago P, 1980.

Gross, Robert A. "Culture and Cultivation: Agriculture and Society in Thoreau's Concord." *Journal of American History* 69.1 (1982): 42–61.

———. "The Great Bean Field Hoax: Thoreau and the Agricultural Reformers." Myerson, *Critical Essays* 193–202.

———. "'The Most Estimable Place in All the World': A Debate on Progress in Nineteenth-Century Concord." *Studies in the American Renaissance* (1978): 1–15.

Gura, Philip. "Thoreau's Maine Woods Indians: More Representative Men." *American Literature* 49 (1977): 366–84.

———. *The Wisdom of Words: Language, Theology, and Literature in the New England Renaissance*. Middletown: Wesleyan UP, 1981.

Gura, Philip F., and Joel Myerson, eds. *Critical Essays on American Transcendentalism*. Boston: Hall, 1982.

Guth, Hans. *Words and Ideas: A Handbook for College Writing*. 4th ed. Belmont: Wadsworth, 1975.

Hall, Donald. *Writing Well*. Boston: Little, 1973.

Harding, Walter. *The Days of Henry Thoreau*. New York: Dover, 1982.

———. "Five Ways of Looking at *Walden*." *Massachusetts Review* 4 (1962): 149–62. Rpt. in Myerson, *Critical Essays* 85–96.

———, ed. *Henry David Thoreau: A Profile*. New York: Hill, 1971.

———. Introduction. *The Variorum "Civil Disobedience."* By Henry David Thoreau. Twayne, 1967. 11–28.

———. "On Teaching *Walden*." *Emerson Society Quarterly* 18 (1960): 11–12.

———, ed. *Thoreau: A Century of Criticism*. Dallas: Southern Methodist UP, 1954.

———. *A Thoreau Handbook*. New York: New York UP, 1959.

———, ed. *Thoreau: Man of Concord*. New York: Holt, Rinehart, 1960. Rpt. as *Thoreau As Seen by His Contemporaries*. New York: Dover, 1989.

———. "Thoreau's Sexuality." *Journal of Homosexuality* 21.3 (1991): 23–45.

———. "*Walden*'s Man of Science." *Virginia Quarterly Review* 57 (1981): 45–61.

———. "Was It Legal? Thoreau in Jail." *American Heritage* Aug. 1975: 36–37.

Harding, Walter, and Michael Meyer. *The New Thoreau Handbook*. New York: New York UP, 1980.

Harrington, Robert Pogue. *Forests: The Shadow of Civilization*. Chicago: U of Chicago P, 1992.

"Has Our Living Standard Stalled?" *Consumer Reports* June 1992: 392–93.

Hawthorne, Nathaniel. *The Letters, 1853–1856*. Ed. Thomas Woodson et al. Columbus: Ohio State UP, 1987. Vol. 17 of *The Centenary Edition of the Works of Nathaniel Hawthorne*. 1962–   .

———. *The Scarlet Letter*. 3rd ed. Ed. Seymour Gross et al. New York: Norton, 1988.

Henley, Don, and Dave Marsh, eds. *Heaven Is under Our Feet*. Stamford: Long-meadow, 1991.

Hernadi, Paul. *Beyond Genre: New Directions in Literary Classification*. Ithaca: Cornell UP, 1972.

Herr, William. "A More Perfect State: Thoreau's Concept of Civil Government." *Massachusetts Review* 16 (1975): 470–87.

———. "Thoreau: A Civil Disobedient?" *Ethics* 85 (1974): 87–91.

Hicks, John, ed. *Thoreau in Our Season*. Amherst: U of Massachusetts P, 1966. Expanded ed. of "Thoreau: A Centennial Gathering." *Massachusetts Review* 4 (1962): 41–172.

Hicks, Philip M. *The Development of the Natural History Essay in American Literature*. Philadelphia: U of Pennsylvania, 1924.

Hildebidle, John. *Thoreau: A Naturalist's Liberty*. Cambridge: Harvard UP, 1983.

Hoag, Ronald. "The Mark on the Wilderness: Thoreau's Contact with Ktaadn." *Texas Studies in Literature and Language* 24 (1982): 23–46.

Hoch, David G. "Theory of History in *A Week*: Annuals and Perennials." *Emerson Society Quarterly* 56 (1969): 32–35.

Hochfield, George. "Anti-Thoreau." *Sewanee Review* 96 (1988): 433–43.

———. "New England Transcendentalism." *American Literature to 1900*. Ed. Marcus Cunliffe. 1973. New York: Penguin, 1993. 135–67.

———, ed. *Selected Writings of the American Transcendentalists*. New York: NAL, 1966.

Holman, C. Hugh, and William Harmon. *A Handbook to Literature*. 5th ed. New York: Macmillan, 1986.

Hosmer, Horace. *Remembrances of Concord and the Thoreaus: Letters of Horace Hosmer to Dr. S. A. Jones*. Ed. George Hendrick. Urbana: U of Illinois P, 1977.

Hovde, Carl. "Literary Materials in Thoreau's *A Week*." PMLA 80 (1965): 76–83.

———. "Nature into Art: Thoreau's Use of His Journals in *A Week*." *American Literature* 30 (1958): 165–84.

Howarth, William. *The Book of Concord: Thoreau's Life as a Writer*. New York: Viking, 1982.

———. *The Literary Manuscripts of Henry David Thoreau*. Columbus: Ohio State UP, 1974.

Howat, John K. *The Hudson River and Its Painters*. New York: Penguin, 1972.

Howe, Irving. *The American Newness: Culture and Politics in the Age of Emerson*. Cambridge: Harvard UP, 1986.

Huber, Bettina J. "Today's Literature Classroom: Findings from the MLA's 1990 Survey of Upper-Division Courses." *ADE Bulletin* 101 (1992): 36–60.

Huber, J. Parker. *The Wildest Country: A Guide to Thoreau's Maine*. Boston: Appalachian Mountain Club, 1982.

Hutchinson, Jamie. "'The Lapse of the Current': Thoreau's Historical Vision in *A Week on the Concord and Merrimack Rivers*." *ESQ: A Journal of the American Renaissance* 25 (1979): 211–23.

Hyman, Stanley Edgar. "Henry Thoreau in Our Time." *Atlantic Monthly* Nov. 1946: 137–46. Rpt. in Paul, *Thoreau* 23–36.

Inge, M. Thomas. "Thoreau's Humor in *Walden*." *Randolph-Macon Magazine* Mar. 1966: 33–44.

ISLE (Interdisciplinary Studies in Literature and Environment) 1 (Spring 1993).

Jackson, John Brinkerhoff. *Discovering the Vernacular Landscape*. New Haven: Yale UP, 1984.

James, David L. "Movement and Growth in 'Walking.'" *Thoreau Journal Quarterly* 4.3 (1972): 16–21.

Johnson, Barbara. "A Hound, a Bay Horse, and a Turtle-Dove: Obscurity in *Walden*." *A World of Difference*. Ed. William Rossi. Baltimore: Johns Hopkins UP, 1987. 49–56. Rpt. in Thoreau, Walden *and "Civil Disobedience"* (Norton) 444–50.

Johnson, Linck C. "Into History: Thoreau's Earliest 'Indian Book' and His First Trip to Cape Cod." *ESQ: A Journal of the American Renaissance* 28 (1982): 74–88.

———. "Revolution and Renewal: The Genres of *Walden*." Myerson, *Critical Essays* 215–35.

———. *Thoreau's Complex Weave: The Writing of* A Week on the Concord and Merrimack Rivers *with Text of the First Draft*. Charlottesville: UP of Virginia, 1986.

Johnson, William C., Jr. *What Thoreau Said:* Walden *and the Unsayable*. Moscow: U of Idaho P, 1991.

Joy, Neill R. "Two Possible Analogies for 'The Ponds' in *Walden*: Jonathan Carver and Wordsworth." *ESQ: A Journal of the American Renaissance* 24 (1978): 197–205.

Kazin, Alfred. "Thoreau and American Power." *Atlantic Monthly* May 1969: 60–68.

———. "Thoreau's Journals." Harding, *Thoreau: A Century* 187–91.

Keats, John. *The Poems of John Keats*. Ed. Jack Stillinger. Cambridge: Belknap–Harvard UP, 1978.

Kern, Alexander C. "The Rise of Transcendentalism, 1815–1860." *Transitions in American Literary History*. Ed. Harry Hayden Clark. Durham: Duke UP, 1954. 245–314.

Ketcham, Ralph L. "Reply to Buranelli's Case against Thoreau." *Ethics* 69 (1959): 206–09.

King, Martin Luther, Jr. "A Legacy of Creative Protest." J. Hicks 13.

———. "Letter from Birmingham Jail." *Why We Can't Wait*. New York: Mentor–NAL, 1964. 76–95.

Kirkland, Leigh. "Sexual Chaos in Walden Pond." *ISLE* 131–36.

Knobel, Dale T. *Paddy and the Republic: Ethnicity and Nationality in Antebellum America*. Middletown: Wesleyan UP, 1986.

Koslow, Francine Amy, and Walter Harding. *Henry David Thoreau as a Source of Artistic Inspiration*. Lincoln: DeCordova and Dana Museum, 1984.

Kritzberg, Barry. "Thoreau, Slavery, and Resistance to Civil Government." *Massachusetts Review* 30 (1989): 535–65.

Krutch, Joseph Wood. *Henry David Thoreau*. New York: Sloane, 1948.

Lane, Lauriat, Jr., ed. *Approaches to* Walden. San Francisco: Wadsworth, 1961.

———. "On the Organic Structure of *Walden*." *College English* 21 (1960): 195–202.

———. "Thoreau's Autumnal Archetypal Hero: Captain John Brown." *Ariel* 6.1 (1975): 41–49.

———. "Thoreau's Autumnal Indians." *Canadian Review of American Studies* 6 (1975): 228–36.

———. "Thoreau's *Walden*, I, Paragraphs 1–3." *Explicator* 29.4 (1971): 35.

Lauter, Paul, et al., eds. *The Heath Anthology of American Literature*. 2nd ed. Vol. 1. Lexington: Heath, 1994.

Lebeaux, Richard. *Thoreau's Seasons*. Amherst: U of Massachusetts P, 1984.

———. *Young Man Thoreau*. Amherst: U of Massachusetts P, 1977.

Leitch, Vincent. *Deconstructive Criticism: An Advanced Introduction*. New York: Columbia UP, 1983.

Leopold, Aldo. "The Land Ethic." *A Sand County Almanac, with Essays on Conservation from Round River*. New York: Ballantine, 1989. 237–64.

Leverenz, David. *Manhood in the American Renaissance*. Ithaca: Cornell UP, 1989.

Levering, Frank, and Wanda Urbanska. *Simple Living: One Couple's Search for a Better Life*. New York: Viking, 1992.

Lewis, R. W. B. *The American Adam*. Chicago: U of Chicago P, 1955.

Lipsitz, Lewis. "If, As Verba Says, the State Functions as a Religion, What Are We to Do Then to Save Our Souls?" *American Political Science Review* 62 (1968): 527–35.

Lowell, James Russell. Rev. of *A Week on the Concord and Merrimack Rivers*. *Massachusetts Quarterly Review* 3 (1849): 40–51.

———. "Thoreau's Letters." *North American Review* 101 (1865): 597–608. Rpt. in Thoreau, Walden *and "Civil Disobedience"* (Norton) 334–41.

Lyon, Melvin E. "Walden Pond as a Symbol." *PMLA* 82 (1967): 289–300.

Lyon, Thomas, ed. *This Incomperable Lande: A Book of American Nature Writing*. Boston: Houghton, 1989.

Maddox, Lucy. *Removals: Nineteenth-Century American Literature and the Politics of Indian Affairs*. New York: Oxford UP, 1991.

Manegold, C. S., and Lenore Magida. "The Roots of the Revolt." *Newsweek* 29 May 1989: 21.

Marble, Annie Russell. *Thoreau: His Home, Friends, and Books*. New York: Crowell, 1902.

Marx, Leo. *The Machine in the Garden: Technology and the Pastoral Ideal in America*. New York: Oxford UP, 1964.

———. "Thoreau's Excursions." *Yale Review* 51 (1962): 363–69.

Masteller, Richard N., and Jean Carwile Masteller. "Rural Architecture in Andrew Jackson Downing and Henry David Thoreau: Pattern Book Parody in *Walden*." *New England Quarterly* 57 (1984): 483–510.

Matthiessen, F. O. *The American Renaissance: Art and Expression in the Age of Emerson and Whitman*. New York: Oxford UP, 1941.

McCarthy, Paul. "Houses in *Walden*: Thoreau as 'Real-Estate Broker,' Social Critic, Idealist." *Midwest Quarterly* 28 (1987): 323–39.

McCrimmon, James M., Joseph Trimmer, and Nancy Sommers. *Writing with a Purpose*. 8th ed. Boston: Houghton, 1984.

McDowell, Deborah E., and Arnold Rampersad, eds. *Slavery and the Literary Imagination*. Baltimore: Johns Hopkins UP, 1989.

McIntosh, James. *Thoreau as Romantic Naturalist: His Shifting Stance toward Nature.* Ithaca: Cornell UP, 1974.

McLean, Albert. "Thoreau's True Meridian: Natural Fact and Metaphor." *American Quarterly* 20 (1968): 567–79.

McPhee, John. *The Survival of the Birch Bark Canoe.* New York: Farrar, 1975.

McQuade, Donald, et al., eds. *The Harper American Literature.* Vol. 1. New York: Harper, 1987.

Mellor, Anne K. *English Romantic Irony.* Cambridge: Harvard UP, 1980.

Meltzer, Milton, and Walter Harding. *A Thoreau Profile.* New York: Crowell, 1962.

Meyer, Michael. *Several More Lives to Live: Thoreau's Political Reputation in America.* Westport: Greenwood, 1977.

———. "Thoreau." Myerson, *Transcendentalists* 260–85.

———. "Thoreau and Black Emigration." *American Literature* 53 (1981): 380–96.

———. "Thoreau's Rescue of John Brown from History." *Studies in the American Renaissance* (1980): 301–16.

Michaels, Walter Benn. "*Walden's* False Bottoms." *Glyph* 1 (1977): 132–49. Rpt. in Thoreau, Walden *and "Civil Disobedience"* (Norton) 405–21.

Milder, Robert. "'An Errand to Mankind': Thoreau's Problem of Vocation." *ESQ: A Journal of the American Renaissance* 37 (1991): 91–139.

Miller, James E., Jr. *Heritage of American Literature.* Vol. 1. San Diego: Harcourt, 1991.

Miller, Perry, ed. *The American Transcendentalists: Their Prose and Poetry.* New York: Doubleday, 1957.

———. *Consciousness in Concord: The Text of Thoreau's Hitherto "Lost Journal" (1840–41) Together with Notes and a Commentary.* Boston: Houghton, 1958.

———. "Thoreau in the Context of International Romanticism." *New England Quarterly* 34 (1961): 147–59.

———, ed. *The Transcendentalists: An Anthology.* Cambridge: Harvard UP, 1950.

Mills, Eugene S. *The Story of Elderhostel.* Hanover: UP of New England, 1993.

MLA. *MLA Elections: Candidate Information Booklet.* New York: MLA, 1991.

Moldenhauer, Joseph J. "Images of Circularity in Thoreau's Prose." *Texas Studies in Literature and Language* 1 (1959): 245–63.

———, ed. *The Merrill Studies in* Walden. Columbus: Merrill, 1971.

———. "Paradox in *Walden.*" *Graduate Journal* 6 (1964): 132–46. Rpt. in Ruland 73–84.

———. "The Rhetoric of *Walden.*" Diss. Columbia U, 1967.

Moller, Mary Elkins. *Thoreau in the Human Community.* Amherst: U of Massachusetts P, 1980.

Murfin, Ross C., ed. *Nathaniel Hawthorne:* The Scarlet Letter. Boston: Bedford, 1991.

Murray, Donald M. "Thoreau's Indians and His Developing Art of Characterization." *ESQ: A Journal of the American Renaissance* 21 (1975): 222–29.

Murray, Meg McGavran. "Thoreau's Moon Mythology: Lunar Clues to the Hieroglyphics of Walden." *American Literature* 58.1 (1986): 15–32.

Muscatine, Charles, and Marlene Griffith, eds. *The Borzoi College Reader*. 2nd ed. New York: Knopf, 1971.

Myerson, Joel, ed. *Critical Essays on Henry David Thoreau's* Walden. Boston: Hall, 1988.

———, ed. *The Transcendentalists: A Review of Research and Criticism*. New York: MLA, 1984.

Nash, Roderick. *The Rights of Nature: A History of Environmental Ethics*. Madison: U of Wisconsin P, 1989.

———. *Wilderness and the American Mind*. New Haven: Yale UP, 1967.

Nelson, Truman. "Thoreau and John Brown." J. Hicks 134–53.

Neufeldt, Leonard. *The Economist: Henry Thoreau and Enterprise*. New York: Oxford UP, 1989.

———. "*Praetextus* as Text: Editor-Critic Responses to Thoreau's Journal." *Arizona Quarterly* 46.4 (1990): 27–72.

———. "Thoreau's Enterprise of Self-Culture in a Culture of Enterprise." *American Quarterly* 39 (1987): 231–51.

Norton, Andrews. *A Discourse on the Latest Form of Infidelity*. Cambridge: Owen, 1839.

Novak, Barbara. *American Painting of the Nineteenth Century: Realism, Idealism, and the American Experience*. New York: Praeger, 1969.

———. *Nature and Culture*. New York: Oxford UP, 1980.

Nozick, Robert. *The Examined Life*. New York: Simon, 1989.

Nye, Russel Blaine. *Society and Culture in America, 1830–1860*. New York: Harper, 1974.

Oates, Joyce Carol. "The Mysterious Mr. Thoreau." *New York Times Book Review* 1 May 1988: 1+.

Oehlschlaeger, Fritz. "Another Look at the Text and Title of Thoreau's 'Civil Disobedience.'" *ESQ: A Journal of the American Renaissance* 36 (1990): 239–54.

Oelschlaeger, Max. *The Idea of Wilderness: From Prehistory to the Age of Ecology*. New Haven: Yale UP, 1991.

Orth, Michael. "The Prose Style of Henry Thoreau." *Language and Style* 7 (1974): 36–52.

Orwell, George. "Politics and the English Language." *The Collected Essays, Journalism, and Letters of George Orwell*. Ed. Sonia Orwell and Ian Angus. Vol. 4. New York: Harcourt, 1968. 127–40.

Paine, Charles. "Relativism, Radical Pedagogy, and the Ideology of Paralysis." *College English* 51 (1989): 557–70.

Paul, Sherman. *The Shores of America: Thoreau's Inward Exploration*. Urbana: U of Illinois P, 1958.

———. "Thinking with Thoreau." *Thoreau Quarterly* 14 (1982): 18–25.

———, ed. *Thoreau: A Collection of Critical Essays*. Englewood Cliffs: Prentice, 1962.

———. "The Wise Silence: Sound as the Agency of Correspondence in Thoreau." *New England Quarterly* 23 (1950): 511–27.

Payne, F. Anne. *Chaucer and Menippean Satire*. Madison: U of Wisconsin P, 1981.

Peabody, Elizabeth. *Aesthetic Papers*. Boston: Peabody, 1849.

Peck, H. Daniel. "Better Mythology: Perception and Emergence in Thoreau's Journal." *North Dakota Quarterly* 59.2 (1991): 33–44.

———. "The Crosscurrents of *Walden's* Pastoral." Sayre 73–94.

———. "Killing Time / Keeping Time: Thoreau's Journal and the Art of Memory." *The Green American Tradition: Essays and Poems for Sherman Paul*. Ed. Peck. Baton Rouge: Louisiana State UP, 1989. 39–57.

———. *Thoreau's Morning Work: Memory and Perception in* A Week on the Concord and Merrimack Rivers, *the Journal, and* Walden. New Haven: Yale UP, 1990.

Perry, William G. *Forms of Intellectual and Ethical Development in the College Years*. New York: Holt, Rinehart, 1970.

Petroski, Henry. "An American Pencil-Making Family." *The Pencil: A History of Design and Circumstance*. New York: Knopf, 1990. 104–25.

———. "H. D. Thoreau, Engineer." *American Heritage of Invention and Technology* 5.2 (1989): 8–16.

Poe, Edgar Allan. "The Philosophy of Composition." *The Complete Works of Edgar Allan Poe*. Virginia edition. Ed. James A. Harrison. Vol. 16. New York, 1902. 193–208.

Poirier, Richard. *The Renewal of Literature: Emersonian Reflections*. New York: Random, 1987.

Porte, Joel. *Emerson and Thoreau: Transcendentalists in Conflict*. Middletown: Wesleyan UP, 1966.

———. *Representative Man: Ralph Waldo Emerson in His Time*. New York: Oxford UP, 1979.

Radaker, Kevin. "'A Separate Intention of the Eye': Luminist Eternity in Thoreau's *A Week on the Concord and Merrimack Rivers*." *Canadian Review of American Studies* 18 (1987): 41–60.

Railton, Stephen. *Authorship and Audience: Literary Performance in the American Renaissance*. Princeton: Princeton UP, 1991.

Ramsey, Jarold. "Thoreau's Last Words—and America's First Literatures." *Redefining American Literary History*. Ed. A. LaVonne Brown Ruoff and Jerry W. Ward, Jr. New York: MLA, 1990.

Reed, Sampson. "On Genius." Hochfield, *Selected Writings* 67–72.

Reynolds, David S. *Beneath the American Renaissance: The Subversive Imagination in the Age of Emerson and Melville*. New York: Knopf, 1988.

Rich, Adrienne. "Disloyal to Civilization: Feminism, Racism, Gynephobia." *On Lies, Secrets, and Silence: Selected Prose, 1966–1978*. New York: Norton, 1979. 275–310.

———. "When We Dead Awaken: Writing as Re-vision." *Adrienne Rich's Poetry*. New York: Norton, 1975. 90–98.

Richards, I. A. *Practical Criticism*. New York: Harcourt, 1929.

Richardson, Robert D. *Henry David Thoreau: A Life of the Mind*. Berkeley: U of California P, 1986.

Rodgers, Robert F. Remarks at workshop. Wartburg Coll. 4 Jan. 1993.

———. "Teaching to Facilitate Critical Thinking: A Cognitive-Developmental Perspective." *Critical Thinking, Interactive Learning, and Technology.* Ed. Thomas J. Freca. Chicago: Anderson, 1992. 91–113.

Rose, Edward J. "'A World of Full and Fair Proportions': The Aesthetics and the Politics of Vision." *Thoreau Society Bulletin Booklet* 19 (1963): 45–53.

Rose, Mike. *Writer's Block: The Cognitive Dimension.* Carbondale: Southern Illinois UP, 1984.

Rose, Suzanne D. "Following the Trail of Footsteps: From the Indian Notebooks to *Walden.*" *New England Quarterly* 67 (1994): 77–91.

Rosmarin, Adena. *The Power of Genre.* Minneapolis: U of Minnesota P, 1985.

Rossi, William. "'The Limits of an Afternoon Walk': Coleridgean Polarity in Thoreau's 'Walking.'" *ESQ: A Journal of the American Renaissance* 33 (1977): 110–19.

———. "Roots, Leaves, and Method: Henry Thoreau and Nineteenth-Century Natural Science." *Journal of the American Studies Association of Texas* 19 (Oct. 1988): 1–21.

Ruland, Richard, ed. *Twentieth Century Interpretations of* Walden: *A Collection of Critical Essays.* Englewood Cliffs: Prentice, 1968.

Ryan, George E. "Shanties and Shiftlessness: The Immigrant Irish of Henry Thoreau." *Eire* 13 (1978): 54–78.

Salomon, Louis B. "The Practical Thoreau." *College English* 17 (1956): 229–32.

Sattelmeyer, Robert. "Away from Concord: The Travel Writings of Henry David Thoreau." Diss. U of New Mexico, 1975.

———. "The Remaking of *Walden.*" *Writing the American Classics.* Ed. James Barbour and Tom Quirk. Chapel Hill: U of North Carolina P, 1990. 53–78. Rpt. in Thoreau, Walden *and "Civil Disobedience"* (Norton) 428–44.

———. "'The True Industry for Poets': Fishing with Thoreau." *ESQ: A Journal of the American Renaissance* 33 (1987): 189–201.

———. *Thoreau's Reading.* Princeton: Princeton UP, 1988.

Sattelmeyer, Robert, and Richard Hocks. "Thoreau and Coleridge's *Theory of Life.*" *Studies in the American Renaissance* (1985): 269–84.

Saunders, Judith P. "'A Different Angle': Thoreau and the Problem of Perspective." *Massachusetts Studies in English* 10 (1986): 184–96.

Sayre, Robert F., ed. *New Essays on* Walden. Cambridge: Cambridge UP, 1992.

———. *Thoreau and the American Indians.* Princeton: Princeton UP, 1977.

Scanlon, Lawrence. "Thoreau's Parable of Baker Farm." *Emerson Society Quarterly* 47 (1967): 19–21.

Schneider, Richard J. "*Cape Cod*: Thoreau's Wilderness of Illusion." *ESQ: A Journal of the American Renaissance* 26 (1980): 184–96.

———. *Henry David Thoreau.* Boston: Twayne, 1987.

———. "Reflections in Walden Pond: Thoreau's Optics." *ESQ: A Journal of the American Renaissance* 21 (1975): 65–75. Rpt. in Myerson, *Critical Essays* 110–24.

———. "Thoreau and Nineteenth-Century American Landscape Painting." *ESQ: A Journal of the American Renaissance* 31 (1985): 67–88.

Schrag, Calvin O. *The Resources of Rationality: A Response to the Postmodern Challenge*. Bloomington: Indiana UP, 1992.

Schueller, Malini. "Carnival Rhetoric and Extra-Vagance in Thoreau's *Walden*." *American Literature* 58 (1986): 33–45.

Schuster, Eunice M. "Native American Anarchism." *Smith College Studies in History* 17 (1931): 46–51.

Scigaj, Leonard, and Nancy Craig Simmons. "Ecofeminist Cosmology in Thoreau's *Walden*." *ISLE* 121–29.

Shanley, J. Lyndon. *The Making of* Walden. Chicago: U of Chicago P, 1957.

Sherwood, Mary P. "Fanny Eckstorm's Bias." *Massachusetts Review* (1962): 139–47. Rpt. in J. Hicks 58–66.

Shi, David. *The Simple Life: Plain Living and High Thinking in American Culture*. New York: Oxford UP, 1985.

———. "Thoreau for Commuters." *North American Review* 272.2 (1987): 65–69.

Shor, Ira. *Critical Teaching and Everyday Life*. Chicago: U of Chicago P, 1987.

Skwire, David. "A Checklist of Wordplay in *Walden*." *American Literature* 31 (1959): 282–89.

Slotkin, Richard. *Regeneration through Violence: The Mythology of the American Frontier, 1600–1860*. Middletown: Wesleyan UP, 1973.

Slovic, Scott. *Seeking Awareness in American Nature Writing: Henry Thoreau, Annie Dillard, Edward Abbey, Wendell Berry, Barry Lopez*. Salt Lake City: U of Utah P, 1992.

Smith, Herbert F. "Thoreau among the Classical Economists." *ESQ: A Journal of the American Renaissance* 23 (1977): 114–22.

Smith, Lorrie. "Walking from England to America: Re-viewing Thoreau's Romanticism." *New England Quarterly* (1985): 221–41.

Snyder, Gary. *The Practice of the Wild*. San Francisco: North Point, 1990.

Spengemann, William. *A Mirror for Americanists: Reflections on the Idea of American Literature*. Hanover: UP of New England, 1988.

Sporn, Paul. "The Politics of Literacy and the Radical Teacher." *Radical Teacher* May 1978: 5–7.

St. Armand, Barton Levi. "Luminism in the Work of Henry David Thoreau: The Dark and the Light." *Canadian Review of American Studies* 32 (1980): 143–66.

Stoehr, Taylor. *Nay-Saying in Concord*. Hamden: Archon, 1979.

Stoller, Leo. *After* Walden: *Thoreau's Changing Views on Economic Man*. Stanford: Stanford UP, 1957.

Stowe, Harriet Beecher. *Uncle Tom's Cabin*. New York: Washington Square, 1977.

Stowell, Robert F. *A Thoreau Gazeteer*. Princeton: Princeton UP, 1970.

Sundquist, Eric J. *Home as Found: Authority and Genealogy in Nineteenth-Century American Literature*. Baltimore: Johns Hopkins UP, 1979.

Tanner, Tony. "Thoreau and the Sauntering Eye." *The Reign of Wonder: Naivete and Reality in American Literature*. Cambridge: Cambridge UP, 1965. 46–63.

Taylor, J. Golden. *Neighbor Thoreau's Critical Humor*. Logan: Utah State UP, 1958.

Thompson, Wade C. "The Impractical Thoreau: A Rebuttal." *College English* 19 (1957): 67–70. Rpt. in Lane, *Approaches* 56–61.

Thoreau, Henry David. *The Annotated* Walden: Walden; or, Life in the Woods. Ed. Philip Van Doren Stern. New York: Potter, 1970.

———. "Autumnal Tints." Thoreau, *Excursions* 215–65.

———. *Cape Cod.* Ed. Joseph J. Moldenhauer. Princeton: Princeton UP, 1988.

———. *Collected Poems of Henry Thoreau.* Ed. Carl Bode. Enl. ed. Baltimore: Johns Hopkins UP, 1964.

———. *The Correspondence of Henry David Thoreau.* Ed. Walter Harding and Carl Bode. New York: New York UP, 1958.

———. *Early Essays and Miscellanies.* Ed. Joseph J. Moldenhauer and Edwin Moser, with Alexander C. Kern. Princeton: Princeton UP, 1975.

———. *The Essays of Henry David Thoreau.* Ed. Richard Dillman. Albany: NCUP, 1990.

———. *Excursions.* 1863. New York: Corinth, 1962.

———. *Faith in a Seed: "The Dispersion of Seeds" and Other Late Natural History Writings.* Ed. Bradley P. Dean. Washington: Island, 1993.

———. *Great Short Works of Henry David Thoreau.* Ed. Wendell Glick. New York: Harper, 1982.

———. *The Heart of Thoreau's Journals.* Ed. Odell Shepard. 1927. New York: Dover, 1961.

———. *Henry David Thoreau: An American Landscape.* Ed. Robert L. Rothwell. New York: Paragon, 1991.

———. *Henry David Thoreau: A Writer's Journal.* Ed. Laurence Stapleton. New York: Dover, 1960.

———. *The Journal of Henry David Thoreau.* Ed. Bradford Torrey and Francis H. Allen. 1906. 14 vols. [Vols. 7–20 of Thoreau, *Writings.*] New York: AMS, 1968. 2 vols. New York: Dover, 1962.

———. *Journal 1: 1837–1844.* Ed. Elizabeth Hall Witherell et al. Princeton: Princeton UP, 1981.

———. *Journal 2: 1842–1848.* Ed. Robert Sattelmeyer. Princeton: Princeton UP, 1984.

———. *Journal 3: 1848–1851.* Ed. Robert Sattelmeyer, Mark R. Patterson, and William Rossi. Princeton: Princeton UP, 1990.

———. *Journal 4: 1851–1852.* Ed. Leonard N. Neufeldt and Nancy Craig Simmons. Princeton: Princeton UP, 1992.

———. *Journal 5: 1852–1853.* Ed. Patrick F. O'Connell. Princeton: Princeton UP, 1995.

———. *Journal 6: 1853.* Ed. William Rossi and Heather Kirk Thomas. Princeton: Princeton UP, forthcoming 1997.

———. *The Maine Woods.* Ed. Joseph J. Moldenhauer. Princeton: Princeton UP, 1972.

———. *The Natural History Essays.* Ed. Robert Sattelmeyer. Salt Lake City: Smith, 1984.

———. *Notes on New England Birds.* Ed. Francis H. Allen. Boston: Houghton, 1910.

———. *The Portable Thoreau.* Ed. Carl Bode. New York: Penguin, 1977.

———. *Reform Papers.* Ed. Wendell Glick. Princeton: Princeton UP, 1973.

———. *The Selected Journals of Henry D. Thoreau*. Ed. Carl Bode. New York: Signet-NAL, 1967.

———. *Thoreau: A Week on the Concord and Merrimack Rivers; Walden; or, Life in the Woods; the Maine Woods; and Cape Cod*. Ed. and notes by Robert Sayre. New York: Library of America, 1985.

———. *Thoreau in the Mountains*. Ed. William Howarth. New York: Farrar, 1982.

———. *The Variorum* Walden *and "Civil Disobedience."* Ed. and introd. Walter Harding. New York: Washington Square, 1968.

———. *Walden*. Ed. J. Lyndon Shanley. Introd. Joyce Carol Oates. Princeton: Princeton UP, 1989.

———. Walden *and "Civil Disobedience."* Ed. Sherman Paul. Riverside ed. Boston: Houghton, 1960.

———. Walden *and "Civil Disobedience."* Ed. Michael Meyer. New York: Penguin, 1983.

———. Walden *and "Civil Disobedience."* Norton Critical Edition. 2nd ed. Ed. William Rossi. New York: Norton, 1992.

———. Walden *and Other Writings*. Ed. William Howarth. New York: Modern Library, 1981.

———. "Walking." *Excursions and Poems*. Boston: Houghton, 1906. 205–48. Vol. 5 of *Writings*.

———. *A Week on the Concord and Merrimack Rivers*. Ed. Carl F. Hovde, William L. Howarth, and Elizabeth Hall Witherell. Princeton: Princeton UP, 1980.

———. *The Writings of Henry David Thoreau*. "Walden" ed. 20 vols. Boston: Houghton, 1906.

———. *A Year in Thoreau's Journal: 1851*. Ed. H. Daniel Peck. New York: Penguin, 1993.

———. "A Yankee in Canada." *Excursions and Poems*. Boston: Houghton, 1906. 3–101. Vol. 5 of *Writings*.

Tichi, Cecilia. *New World, New Earth: Environmental Reform in American Literature from the Puritans through Whitman*. New Haven: Yale UP, 1979.

Todorov, Tzvetan. *Genres in Discourse*. Trans. Catherine Porter. Cambridge: Cambridge UP, 1990.

Van Dusen, Lewis, Jr. "Civil Disobedience: Destroyer of Democracy." *American Bar Association Journal* 55 (1969): 123–26.

Vinaver, Eugene. *The Rise of Romance*. New York: Oxford UP, 1971.

Wagenknecht, Edward. *Henry David Thoreau: What Manner of Man?* Amherst: U of Massachusetts P, 1981.

Walls, Laura Dassow. "*Walden* as Feminist Manifesto." *ISLE* 137–44.

Warren, Joyce W. Introduction. *Fern* ix–xxxix.

Warren, Robert Penn. *New and Selected Poems, 1923–1985*. New York: Random, 1985.

Weisbuch, Robert. *Atlantic Double Cross: American Literature and British Influence in the Age of Emerson*. Chicago: U of Chicago P, 1986.

West, Michael. "Analogy, Metaphor, and Etymology in Thinking." *Collective Wisdom: A Sourcebook of Lessons for Writing Teachers*. Ed. Sondra J. Stang and Robert Wiltenburg. New York: Random, 1988. 288–92.

———. "Scatology and Eschatology: The Heroic Dimensions of Thoreau's Wordplay." *PMLA* 89 (1974): 1043–64.

————. "Spellers and Punsters." *Southwest Review* 42 (1987): 492–511.

Westling, Louise. "Thoreau's Ambivalence toward Mother Nature." *ISLE* 145–50.

Whitaker, Rosemary. "*A Week* and *Walden*: The River vs. the Pond." *American Transcendental Quarterly* 17 (1973): 9–13.

White, E. B. "Henry Thoreau." *New Yorker* 7 May 1949: 23. Rpt. in Ruland 113–14.

————. "The Retort Transcendental." *The Second Tree from the Corner*. New York: Harper, 1953. 94–96. Rpt. in Lane, *Approaches* 84–86.

————. "A Slight Sound at Evening (Walden—1954)." *The Points of My Compass*. New York: Harper, 1954. 15–25. Rpt. in Thoreau, Walden *and "Civil Disobedience"* (Norton) 359–66.

Whitford, Kathryn. "Thoreau and the Woodlots of Concord." *New England Quarterly* 23 (1950): 291–306.

Whitford, Philip, and Kathryn Whitford. "Thoreau: Pioneer Ecologist and Conservationist." *Scientific Monthly* Nov. 1951: 291–96. Rpt. in Harding, *Thoreau: A Century* 192–205.

Williams, Paul O. "The Influence of Thoreau on the American Nature Essay." *Thoreau Society Bulletin* 145 (1978): 1–5.

Williams, Raymond. *Keywords: A Vocabulary of Culture and Society*. Rev. ed. New York: Oxford UP, 1983.

Willson, Lawrence. "Thoreau and New England's Weather." *Weatherwise* June 1959: 91–94.

Wilmerding, John. *American Light: The Luminist Movement 1850–1875*. Washington: Natl. Gallery of Art, 1980.

Wolf, William J. *Thoreau: Mystic, Prophet, Ecologist*. Philadelphia: Pilgrim, 1974.

Wood, Ann D. "The 'Scribbling Women' and Fanny Fern: Why Women Wrote." *American Quarterly* 23 (1971): 1–24.

Wood, Barry. "Thoreau's Narrative Art in 'Civil Disobedience.'" *Philological Quarterly* 60 (1981): 105–15. Rpt. in Thoreau, Walden *and "Civil Disobedience"* (Norton) 421–28.

Woodlief, Annette. "The Influence of Theories of Rhetoric on Thoreau." *Thoreau Journal Quarterly* 7.1 (1975): 13–22.

————. "*Walden*: A Checklist of Literary Criticism through 1973." *Resources for American Literary Study* 5 (1975): 15–57.

Woodruff, Stuart. "Thoreau as Water-Gazer: 'The Ponds.'" *Emerson Society Quarterly* 47 (1967): 16–17.

Woodson, Thomas. "Thoreau on Poverty and Magnanimity." *PMLA* 85 (1970): 21–34.

————. "The Title and Text of Thoreau's 'Civil Disobedience.'" *Bulletin of Research in the Humanities* 81 (1978): 103–12.

————. "The Two Beginnings of *Walden*: A Distinction of Styles." *English Literary History* 35 (1968): 440–73.

Wordsworth, William. *The Poems*. Ed. John O. Hayden. New Haven: Yale UP, 1981.

Worster, Donald. *Nature's Economy: A History of Ecological Ideas*. Cambridge: Cambridge UP, 1977.

Ziff, Larzer. *Literary Democracy*. New York: Viking, 1981.

Zinn, Howard. *A People's History of the United States*. New York: Harper, 1980.

INDEX

Modern Language Association of America
Approaches to Teaching World Literature
Joseph Gibaldi, series editor

Achebe's Things Fall Apart. Ed. Bernth Lindfors. 1991.
Arthurian Tradition. Ed. Maureen Fries and Jeanie Watson. 1992.
Austen's Pride and Prejudice. Ed. Marcia McClintock Folsom. 1993.
Beckett's Waiting for Godot. Ed. June Schlueter and Enoch Brater. 1991.
Beowulf. Ed. Jess B. Bessinger, Jr., and Robert F. Yeager. 1984.
Blake's Songs of Innocence and of Experience. Ed. Robert F. Gleckner and
    Mark L. Greenberg. 1989.
Brontë's Jane Eyre. Ed. Diane Long Hoeveler and Beth Lau. 1993.
Byron's Poetry. Ed. Frederick W. Shilstone. 1991.
Camus's The Plague. Ed. Steven G. Kellman. 1985.
Cather's My Ántonia. Ed. Susan J. Rosowski. 1989.
Cervantes' Don Quixote. Ed. Richard Bjornson. 1984.
Chaucer's Canterbury Tales. Ed. Joseph Gibaldi. 1980.
Chopin's The Awakening. Ed. Bernard Koloski. 1988.
Coleridge's Poetry and Prose. Ed. Richard E. Matlak. 1991.
Dante's Divine Comedy. Ed. Carole Slade. 1982.
Dickens' David Copperfield. Ed. Richard J. Dunn. 1984.
Dickinson's Poetry. Ed. Robin Riley Fast and Christine Mack Gordon. 1989.
Eliot's Middlemarch. Ed. Kathleen Blake. 1990.
Eliot's Poetry and Plays. Ed. Jewel Spears Brooker. 1988.
Ellison's Invisible Man. Ed. Susan Resneck Parr and Pancho Savery. 1989.
Flaubert's Madame Bovary. Ed. Laurence M. Porter and Eugene F. Gray. 1995.
García Márquez's One Hundred Years of Solitude. Ed. María Elena de Valdés and
    Mario J. Valdés. 1990.
Goethe's Faust. Ed. Douglas J. McMillan. 1987.
Hebrew Bible as Literature in Translation. Ed. Barry N. Olshen and
    Yael S. Feldman. 1989.
Homer's Iliad *and* Odyssey. Ed. Kostas Myrsiades. 1987.
Ibsen's A Doll House. Ed. Yvonne Shafer. 1985.
Works of Samuel Johnson. Ed. David R. Anderson and Gwin J. Kolb. 1993.
Joyce's Ulysses. Ed. Kathleen McCormick and Erwin R. Steinberg. 1993.
Kafka's Short Fiction. Ed. Richard T. Gray. 1995.
Keats's Poetry. Ed. Walter H. Evert and Jack W. Rhodes. 1991.
Kingston's The Woman Warrior. Ed. Shirley Geok-lin Lim. 1991.
Lessing's The Golden Notebook. Ed. Carey Kaplan and Ellen Cronan Rose. 1989.
Mann's Death in Venice *and Other Short Fiction.* Ed. Jeffrey B. Berlin. 1992.
Medieval English Drama. Ed. Richard K. Emmerson. 1990.
Melville's Moby-Dick. Ed. Martin Bickman. 1985.
Metaphysical Poets. Ed. Sidney Gottlieb. 1990.
Miller's Death of a Salesman. Ed. Matthew C. Roudané. 1995.
Milton's Paradise Lost. Ed. Galbraith M. Crump. 1986.

Molière's Tartuffe *and Other Plays*. Ed. James F. Gaines and
    Michael S. Koppisch. 1995.
Momaday's The Way to Rainy Mountain. Ed. Kenneth M. Roemer. 1988.
Montaigne's Essays. Ed. Patrick Henry. 1994.
Murasaki Shikibu's The Tale of Genji. Ed. Edward Kamens. 1993.
Pope's Poetry. Ed. Wallace Jackson and R. Paul Yoder. 1993.
Shakespeare's King Lear. Ed. Robert H. Ray. 1986.
Shakespeare's The Tempest *and Other Late Romances*. Ed. Maurice Hunt. 1992.
Shelley's Frankenstein. Ed. Stephen C. Behrendt. 1990.
Shelley's Poetry. Ed. Spencer Hall. 1990.
Sir Gawain and the Green Knight. Ed. Miriam Youngerman Miller and
    Jane Chance. 1986.
Spenser's Faerie Queene. Ed. David Lee Miller and Alexander Dunlop. 1994.
Sterne's Tristram Shandy. Ed. Melvyn New. 1989.
Swift's Gulliver's Travels. Ed. Edward J. Rielly. 1988.
Thoreau's Walden *and Other Works*. Ed. Richard J. Schneider. 1996.
Voltaire's Candide. Ed. Renée Waldinger. 1987.
Whitman's Leaves of Grass. Ed. Donald D. Kummings. 1990.
Wordsworth's Poetry. Ed. Spencer Hall, with Jonathan Ramsey. 1986.